A Lady Travels

A Lady Travels

JOURNEYS IN ENGLAND AND SCOTLAND
FROM THE DIARIES OF
JOHANNA SCHOPENHAUER

Translated from the German and edited by
Ruth Michaelis-Jena and Willy Merson

ROUTLEDGE
London

First published in 1988 by
Routledge
11 New Fetter Lane, London EC4P 4EE

Set in 10 on 12 point Bembo
by Columns of Reading
and printed in Great Britain
by T. J. Press (Padstow) Ltd
Padstow, Cornwall

British Library Cataloguing in Publication Data
Schopenhauer, Johanna, 1766–1838
    A lady travels: journeys in England and
    Scotland.
    1. Great Britain. Description & travel,
    1800–1830. Personal observations
    I. Title   II. Michaelis-Jena, Ruth, 1905–
    III. Merson, Willy
    914.1'0473

ISBN 0–415–00616–3

CONTENTS

Contents

ILLUSTRATIONS

Illustrations

ACKNOWLEDGMENTS

We would like to express our thanks to Ms Margaret Deas of the Reference Department at the National Library of Scotland for her special help.

The authors and publishers would like to thank The Trustees of the National Library of Scotland for permission to reproduce all the illustrations except for The Bridge over the Wear at Sunderland which is reproduced courtesy of the Tyne and Wear Museums. Two lines from 'ZIP', lyrics by Lorenz Hart from the musical production *Pal Joey* (c) 1951 Chappell & Co Inc are reproduced by permission of Chappell Music Limited, London.

INTRODUCTION

'Zip! I was reading Schopenhauer last night.
Zip! And I think that Schopenhauer was right.'

'Who was Johanna Schopenhauer?' 'She was the mother of the great philosopher, Arthur'. The reaction to this answer is either to quote immediately some paragraph from his pessimistic works or, more often, to ask blankly, 'Who?' Yet in the materialistic 1930s his name was considered well enough known, albeit somewhat awesome, for Lorenz Hart to refer to him casually in one of his brilliant Broadway lyrics. His mother's travels make considerably easier and more enjoyable reading, but they do reveal enough of her indomitable character to account, to some extent at least, for the gloomy misogynous outlook of her son. While he expected his weighty writings to be read earnestly, his mother, in the introduction to the second edition of her diaries, remarked:

> I repeat my request to the reader, not to take up this book with too great expectation. It contains a woman's simple tales of what she has seen and observed, written to entertain pleasingly, not to instruct deeply.

Johanna Schopenhauer was born in Danzig on 9 July 1766, the daughter of a merchant and a Senator, Christian Heinrich Trosiener. A man of progressive ideas, proud of his city's republican institutions, he had travelled widely, spoke several languages and showed a great preference for all things English. He saw to it that his daughter received a liberal education, and at her father's insistence, she learnt languages at an early age, acquiring an ease in Polish from her nurse and the servants, even before she could speak German. Her first formal education was at a small establishment, presided over by the mother and the sister of the painter and engraver, Daniel Chodowiecki. She enjoyed watching the artist at work in his studio and it is possible that he first aroused her interest in painting, which manifests itself so clearly in her diaries. Although her ardent wish to make painting her career was received with a degree of scorn by her family, the fascination with this branch of the arts remained with her for life.

Johanna was, by all accounts, a happy child, bright and eager to learn. At the age of six she was given a private tutor called Kuschel who, when she was only thirteen years old, in a fit of mistaken enthusiasm, proposed marriage to her. Thereafter she was put on safer ground with a friend of the family, the Rev. Richard Jamieson, Minister to the English Community of Danzig, who became her special mentor. From him she absorbed a knowledge of English literature and the English scene, and the fact that Jamieson was, in fact, a Scot, with a fervent love for his homeland, kindled in Johanna the interest in that country which influenced her later travels.

A dancing master taught her deportment, while she learnt French from a Mamsell Ackermann. This lady, who came from Berlin, had tutored a Swedish princess and now kept a small educational institution in Danzig, the *Société des Jeunes Dames*, where the daughters of good families could study French, a necessary attribute in polite society, and acquire that 'finish' considered so important. Here, for the first time, Johanna enjoyed the company of people of her own generation.

In 1784, when she was just eighteen years old, Johanna met Heinrich Floris Schopenhauer, a man twenty years her senior. He was a well-respected figure among the citizens of Danzig, head of a large merchant house, wealthy, much travelled, fiercely patriotic, anti-Prussian and, above all, an Anglophile. Her carefree liveliness must have attracted him, while his style and knowledge of the ways of the world made him, in her eyes, superior to men of her own age. They were married after a short courtship and although Johanna never pretended passionate love, they got on well together, had many tastes in common and were particularly united in their love of travel and acquiring a knowledge of new people and places. She gladly overlooked his irritable and occasionally depressed moods and spent happy times at her husband's country house near Oliva, where, in an elegant and English atmosphere, she enjoyed the beauty of the countryside, his fine collection of paintings and sculptures, and well-stocked library.

The couple made a long journey through several countries of Europe in 1787, meeting many prominent figures of the German Enlightenment in Berlin and experiencing the last splendours of the French court in Paris. Johanna became pregnant and for a while her husband seemed eager to have his first child born on English soil and so be a British citizen. To this end they spent some time in London, but he eventually changed his mind and they undertook the arduous journey back to Danzig, where on 22 February 1788 their son, Arthur, was born.

When Danzig was annexed by Prussia in 1793, the liberal-minded Heinrich Floris felt impelled to seek refuge in the Free City of Hamburg, where a daughter, Adele, was born in 1797. He soon considered himself to be a foreigner there and began to suffer from bouts of depression. They both grew restless and once again travelled in several parts of Europe. Between 1803 and 1805 those travels included England and Scotland. Johanna kept diaries wherever she went and was to use them later as the basis for her travel books.

After her husband's sudden death in Hamburg – believed by many to have been suicide – Johanna decided, in 1806, to move to Weimar whose *Musenhof* had become a cultural centre for writers, musicians and artists. There she felt she would be able to have a 'salon', no doubt in the hope of becoming a minor Madame de Staël. She showed a definite desire to shine and to please, and was fortunate in being accepted quickly into Weimar society. This was partly due to the great courage she showed during the sacking of Weimar by Napoleon's armies. Her fluency in French and her ability to deal with strangers saved her home from destruction and made it a refuge for others less fortunate. She enjoyed the friendship of Goethe and particularly endeared herself to him by 'receiving' Christiane Vulpius when, at long last, she became Frau Geheimrat

Goethe. The ladies of Weimar had been reluctant to include her in their circles, but Johanna is said to have remarked: 'If Goethe can give her his name, we can surely offer her a cup of tea.' The establishment of her modest salon naturally gave rein to her literary ambitions. She wrote novels, worked at translations and contributed to periodicals and almanacs. As she had kept diaries of all her travels, the obvious sequel was a series of books based on her experiences abroad. She published volumes on Italy and France before undertaking the present work. The opening chapter of her travels in the United Kingdom, not included here, does in fact take her through Holland on her way to these shores, something to which she makes reference when she meets the little Dutch girls at an English school.

The Edinburgh Review said of Johanna's writings that they 'have all the charm and vivacity of truth . . . '. Indeed, she did not follow the usual pattern of those travellers of her time who arrived in a foreign country, armed with sheaves of introductions to the nobility and the great men in politics and the arts. Apart from her countryman, the astronomer Herschel, she does not, in fact, recount presenting credentials to anyone of importance. Instead she was recommended to industrialists who showed her round the most unlikely places for a lady of the period: a coal-mine, an armaments factory, a mint, a steel foundry. This could of course have been partly due to her husband's strong republican ideas and his indifference to high society. While she notes the splendours and niceties of the aristocracy and their grand houses, seen more or less as a tourist, it is a day in the life of a well-to-do merchant and his family which she chooses to describe in minute and amusing detail.

Johanna did at times get carried away by her enthusiasms. It was only natural that the great wave of interest in the Ossianic legends which had swept Europe and had particularly influenced Germany, should have been strongly felt by her. Once let loose in the Scottish Highlands, therefore, she was quick to rhapsodize on almost every moor, glen, rocky mountain and mist-shrouded stretch of water upon which she came. Occasionally it proved excessive, just as her love of the English garden, first felt on her husband's Danzig estate, brought forth a stream of adulative adjectives on trees, shrubs, lawns and follies, each time she visited some great estate. She had a tremendous liking for the 'unfortunate' Mary, Queen of Scots, but no great love for Elizabeth. These extravagances aside, what clearly emerges is a picture of a woman with a keenly observant eye, noticing those things around her not usually associated with the women of her time. She was perceptive and critical of social conditions and cast an inquisitive look on the achievements in industry and technology. She was intrepid, to say the least, in her expeditions, traversing rough, precipitous roads well off the beaten track, watching a cannon being made, making the alarming journey through the Peak Caves and, save on one or two occasions, remaining cool-tempered when things did not work out as she had planned.

Many interesting points emerge – that the great houses, for instance, were opened to the public at certain times by arrangement, that in fact Blenheim was organized for this purpose almost as a stately house is today, and that Royal Walkabouts are not a modern innovation.

There are a number of inaccuracies to be found in her recollections. These are probably due in part to the fact that certain places were visited on more than one occasion, but mainly that she was drawing on diaries written some ten years earlier as well as on her own, perhaps over-vivid, memories. She is somewhat confused, for example, on the history of the Glencoe massacre and somehow manages to see that scene from Rest and Be Thankful, near Arrochar. Ben Mhor is the highest peak in Scotland and Holyrood is situated on a rock, but on the whole her facts are accurate and even her legends, authentically legendary.

The present text is based mainly on the second edition of the book she wrote on her journeys through England and Scotland, which was published in 1816. Her later years were marred by a loss of investments and declining health. This caused her to leave Weimar for the milder climate of the Rhine at Bonn. In 1837 the Grand Duke of Weimar granted her a pension and she returned, together with her daughter, to Thuringia which had become her second home. Alas, she did not live long to enjoy it, dying in Jena in 1838.

1 ENGLAND

SOME PRELIMINARY REMARKS ON ENGLAND

Travel in England is truly enjoyable. The parks are as beautiful as the finest landscape paintings, the houses are comfortably equipped and offer refined luxury and a feeling of orderliness where even the most basic of household utensils are not only useful, but elegant and pleasing to the eye. One does not desire to possess all these things because one has no need for them, sometimes does not even know what they are, but they give an admirable sense of well-being. On the other hand one should beware of a desire to take pleasure in works of art by studying or even copying them, for in this country one would face so many obstacles that the whole project would become quite impracticable.

Much has been written about the beauty of the countryside, the excellent roads, the comfortable inns to be found even in the remotest places – where nothing but a well-filled purse is needed to feel at home – and the excellence of the mail-coach service. Nobody, however, has sufficiently praised the perfect whole which it all forms.

For the present we shall be content to draw a general picture of a large English country house and its surroundings, and at the same time tell of what we observed on a journey from London through the north of England and Scotland. An English park is quite different from what we consider to be a park in Germany. It includes all the land around a house or castle, usually of considerable size. Within this area there are fields and meadows, pleasantly enclosed by hedges and crossed by gravel-strewn paths, well-kept for walking or driving. There are farm buildings and outhouses, agreeable to look at yet practical for their purpose, for a picturesque effect is always sought, helped by the undulating nature of the countryside. Everywhere we find the useful combined with the beautiful.

The finest adornment of these parks is their luxuriant vegetation, a combination of well-cultivated fields, incomparably green meadows and splendid trees, mostly oak or beech, planted in groups. In England small trees grow in a special way as more than in other countries, their branches sprout straight out from the base. Thus one does not find narrow paths winding their way through heavily shaded shrubberies and copses, and in fact one might say there is a lack of shade. In a country where the air is mild but the sun seldom too hot or bright, shade is not so vital as elsewhere. The pavilions, temples and hermitages are not, as with ours on the Continent, spaced out in the park but are in the so-called pleasure grounds close to the house. An obelisk, a pyramid or a tower is found only in the great parks of, say, Blenheim or Stowe, where they are intended to form part of a vista from the house.

There must never be an absence of water. While artificial waterfalls are practically unknown, with fountains even less common, a small river or even a sizeable stream will, at considerable expense, be diverted to wind its way through the park. Should there be no running water, a canal is used by giving it a slight, apparently natural, bend and hiding its beginning and end by planting overhanging bushes or deceiving the eye by throwing a handsome bridge across it. Similarly the banks of a pond may be reformed irregularly, thus giving the impression that they are the shores of a small lake. Everywhere the aim is beauty, avoiding the artificial, the stiff and the pretentious.

The wild life of the countryside completes the picture. Hundreds of half-tame stags and roedeer graze in paddocks, almost fearlesly, on the greenest grass in the world. With them are the finest horses, cows and goats, and the handsome appearance of these animals, their free and easy movements and their contentedness lend a unique attraction to the whole scene.

The house is always situated on a slight incline with no trees near it, so that light, air and sun are not kept out, and close to it lawns are spread out like green carpets. All the same, the rooms of the house are never too hot because it is actually rarely very hot in England, and anyway the windows of the house are so well placed that there is sufficient light everywhere.

The external appearance of English country houses is well known from engravings. The houses are seldom in one pure style as they tend to be overloaded with decoration. The front of the house is usually embellished with columns. The proportions of these are not always satisfactory and often seem to serve no purpose, yet they provide an agreeable place in front of the house for comfortably contemplating the green lawns beyond. At the foot of these columns stand many shrubs, greenery and flowers in urns, some on beautiful stands, one above the other, some prettily arranged on the entrance steps and on balustrades. The mere luxury which this love of plants engenders is most enjoyable. Every day, plants past their best are removed and replaced with fresh ones.

The sight of this greenery is charming. Flora's treasures from all over the world are brought here as if by magic, but in England they are also subject to the iron rule of fashion. At the time of writing this, ericas or heathers are great favourites and people have paid fifty and more guineas for this scentless plant which often does not even have much colour. The main criterion is that a plant should come from a distant corner of the globe. Large orangeries are seldom found in England except in the Royal Gardens.

The interior of the houses, here as elsewhere, depends on the wealth and taste of the builder, the present owner and the period in which it was created. Most houses have large, well-lit basements, containing the kitchen and rooms for keeping provisions, as well as accommodation for the servants. The rooms are well furnished, indeed the housekeeper's and butler's are even elegant, with pretty wallpapers, mahogany furniture and good carpets. They, too, enjoy the English custom of having, apart from their bedroom, a sitting- and dining-room.

From the garden one usually enters a large, high hall, often lit from above. It is decorated with paintings, statues, bas-reliefs or vases. Reception- and drawing-rooms are on each side of the hall. One long room contains the library and the beautiful book-cases and fine bindings make this one of the most elegant rooms in the house. It is the custom in many places for the family to assemble here for breakfast. There are, too, a breakfast-room, a study, a music-room, drawing-rooms, parlours, dining-rooms, and rooms for games in plenty, not always very large. Everywhere one finds elegance without ostentation.

In many houses warm winter carpets are changed in the summer to cooler coverings, druggets of painted or waxed linen, made especially for the purpose and quite heavy. Mahogany is used mainly for bannisters, large dining-tables and beds. The furniture in the more fashionable rooms is made of costly, exotic or finely lacquered woods.

It is considered 'bourgeois', even ridiculous, to place furniture against the walls as is the custom in Germany. In parlours and reception-rooms things are arranged in a wide circle so that there is enough space to walk about in between chairs, sofas and tables. Writing desks and pianos stand freely in the rooms, wherever the light is best, and where there is not too much heat from the fireplaces, which are skilfully made of marble or decorated with polished steel. The fireplace is the finest ornament in each room. Beautiful vases and fine candelabra stand on their mantels. The bedrooms are on the second floor and seldom shown to a stranger. These bedrooms, particularly those of the ladies of the house, are a sanctum which no alien eye may penetrate. Quite often we heard English women talk with disgust of the habit of French ladies who turn their bedrooms into a favourite meeting-place for visitors. So much for the interior of English country houses in general: let us now return to the immediate surroundings.

The fruit and vegetable gardens, the hothouses and all other buildings needed for the domestic economy of the house are near at hand, but are hidden from the onlooker in a number of ways. These areas near the house are considered 'gardens' by the English. The Pleasure Ground for 'taking the air' is closest to the house. Here there are certain similarities with a German park, their walks being heavily shaded or winding their way in the open. There are temples, columns, monuments, seats and

[4]

all the wealth of things modern garden architecture provides. Buildings are made of stone and the gates of finely wrought ironwork. Many indigenous shrubs, trees and flowers grow here in profusion, as well as some brought from foreign parts and hardy enough to endure a winter in the open.

Many plants needing careful protection from the cold in Germany, stand up well to the English winter, which is made less harsh by the flow of sea air. Examples are *laurus tinus*, the *heliotropium* and *jasmin officinale*. The last two we saw often growing up to a height of 6 or 8 feet against walls. Fruit trees of all kinds are banished from the area near the house. The aesthetic way in which trees are planted according to their height, the form of their growth, the darker or lighter shade of their foliage, makes for a magic which one senses but cannot explain. Everything aims at making a beautiful and satisfying whole. The eye is sometimes deluded when it comes to judging distances, for English gardeners are genuine landscape painters on a large scale. We might even call them the true artists of their nation. They know well how to use the rules of perspective and to dispense with too much tiresome detail. Using conifers of all kinds, some unknown to us in Germany, and evergreen shrubs, some of which flower into December, they achieve pleasing effects. Usually one sees an arrangement of these close to the house, where one can stroll in the winter sunshine and dream that one is already in spring. Such an illusion is more necessary here than with us, for this strange inclination which causes the English to turn night into day also causes confusion in the seasons. In dress and entertainment, winter rules beyond the middle of June, and only then does spring arrive. Thus summer, only happening in August, has to be prolonged until Christmas, so that justice is done to the seasons and to the people.

The main entrance to the park, usually a very splendid gate, is flanked by two small buildings, the home of the caretaker, and here one must ring a bell if seeking admission. The gate with its buildings is called a lodge and is one of the chief ornaments of the park. The two pavilions may be built in the Gothic or even Egyptian style, they may represent towers, Greek temples or just pretty little garden cottages, according to the particular taste of the owner. The caretaker always has a pleasant home there, well furnished, with kitchen and cellar, in fact everything he needs, and many a good family in Germany would be happy to have such a place for a summer holiday.

WOBURN ABBEY

Woburn Abbey, the seat of the Duke of Bedford, was the first great house we visited. The Duke is the richest landowner and biggest farmer in England. His brother, an even keener farmer, died a few years ago, aged only thirty-six, leaving a large fortune to the present owner, who had earlier entered the Church.

Woburn is a day's journey from London. The farm buildings, especially the cattle sheds, were, quite naturally, the first things we had to see for the Duke, like his predecessor, is particularly interested in animal husbandry. His four-legged charges are certainly a credit to him and at agricultural shows, so popular in England, they usually carry off the major trophies because of their size, fine appearance and general air of well-being. Certainly everything is done here to keep their memory green after their, alas, nearly always violent death, for the house abounds in painted and sculpted likenesses of the finest of them. Many have even been engraved and their portraits are to be found displayed in London art shops next to those of great scholars or Ministers of the Crown.

Although we understand little of agriculture and husbandry, it is quite impossible not to take pleasure in the orderliness all around and the efficient way in which everything is arranged. We were shown many mechanical devices, invented in this country of industry, designed to make rural tasks more simple, easy and profitable. There were, for example, a threshing machine, another for taking off the husks so that no flour should be lost in the bran, yet another for sifting four kinds of flour at the same time, and many other such contraptions.

The cleanliness of the byres was almost unbelievable, especially where we least expected it, in the pig-sty. Its inhabitants were thriving although they were so large that the burden of their weight tended to give them a dejected appearance, as though weary and tired of life. We were also shown bulls, famed for their great qualities, and some cows of American-Indian origin. These have a straighter back and a smaller head but otherwise do not differ much from the ordinary animal.

The park with its magnificent grasslands and fine old trees has a picturesque beauty of its own. Herds of tame deer graze there and among them roam the most beautiful large sheep, some of them from the Orient, with thick fat tails. The sense of security and lack of fear among these different animals living together charmed us whenever we looked at them, conjuring up an image of the Golden Age.

The house itself does not excel in either splendour or beauty. It is too new to be viewed with respect and too old to be elegant. It is open to the public on Mondays only and we were lucky on this occasion to be admitted. We walked through a number of rooms full of paintings, mainly portraits. There were six very fine van Dycks, full-length life-size figures, which caught our special attention. We also saw a portrait of the hapless Earl of Essex, life-size too. He has about him an unforgettably cunning look, and a very red beard. Opposite him hangs a portrait of Queen Elizabeth, clad in the most tasteless and exaggerated finery and without any feminine charm at all. Historical paintings and landscapes, mostly belonging to the Dutch school, are there in plenty and certainly some are of great value. There is, too, a very elegant library.

The orangery is simply splendid. In its centre are eight large marble columns supporting a cupola, which gives light from above, and surrounding an antique marble urn, decorated with bas-relief. One could write a whole book about this urn alone, but alas we had to hurry past it. The orangery is flanked on both sides by a roofed promenade in the shape of a semi-circle, which allows one to stroll there in inclement weather and in winter. Honeysuckle, roses, true jasmine, heliotrope and many similar plants cling to the pillars and the arches of the roof which rest upon them, and many rare flowers and plants grow in urns along the promenade.

Quite near to this are the riding school, an area for ball games, and a 'model dairy' with stained-glass windows. All the utensils used in dairying are on display and are made of rare Japanese or Chinese porcelain. The walks at Woburn are elegantly laid out, but seem not to have been planned on a grand scale, when compared to others we have seen on our many travels.

THE GARDENS AT STOWE

The gardens at Stowe, which are rightly considered the most beautiful and magnificent in England, lie not far from Woburn, which we had left in the afternoon. We arrived in the evening and were fortunate in finding an inn with excellent service very close to the gardens.

The grounds abound in temples, obelisks, columns and pavilions of all kinds. While in a restricted space it is wise to limit such embellishments, in this vast expanse the variety of the buildings becomes striking. One has to admire the felicitous choice of location for each and marvel at the wealth which made it possible to create such splendid beauty in a countryside already richly endowed by nature. It is impossible to describe these gardens in mere words! Only when seen can one conjure up again the picture in one's mind, and ask, who but a poet could have devised so lovely a scene. One treads on ground made interesting by association, for Lord Cobham, to whom the gardens largely owe their development, lived here during one of the most brilliant periods in English literature. The finest minds of Britain were his friends and shared happy days with him in this enchanting place.

Everything has been done to keep fresh the memory of Lord Cobham and his friends. Their busts, hewn in marble, stand in a temple, while a half-open rotunda contains the likenesses of King Alfred, Queen Elizabeth, Newton, Francis Drake and several others who, though separated by many years, had one common virtue: they served their country well.

A high column, begun by Lord Cobham, was finished by his successor, Lord Temple, and is dedicated to his memory. It is hollow inside and contains a winding staircase of 170 steps, and mounting to the top one can enjoy a fine view towards Oxford. Another column is dedicated to the memory of General Wolfe, while a smaller one, decorated with a globe,

1 *Stowe House, Buckinghamshire*

has been erected in honour of Captain Cook who circum-
navigated the world.

Memorable too is a Gothic temple with stained-glass
windows through which the surrounding landscape looks quite
magical. There are many fine old trees in the grounds,
especially oaks and cypresses and a remarkable large yew.
Shady walks wind round a small lake and natural waterfalls and
picturesque bridges all combine to enhance the scene further.

The house itself consists of a two-storey building with two
wings of one storey only. The rarest plants grow in pots in an
attica, a structure supported by marble columns in the Athenian
style. From here one enters a magnificent hall, lit from a cupola
above. Its marble frieze depicts a Roman triumphal procession
while the hall itself is adorned with marble columns, a statue
placed between each. Through this main hall one reaches a
smaller inner one, decorated with antique busts. There is a
beautiful Apollo in the centre of the room and this and most of
the others are of great age.

The rooms, not exactly decorated in the height of fashion,
contain many paintings, mostly by Dutch masters and in
particular, Rembrandt. Among them is a self-portrait of this
painter whose works are so much appreciated in England. One
small room full of portraits is well worth looking at, as these
represent a remarkable circle which Lord Cobham gathered
around him: Pope, Swift, Steele, Addison (who has a very kind
face), and many others. There is also one of the unhappy Mary
Stuart. She is strangely dressed, wearing a very high collar, and
seems much less beautiful than one is apt to think of her.
Perhaps the not very great skill of the artist is to blame. Lady
Buckingham and her daughter also paint: the mother in oil and
the daughter in crayon. A whole room is decorated with their
work, of which no more will be said, save that it is
praiseworthy for such ladies to spend their time so.

The night after we had looked at Stowe we continued to
Woodstock, a little town notable for a number of things. Quite
near is the splendid palace of Blenheim, which Queen Anne
gave to her favourite, the Duke of Marlborough, as a reward
for his victories, and named after one of the most celebrated.
Excellent steelware, popular all over England, is made in the

town, not in factories but by workers in their own homes. We visited one of the most skilled in order to buy some things from him. Like a painter, who for gold must part with his favourite picture, the old man looked at his finest scissors and knives in a manner expressing the artist's distress, before he eventually handed them over to us. On parting he cautioned us to take good care of them and to rub them down twice a day with a woollen cloth, for to him it seemed that looking after them should be our prime concern.

From a historical point of view, Woodstock is especially remarkable. In a meadow now incorporated in the park of Blenheim, there once stood a country house where Queen Elizabeth was educated in her youth, held practically a prisoner. She could not expect, at that time, that her claim to the English crown would ever succeed. This claim must have often caused her sorrow and bitter tears, robbing her, as it did, of her freedom, social life and all the pleasures to which youth is entitled. Here at Woodstock, however, Elizabeth gained the knowledge, firmness and intellectual qualities which later made her a great ruler. One wonders how it was possible that this early experience, of unhappiness and loneliness on the one hand and her learning and knowledge of what the wise men of her time thought and wrote on the other, made her clever but not good. Having herself once been a prisoner in fear of her life, since she stood in the way of the ambitious plans of others, how could she inflict such sorrow on one so close to her, sorrow she had known only too well from experience, and in the end let the unhappy woman die on the scaffold? Posterity, however, has been fair. Every Englishman will, even today, speak with admiration of Elizabeth the ruler, but with contempt of Elizabeth the woman, while the name of the unhappy Mary is remembered everywhere with love and pity. Mary's shortcomings are forgotten while her ill luck and charm live on in every heart.

BLENHEIM

In Woodstock we had intended to follow our rule, that is first of all to walk through the park, when to our astonishment we saw a phaeton drawn by two rather fierce-looking white horses, waiting for us in front of the inn. Our hostess assured us with much eloquence that it was practically impossible to tour the park on foot, so we accepted her arrangements, mounted the dangerous-looking vehicle and had every reason to be satisfied with our decision. The park is so large that one-and-a-half hours were barely enough to complete the trip. The white horses were less wild than they had seemed at first and the considerable height of this, no longer fashionable, uncovered vehicle made it easy to look around in all directions and enjoy to the full the varied views.

Blenheim, by the way, is shown in a more expansive, and hence a more expensive, manner than is the custom with other great houses. The spirit of the proudest woman of her day, Lady Sarah, Marlborough's wife, seems even now to influence the government of her one-time home.

A large and splendid gate with two lodges, the home of the gatekeeper, forms the park's main entrance. An inscription on the marble plaque above it explains that Lady Sarah had this triumphal arch built in honour of her late husband. We were greeted by the gatekeeper with a speech which most likely he had learnt by heart for just such occasions. Very sedately he walked for some fifty steps alongside our carriage and then stopped it. 'This is the first view', he proclaimed, 'over there you can see water with a fine straight bridge across it and to the right of it is a high column on which you can read about the Duke's exploits, the battles he fought and won. On top of the column stands his statue which looks small but is in fact 10 feet high.' He went on in this way for some time until we got rather bored. Everything we were to see later on at close quarters was now being shown to us from a distance, instead of allowing us time to admire the truly varied and charming views from the entrance. Alas it was impossible to stop the stream of his obviously prepared speech.

At long last we reached the point where the wearisome guide had to take his leave according to the rules of the house. He handed us over to a forester who accompanied us on horseback. At this point, in spite of the ducal livery the guide was wearing, he drew our attention to the real purpose behind his discourse, a good *pourboire*, and only left us when we had dealt with the matter satisfactorily. Fortunately his successor was less talkative and, riding next to us, spoke only when necessary.

The park is one of the most splendid in England. Gentle slopes and valleys alternate in delightful variety. All is covered with the finest grass and the whole scene enlivened by movements of many hundreds of deer. Several handsome stone bridges cross a canal which has been carefully laid out to give the illusion of a quietly winding stream. Temples and other buildings, the column with the statue of the great Marlborough, and many beautiful trees combine to give the place an indescribable charm. From all around there are different vistas of the house, the water and the bridges, all carefully planned yet modestly hiding the great art which must have gone into its conception. After we had admired everything thoroughly, and had incidentally settled with him, the forester handed us over to the gardener who took us round the gardens close to the house. These are laid out for promenading and are pretty but not nearly as fine as those at Stowe. Their graceful simplicity pleases, although we could not help but feel that they would better suit the smaller and less grand house while the magnificently rich gardens of Stowe might be more in keeping with the splendour of Blenheim. All is further enhanced by cascading waters, a quiet path wandering round a small lake, and the many fine old trees.

When, in the afternoon, we went to see the house, we were received by an elderly woman at the entrance to the second courtyard. At first we took her to be the housekeeper about to · show us the rooms as is the custom in England. She, in the manner of all English women of the lower classes, greeted us with a strange little curtsey, repeated at every word we addressed to her and then proceeded with much eloquence to guide us across the courtyard. At the house, again with innumerable curtsies, she took her leave of us, explaining that it was her duty to receive people of rank (the quality, she called it) with fitting respect and to see that they were conducted safely to the house. Laughing, we gave her a few shillings, assuring her that she had done her job admirably, and so both sides parted content.

2   *Contemporary fashion model with Blenheim behind*

The house is imposing by nature of its sheer size, but it is
heavy and rather mistakenly decorated, or perhaps spoilt, by a
great number of columns, vases, stairs, railings and towers.
The great hall through which one enters is high and spacious
and, like that at Stowe, lit from above. It has a fine painted
ceiling, supported on marble columns, while statues, some of
them of rare antiquity, are set around. The rest of the rooms
are of old-fashioned splendour, everything solid and precious
as one might expect here. French *Haute-lice* work covers the
walls of several rooms, all depicting the victories of the great
Duke, though, alas, the tapestries have faded badly.

There is a large collection of paintings: a Magdalen by Titian and a Holy Family by Leonardo da Vinci; two Marattis, representing beggar boys; a few portraits by van Dyck also lingered vaguely in our minds after the all too quick viewing. We were shown at least half a dozen Raphaels, on none of which the master had probably ever set eyes himself. There are excellent Dutch masters, several paintings by Rubens, cottage interiors, very real and full of life, by Ostade, Steen and others. We had to tear ourselves away from these closely guarded treasures. A large painting by Sir Joshua Reynolds represents the present Duke and his family, but the high quality of the neighbouring pictures and the poor presentation of the costumes in this particular work make it look rather inferior.

Another large lofty hall, also lit from above and very realistically painted by la Guerre, seems worth mentioning. The ceiling shows the Duke's triumphal progress halted by Time and Peace. The walls are painted in a *trompe-l'oeil* fashion to represent an open hall. All around it there are railings and behind them stand figures representing the nations of Europe, showing their characteristic physiognomy and costume. The figures are slightly more than life-size and astonishingly real, seeming to lean out from the railings.

The library, a long narrow room, is said to contain about 70,000 volumes. At the far end stands a marble statue of Queen Anne. She wears full court regalia, her long royal mantle draped over a dress which is stretched over a farthingale, narrow at the waist and widening out below. She wears the high collar of the period and with the crown on her head she looks like a large Christmas doll. The lace and embroidery have been admirably cut from the hard stone. In the library too there are many portraits, including the great Duke and his Sarah. She holds firmly onto her ducal coronet and surveys the world with a dazzling boldness.

In the chapel we were shown the large tomb which Lady Sarah had built, during her lifetime, for herself, her husband and their two children. The family is represented on it, life-size, together with a goodly retinue of Virtues and Muses. The tomb was made in London at great cost, and that is all we can say about it, as neither the idea nor the execution attracted us.

Weary of sightseeing and tired by much standing and walking through so many large rooms, we hurried back to the inn, giving a miss to a collection of old Japanese and Chinese porcelain which we were encouraged to look at as being very remarkable.

BIRMINGHAM AND SOHO

The next day we travelled towards Birmingham, by way of Ditchley, Lord Shrewsbury's estate, and by Heatherup with its beautiful pineapple house and flower gardens. With every mile the countryside grew more and more delightful, hills from where there were expansive views running down to the valleys so steeply that we had to use the brake on the carriage. In Birmingham itself we had to climb a very steep hill which reminded us vividly of the Hradschin in Prague, before we arrived at the large and elegant inn. It is still known as The Hen and Chicks although the landlord has taken pains in these more sophisticated days to change the name to Lloyd's Hotel.

Birmingham is known everywhere for its factories. One might even say that there is not a village in civilized Europe, perhaps not a house, where there cannot be found some industrial product made in that city, if only a button, a needle or a pencil. The hilly position of the town does not make it particularly beautiful. The smoke from its many factories and workshops gives it a gloomy and dirty appearance. Everywhere the sound of hammering and knocking is heard and during the day the population hurries about busily, no one having a second to spare during daylight hours. To make up for all this, the streets at night echo with the shouting and singing of those who have borne the burden of a hard-working life all day. In the few hours when they might benefit from soothing sleep, they stay awake to seize a little pleasure in the taverns and gambling houses, pleasures they are deprived of throughout the day.

Twenty-four hours after our arrival we went to visit the establishment of Mr Boulton, the most remarkable sight of the region, called Soho. In the whole of England, perhaps in the whole of Europe, there is no more striking proof of what can be achieved by industry, diligence and continuous endeavour, than this friendly little place. We were heartily delighted to meet its creator, Matthew Boulton, now eighty years old and still in possession of all his mental faculties even though his body has long since been defeated by illness, age and relentless work. We found him incapacitated by severe pain.

In the house he was carried by two sturdy servants, while out of doors he pushed himself about in a small comfortable carriage, invented in England to assist the lame and infirm who are so numerous there. His infirmity did not hinder him from showing us around personally, for we had been recommended to him by one of his friends. His dark eyes lit up with youthful fire when he told us how he had courageously fought and overcome the many difficulties he encountered. He explained and showed us everything in a most friendly manner. When we arrived at the ornamental grounds which he had created from a barren swamp with the help of the steam engine, his lively grandchildren rushed towards us, then yoked themselves to the little carriage and drew the happy old man along in triumph.

There is work in Soho every day for 800 people. English copper coins are minted here, also coins for the East India Company, for America and a number of foreign courts. There are rumours in Germany that Boulton also made the many counterfeits which flood Germany and originate in England, but this is not true. He has more legitimate work than he can actually cope with and is anyway too honest and too wealthy to become involved in such a dangerous trade. At one time the counterfeiting of foreign coins, if not actually permitted, was at least tolerated in England. These coins were considered to be substitute counters for gaming and were produced quite openly in great numbers, mostly on the orders of speculators in Germany and other countries. But since the gallows is now the reward for this kind of activity, just as it is the punishment for counterfeiting English bank notes and coins, the business is only carried on in great secrecy. It is said, however, that there are quite a few such places in Birmingham, parading as makers of buttons.

Apart from the mint, Soho has a large factory for plated goods of all kinds, a glassworks, and a factory for the making of steam engines. The amazing invention of this engine is specially valuable in a country as rich in coal as England. Its present excellence is due entirely to Boulton's continuous work and effort. He makes steam engines for the whole of Europe and America but does not allow anybody to look over the factory. The decision was forced upon him through people taking advantage of Boulton's hospitality for the sole purpose of stealing his ideas. He thought perhaps that we might have thought it ill-mannered of him to have put up a notice in every inn for miles around Birmingham, stating that no stranger could be shown over his establishment without recommendation. The constant stream of strangers wasted much of his or one of his associates' time and continually disturbed his workmen so that something had to be done, albeit unwillingly. 'Nothing is more unbearable', he said, 'than to own a house which has become a "raree-show" or even to have become one oneself. Both have been my fate, for everyone who saw round Soho, believed that, out of sheer courtesy, he should inspect the owner. So, in the end I had no alternative but to act in that unfriendly manner.'

The dwelling house in Soho is a large, comfortable building, well-kept and elegant. Nowhere is there any ostentation, any attempt to compete with the magnificent houses of the gentry. It stands in an agreeable position: from the front rooms one overlooks a rich scene. In the foreground lies the city with fertile, cultivated hills rising above it. Close to the house is a pretty garden full of flowers and shrubs while behind it runs a charming walk along the banks of a small lake, created by Boulton himself who, with the help of the steam engine, drained the old marshes and dammed the water here. In one corner a waterfall pours down from a hill planted with flowers and trees. Yet twenty years ago all this was a barren, swampy heath.

The factory making plated ware seemed to us specially interesting. It is impossible to see finer shapes and better finish than that given to the silver here. One cannot distinguish plate from pure silver with the naked eye, and as a result of the way they are made, plated articles will wear as well as pure silver.

On to a piece of copper two pieces of silver, only a tenth as thick as the copper, are soldered. Then, through rollers driven by a steam engine, this is made into sheet metal to the thickness required. All the time, silver and copper remain in the same proportion. This sheet metal is then used for the making of candlesticks, tea and coffee pots, jugs and other silverware with a largish surface. For the handles, feet and such things a rod of copper is covered with silver in the same way as we have described. Extrinsic parts of plated ware are often made of pure silver and applied separately, as are most decorations.

The glass-cutting works are equally remarkable. In a long room there are a great number of metal wheels, turning rapidly all the time. A long wooden cylinder, lying horizontally on the floor, is driven by a steam engine located in the room below, the steam power moving the sheets above. With apparent great ease and with admirable precision, not using a pattern, the workmen cut the most beautiful designs in the glass by holding it against the wheel which seems to be driven by magic. All kinds of candelabra, drinking glasses and vases for display, the most brilliant ornaments of many an elegant table, are made here. We were full of admiration when we saw them in the glassware shops of London, glittering at night like fairy castles. The glass is finished by using a wooden disc in place of a wheel.

On the day of our visit the mint was not working, but Mr Boulton had a few small coins specially minted to show us how the mechanism worked. Eight matrices are again driven by a steam engine, and every one of them mints thirty to 120 pieces per minute, according to their size, stamping both sides at the same time. Each mould is fitted with a very ingenious device which – like lighting – carries away the finished coin and injects a new blank one in its place. Everything seems to be operated by invisible spirits. The quality of the coins is good throughout and they are all perfectly round, of even size, and, as far as possible, of even value. There is another room where the metal is cut out before the coins are minted, and another where they are polished after minting. This is done by shaking them around in large linen bags, an operation controlled by a steam engine.

As a farewell we paid a visit to the steam engine itself. In a subterranean vault we saw a pump kept in permanent motion by the steam from a large, closed kettle, set below it in the wall, its water kept constantly on the boil. This pump drove several large wheels which connected with the machines in the upper rooms, thus creating all the wonders which had astonished us. That is as much as we were able to understand by merely looking at this marvellous invention. The water has to be kept boiling all the year round, so that the engine never stops, but Mr Boulton assured us that much less fuel is needed to do this than might appear at first sight.

BURTON AND DERBY

From Birmingham we travelled via Burton to Derby. Burton is a friendly little town, renowned all over the world for its ale which is brewed better here than anywhere else. In times of peace large supplies of it are sent every year to the whole of Europe, especially to Russia. Quantities are also shipped to America. In England ale is laid down for some years and when it has matured, is drunk in middle-class houses with the dessert. It is then equal in potency to any wine and has lost its beery taste altogether.

Although it is a fairly large town, Derby is not very beautiful. It has many factories, including a silk-spinning works. The most excellent, however, is the porcelain factory. In the fineness of clay, the local china is possibly inferior to that of Meissen and Sèvres, but the colour, gilding and beauty of the design of the vases and other vessels leaves nothing to be desired. The biscuit figures on the other hand are inferior to those from Saxony in inventiveness as well as execution. Once again it becomes obvious that the English artistic sense tends to produce best that which is useful and comfortable, and does this to the highest perfection.

For the first time in England we had to wait for our horses. At last, at six o'clock in the evening two appeared, tired after the day's hard work. We planned to leave for Matlock, a spa in the Derbyshire hills, 17 miles away. In England a 17-mile-journey is usually made in two to three hours and so we decided to leave, ignoring the heavy rain which would have kept us indoors anyway. The horses were very tired and all the postilion's urging could hardly get them to move. Very slowly they proceeded, step by step, making us feel as though we were on a post road in the Mark Brandenburg. We really feared that in the end the poor beasts might stop altogether from sheer exhaustion. The rain grew heavier as night fell, dark and gloomy, even though we were in the first half of June. The road was very hilly and high rocks rose in front of us, their huge outlines vaguely visible in the dark. Everywhere the fires from the brick works blazed, hovering in the night air like fiery spectres and making the darkness more evident without actually lighting it up. At times the fires made the horses shy as we travelled up and down steep hills, with the roaring of the torrents reminding us of the precipices by the roadside. The noise of many mills, of all the water-wheels in this area of factories, together with the rushing of the waters, the wind, the rain, the blazing lime kilns, all this combined to make the night a truly frightening one.

Undoubtedly the situation had about it a certain romance, yet we were delighted when after eleven o'clock we reached the end of the journey. In the old spa of Matlock we found all the comfort we had come to associate with the English inn, and our adventurous and tiring journey made us all the more appreciative.

SPAS

England abounds in spas of all kinds; in fact any place by the sea, where the beach and surroundings permit, boasts of some sort of bathing establishment. These spas attract a varied public, according to the dictates of fashion. Society escapes to the bathing places or mineral springs, that is to say, everyone who has not got his own house in the country or has not been invited to one, but still wants to avoid the shame of being seen in London during the summer.

It is well known that London is considered to be empty at that season, even though the streets are crowded with people, and no stranger would ever notice the emptiness. People seen in London from the beginning of July until about Christmas are 'Nobodies', they do not count. Elegant society, the leisured, the wealthy and the fortune hunters, all escape to the country or to a spa. Sea-bathing establishments are on the whole the most popular and best equipped. Mineral springs are preferred by the middle class who tend to look for rural pleasures rather than extravagant entertainment. Bath is an exception: during the summer it is visited by the genuinely sick, the lame and those afflicted with gout, all of whom hope to benefit from the hot springs. The true season, however, begins in December, and lasts until the spring. All the pleasures of London, if on a slightly reduced scale, may be enjoyed more cheaply there. Hence those who wish to live elegantly but are not rich enough to do so in London, flock to Bath. Many great families take to spending winters here and are able by such economy to stabilize their precarious finances.

The spa at Bristol, on the other hand, is not a place for the pleasure-seeker but is frequented by those in need of real help, even though the beautiful surroundings do provide pleasure. It is well known that every year a great number of people fall victim to tuberculosis in England, and doctors, as a last resort, usually recommend the springs at Bristol. Many of the monuments in the local cemetery bear witness to this.

In all spas the daily routine differs widely: at the small ones, such as Matlock, one lives quietly and peacefully, with social etiquette being more relaxed than is usual in England among strangers, yet more strict than in similar circumstances in Germany. In the larger spas which are visited by the upper classes, a strict and rather strange etiquette is enforced, something we hope to discuss at length later. Meanwhile we proceeded to Matlock and its surroundings.

MATLOCK AND KEDDLESTON

This lovely valley, friendly yet vast, lonely yet full of life, is one of the most beautiful in Britain. It may be that Matlock's springs are not very effective, but this is not necessary to the finding of new energy and vitality in this heavenly place. The fifty or sixty visitors we came across certainly did not look as if Asclepius had spirited them here by a wave of his serpent wand. They seemed rather to have fled from the rush of life to find peace, breathe freely, and return refreshed to the daily round.

The actual spa consists of three large inns and two lodging-houses, with the village of Matlock about a mile and a half away. It is impossible to describe the charm of this valley in mere words: it is so peaceful, so intimate, with the Derwent flowing through it, surrounded by high cliffs which stand rugged and bare against the sky, yet usually looking friendly, as their summits are crowned with beautiful trees.

We took a boat on the Derwent as far as it is navigable, which is only a short stretch. After that it becomes a wild torrent, full of rapids and whirlpools. As we sailed along, the cliff walls seemed to draw in upon us as if trying to block our way altogether. Trees on the banks became arches over our boat while the cliffs stood threateningly above us. Then these rocks would recede, revealing friendly cottages perched high on the banks, surrounded by little gardens and meadows, with handsome houses and factory buildings below. Simple paths, which nature herself seemed to have laid out, ran along both banks between the woods and rocks right up to our inn.

Opposite us was the highest cliff in the neighbourhood, which the local people call the High Tor. We climbed it easily, up a shaded path, and from the top we could see on one side the narrow valley in all the glory of its rich vegetation, with the river running through the centre. On the wooded rocks opposite were the fine buildings of the spa, providing a friendly picture of pleasant social life in this otherwise rather lonely scene. On the other side we saw a second valley, looking as if no human foot had ever trod there, so remote and silent was it, enclosed by green hills. Flocks of sheep, with no shepherd, grazed in the high grass. Nowhere else had we seen the wild, simple beauty of nature more happily combined with civilization than here on the banks of the Derwent.

The pleasure for the spa visitor derives mainly from his enjoyment of the natural surroundings, for all that man has dared to contribute in competition are a bowling green and a few billiard tables. Dancing is rare and can only be arranged at the special request of the visitors, as the local innkeepers show little enterprise in this direction. The waters are honoured by being called hot, though we found them no more than tepid. They taste well and are clear, while the bathing establishments are comfortable and clean, something one has come to expect in this country.

Matlock is of special interest to the geologist, owing to the many different kinds of stone, fluorite and pieces of stalactites found in Derbyshire. These are available in great variety in two elegant shops in Matlock where fine examples can be bought or merely inspected in their natural state by the connoisseur and collector. They are also used to make fireplaces, urns, vases, inkwells and many other things. These artifacts are sold here at low prices, beautifully finished and of good design. Alas, as they are so fragile, it was difficult to take them with us on a long journey.

Another remarkable thing here is a petrifying well. Anything put into the water incrustates in a short time, and if it is left lying in the water becomes completely calcified. The keeper of the well showed us a wig and an ordinary broom which had been rendered immortal in that way. Both looked most strange in their new state.

Beyond the Derwent and diagonally opposite the village lies Cromford Hill, the cotton-spinning mill belonging to Sir Richard Arkwright, the inventor of the spinning machine, the mechanism of which borders on the miraculous. It was the first ever to be built. This man, remarkable both for his mechanical skills and his persevering courage, started life as a barber. His enterprise encountered many difficulties to which an ordinary man would have succumbed. He well deserved the powerful friends who stood by him, and in the end his great undertaking succeeded, and he lived long enough to enjoy the material comforts of his success. Up to this day his mill, which now boasts three spinning machines, belongs to the Arkwright family and they live in the fine house of Wellersly nearby. This house, solidly built of white stone, and the large factory on the banks of the river, guarded by high cliffs, both help to enhance the scene. What is even more delightful to see is the prosperity of the people in the valley, brought about by Arkwright's enterprise. We saw with great joy on a Sunday night the neatly turned-out workers with their smartly dressed wives and sweethearts, strolling around in the company of their pretty children.

The English country-girls and young women are generally fine figures, though with age they tend to grow fat. In their finery they manage to look genteel and ladylike. A pretty straw hat decorated with coloured ribbons over a small snow-white cap, fits their bonny, modest faces well. With this they wear large white kerchiefs, a quilted skirt of a light colour, sky-blue or rose-pink for the elegant ones, and a long cotton dress, cut low in front. At the back the dress is carefully hooked up and the whole is immaculately clean down to the fine, white, woven stockings. This is their Sunday dress, from which the everyday one differs only by being of a darker colour and cheaper material.

Large, well laid-out paths for promenading stretch up the hill behind Wellersly House, giving varied views of the valley below. In the gardens are hothouses and a pretty orangery, and everywhere the results of diligence and industry are evident.

As the weather had greatly improved, we decided we should see something of what we had missed during that dark and stormy night of our arrival, and went back on the road to Derby, to see Lord Scarsdale's residence, Keddleston. The large park surrounding this house is excellent both as to position and the way art has improved nature without being too obtrusive. A stream gives the grounds special charm, and nowhere in England did we find greener lawns, more splendid flocks, horses and deer. They grazed together happily in groups under magnificent oaks and beeches, reflected in the stream, just in front of the house. It stands on a slight incline and consists of a main building and two pavilions, connected to it by galleries. Fine Corinthian columns embellish the entrance while the stairs are remarkable for their very broad steps. The walls and the floors of the fine entrance hall, lit by a cupola, and the columns surrounding it are all made of Derbyshire marble.

We did not much admire the collection of antique figures as they had all been treated with white paint to make them look like marble. There was beautiful silverware in the dining-room and many of the large paintings, depicting all kinds of food and drink, with which the English like to surround themselves, even though connoisseurs might not think much of them.

The large library was unremarkable but we admired a picture by Rembrandt and a few other interesting ones. Alas, the catalogue was so full of mistakes that it was impossible to identify them properly. At the end of the gallery the guide opened a door which allowed a view of the well-equipped kitchen. Above the hearth we saw the most appropriate inscription: 'Waste not, want not.'

Not far from Keddleston a spring had been discovered, said to have healing powers, and Lord Scarsdale built a large inn there, where visitors could find all their comforts. Due to its closeness to Matlock, however, the project was not very successful.

Early one morning we reluctantly left friendly Matlock. For quite a while the road ran through the valley by the banks of the Derwent, sometimes flowing quietly, sometimes gushing wildly across boulders. In due course the road wound its way up into high hills from whose summits we had a wide view over the countryside, with its many houses and factories. As the road began to descend again, we saw before us a magnificent building, glittering in the morning sun. It was Chatsworth, for 200 years seat of the noble family of Cavendish, and now that of their descendants, the Dukes of Devonshire. The house stands in a romantic valley with a high cliff behind it. In front of it, the silver Derwent winds its way through the smiling greenery, spanned by a very fine stone bridge. As we drove through the park, its inhabitants, stags and roedeer, examined our coach with great curiosity.

CHATSWORTH

Residence of the Duke of Devonshire

With a frontage of 182 feet, this house, build in the grand style, is one of the finest and most splendid in all England. Nowhere had we seen window-frames thickly gilded on the outside. They glittered in the sunlight and gave the whole building a marvellous fairy-tale appearance. This splendour is far removed from the quiet solitude of the surrounding countryside. It seemed as if some magician had put the house down in this spot for a purpose. And, indeed, it once had a special and sad purpose. It was here that Mary Stuart, for sixteen long years, suffered her loss of freedom, deprived of all life's happiness. Her cruel enemy sent her first to Chatsworth as a closely guarded prisoner, and after sixteen years transferred her to Fotheringhay in Northamptonshire, where she died on the scaffold.

The interior of Chatsworth has little of great interest. Not visited by its owners for many years, the house now shows only traces of its ancient splendour and is, alas, slowly decaying. However it is on the whole well maintained, but as nothing new is ever added, it lacks freshness, that very freshness which makes other English country houses so very attractive. On the second floor of the oldest part of the house is the room of the unhappy Mary Stuart, arranged and furnished exactly as it was when she lived there. It is large and high with old tapestries on the walls which give it an appearance of gloom and sadness. A high prie-dieu stands near the window from where the view is not very cheering, looking onto a beautiful but very desolate scene, shut in by hills. The room is furnished with high chairs and oak and walnut tables, all very heavy, reminding us of those dark days which this beautiful and unhappy woman spent here. Her bed with its red velvet curtains, trimmed with silver lace, stands in its old place and one can almost feel the many lonely tears she must have shed there.

The gardens at Chatsworth are very old and are laid out in a style alien to our day. One might call it 'old French', were its design more regular. It is possible that it had been so at one time, for it is obvious that the many ornamental beds, walks, arbours and so on have fallen into decay. What makes the gardens famous all over the country are its fountains. Although these cannot be compared to St Cloud, Herrenhausen or Wilhelmshöhe near Kassel, their fame rests on the fact that they are unique in this country.

We were first confronted with a huge artificial cascade, 200–300 feet high, graduated in a series of basins over which the water descended, although, alas, as is usual, not in sufficient quantity. In one of them the water shot upwards in

3 Chatsworth, Derbyshire

the shape of a bell. Next to it stood a tree, appearing at first sight to be withered, but on closer inspection we saw that it was in fact made of copper. Water spurted from its branches, giving it the pleasing appearance of being covered with snow and icicles, while all around it little jets played. Two other fountains threw jets some 90 feet upwards to the sky, a pretty and spectacular sight. English people staying in the nearby spas, all make a pilgrimage here to marvel at something they have never seen before, and so consider Chatsworth one of the wonders of the world.

CASTLETON

As we left sad but beautiful Chatsworth, we were still much under the influence of Mary's fate and felt quite proud that in his play *Maria Stuart* our own poet, Friedrich Schiller, had paid homage to her, long before anybody did publicly in Britain. After travelling for a short while, the lonely yet rich scenery disappeared, and we came into a narrow, somewhat forbidding-looking valley. There was no tree, no trace of vegetation, only steep, bare rocks, as we wound our way wearily while it seemed that at any moment these rocks might bar our path completely. At first we saw here and there handsome factory buildings of considerable size. Then they too disappeared, and we travelled through the saddest, most desolate and inhospitable region of England, the lead mines of Derbyshire. There were a great many of them and in between them the poorest cottages, roughly put together of natural stone, where pale figures moved slowly about. They were the inhabitants of this desert, debilitated by the terrible work in those mines.

At noon we arrived in Castleton, a very poor little place, the like of which we had not seen in England. We ordered our lunch in the miserable-looking inn and then hurried to the Peak Cave, taking with us a guide who had seized upon us the moment we stepped off the coach.

4   Dove Dale, Derbyshire

THE PEAK CAVE

This famous cave is only a short distance away. At the entrance, a row of vertical cliffs, their summits crowned with trees, rises in a series of strange and rugged shapes. In one of the rocks nature has created a mysterious opening, 240 feet high and 120 feet wide, through which we seemed to look into impenetrable darkness. Out of the nether regions flows a broad black stream. Huge, fantastically-shaped stalactites hang from the cave's entrance, which is surrounded by a maze of bushes and wreathed in tendrils of ivy. Above us were perched lumps of rock, so precariously that they seemed to threaten certain disaster for the over-inquisitive, who might be too anxious to penetrate the secrets of the depths below.

Once inside the cave, the black night changed to dusk as our eyes grew accustomed to the gloom. We could soon distinguish the figures of women and children, cowering like gnomes, busily spinning. These creatures, as miserable as the imagination can conceive, live out their wretched existence in this cold damp darkness, sleeping at night in little wooden huts which they have built inside the cave. As soon as they became aware of us, they surrounded us, begging noisily, so that we were glad we had followed the advice of our landlady in Castleton and taken a good number of coppers with which to pay our ransom. This is the subterranean town of travellers' tales. The warmth provided by the cavern in winter, making a proper house unnecessary, the pennies they can extract from curious visitors and above all the freedom from having to pay those taxes which are levied in the daylight regions above, these are the factors that make the poor souls choose this unfriendly place as their abode.

As soon as we were able to free ourselves from their turbulent entreating, we bought some lights. As we proceeded into the deep gloom at the back of the cavern, we each had to carry one, while the guide, walking before us, carried two. He drew our attention to some of the enormous stalactites, likening them to this or that, although we confess we could find no resemblance to the things he mentioned. Then

suddenly he opened a small low door and we found ourselves
in a huge cavern from whose ceiling hung great lumps of rock,
seemingly poised even more threateningly above our heads
than before. The glimmer of our flickering lights made them
the more frightening, as they appeared to be moving.

The cave now became quite low. Bent over and unsure of
our steps on the slippery, uneven ground, we had to wind our
way for some time through a narrow passage in the rock.
Surrounded on all sides by projecting stone, sometimes we
mounted steeply, then we quickly descended again. Here and
there we could see a lonely light, making the darkness of the
grave seem even darker.

The air was heavy, almost clammy, and seemed to resist our
intrusion. When at long last we could raise our heads, we had
entered a further small cavern and found ourselves on the bank
of a subterranean water which here, like the Styx, flows cold
and silent through the eternal night, its waves rolling slowly
along. There we found a boat, filled with straw, with just
enough room for two people to lie stretched out, side by side.
We lay on the straw, hardly daring to breathe, as the guide
waded into the water, almost up to his hips, and began to push
the boat along in front of him. We moved under rocks,
scarcely a hand's breadth away from our heads and appearing
to be about to break off at any moment. On the other side
there was not an inch between us and the bank. Never had the
impression of being buried alive seemed clearer to us than in
this coffin-like little boat with the black roof of rock looming
over us. Our guide had to wade along, stooping; one knock
against the rock above would have rendered him unconscious
and we should have found ourselves alone in the most horrible
situation. With these sobering thoughts in our minds, we
moved on, light in hand, until we were eventually able to land.
When at long last we stepped from our coffin, dizzy as a result
of our voyage, it took us a little time to recover. Eventually we
were able to look about us and what we saw made us feel even
more unsteady. Under an enormous dome, according to the
guide 120 feet high, 270 feet long and 210 feet wide, a mass of
scattered lights sparkled like stars. This is the temple of eternal
silence into which no gleam of the sunny upper regions has

ever penetrated, nor the sounds of joy been heard. In this vast cavern we felt even more uneasy than in the small narrow ones for we could more keenly sense how far we were from the living world from which we were now separated.

Wearily we climbed across rough, broken pieces of rock and returned to the water. As we stood still, we seemed to hear the sound of distant music. Our guide again waded into the water and now carried us, one at a time, for quite a distance on his shoulders to a small, round hollow where the water dripped constantly on all sides, called Rodger's Rain House. We found that this continuous dripping of water was the origin of the sounds which, from a distance, we had taken to be music. The floor here was covered with thousands of strange shapes, little stalagmites, which made walking extremely difficult, especially as the constant moisture left the ground slippery. We hurried along as best we could, though the air was even more unpleasant, cold and damp, until at last we reached a higher, vaulted part of the cave where a surprise awaited us. We were greeted by a male choir, slowly and monotonously singing. Holding lights in their hands and waving them about, they stood 50 feet above us in a kind of niche which nature had made in one of the walls. Their singing was simple, consisting of only a few notes, wild and plaintive, yet not unpleasant.

After this strange reception, we crept on our way, bent over, moving anxiously under and across the rock masses to another small cave, even more frightening and gruesome than any of the others, with a black pit yawning at our feet beneath the flicker of our lights. The guide pointed to where the deep and awful footpath led down across the slippery stalagmites. 'This is the Devil's Cellar', he said, suddenly seizing one of us by the arm. 'I am the master here,' he continued with a nasty laugh. 'Here I can do what I please; I wish I had Napoleon here!' It is no use denying that we were frightened, for it was only too clear that here he was indeed the master, and we had long since noticed that he had taken us to be French. However, we soon collected ourselves and told him that we did not grudge him his wish but reminded him that Napoleon always moved in large company. Our own companions, who, as he was bound to know, had stayed outside, would certainly make careful investigations should some misfortune befall us here. This argument made its point with him and he grew somewhat more courteous. Our alarm at the guide's strange behaviour would have been much greater, had we known at the time what we heard later, that several years earlier a lady and gentleman arrived at the cave in a 'whisky', drawn by a single horse and unaccompanied. They fastened the horse outside, went into the cave and were never seen again.

Our guide now held his light over the abyss in front of us. Few visitors dare to take the steep path which leads down a further 150 feet. They let the guide go down carrying the lights and are content to view the awesome sight from above. We did the same. In the flickering light we saw a series of arched cavities and tall columns, formed by the hand of nature, with the water splashing even more noisily in these great depths. Down there the waters were crystal clear, the guide told us. At last he climbed up again and we started on our way back. A distant glint of daylight which our eyes, now accustomed to darkness, discerned in the second cave, filled our hearts with great joy.

We had spent two hours in this world of night and eternal silence. Now, as we stepped into the comforting light of the sun, as the mild caressing summer air, warm and life-giving, welcomed us, we felt as if we had wakened from a nightmare. Everything around us, the whole countryside in its wild splendour, appeared to be steeped in heavenly brightness. And with the poet Schiller we exclaimed:

> How happy are they, who live in the light of day,
> For the nether regions are dark and gruesome.
> Man should not go counter to the will of the gods
> Or strive to see what they have shrouded in grey night.

We continued on our way to Buxton, a spa where we were to spend the night. However we found it worth our while to linger a little on our way and to admire the wide panorama to be seen from the top of the hill behind Castleton, a fertile, cultivated valley surrounded by strangely-shaped, cliff-like hills. One of these is called Win Hill and the other Lose Hill, as a result of a battle said to have been fought here long ago. But the most remarkable of them all is called Mam Tor, also known, not without good reason, as Shivering Hill. It is said that its surface is crumbling away without its ever decreasing in size. It is named Shivering Hill because, seen from the distance, the rippling of its sandy surface really does make it appear to be shivering. The truth is, however, that through the years the harsh elements have caused fragments of its slopes, which are rugged and steep, to loosen and careful observation has shown that it is in fact actually shrinking. The local people none the less prefer to maintain their belief in the legend and count it among the seven wonders of the Peak District. After pausing here a while, we then proceeded on our way across the bare rocky heaths to Buxton, which we reached in good time before dark.

BUXTON

Buxton is another spa but very different from magically pretty Matlock. Surrounded by bare rocks, it lies in a basin, with the countryside around it wild and sad. The well-known site of the Pool's Cave is a mile away from the town, but we were assured that after seeing Castleton's cave it was hardly worth looking at and, moreover, it was even more difficult to visit. It did not take much to discourage us from this particular enterprise. From an insignificant village, Buxton has become quite a popular place due to its hot spring which was known as early as Roman times. The waters are lukewarm, taste quite pleasant and are used for both drinking and bathing in the treatment of gout, scurvy and many other ills.

The daily routine here is simple and boring. The mornings are spent promenading in the Crescent, a row of fine houses built in a semi-circle. They contain pleasant lodgings for spa visitors and a few elegant inns which provide rooms for balls and assemblies. The whole crescent has the appearance of one single fine building with more than three hundred windows in its façade. The ground floors contain elegant shops, some lending libraries where according to English custom one takes a rest after the promenade and a few coffee shops, while a covered columned walk protects the strollers from the rain which is so common here. The pump-room and baths are nearby. After the morning's promenade the rest of the day is taken up with carriage drives or horse riding, even though the countryside is not very enticing.

Shooting is the gentlemen's chief entertainment. Patrons of the sport may hire a leash of gun dogs, kept specially for the purpose. Game is very scarce in England but in this wilderness there are some hares and foxes, with wild duck and other water fowl abounding on the nearby marshy stretches of the river Wye. In the evenings, there may be a ball or a card party while a play is performed three times a week in a barn, pleasantly fitted for the purpose.

Buxton's most remarkable sight is the set of magnificent stables built by the Duke of Devonshire, said to be the finest and most perfect of their kind in Europe, and, as far as we know, they may well deserve that fame. Built in a circle, they are surrounded by a colonnade where, as is the custom in England, the horses are protected from the wind and rain and can be taken care of and groomed throughout the day. In the centre of this is a beautiful and commodious riding school. There are also coach-houses, and the whole is of considerable size, almost suggesting that the four-footed spa guests are of prime importance here. A small stream running alongside makes it easy to keep these magnificent stables clean, so doing away with any unpleasant smells.

To us the most interesting thing in Buxton was a window-pane in the oldest lodging-house, where Mary Stuart stayed on her ill-fated journey from Scotland. With prophetic perception she had scratched on the pane:

> Buxton! whose fame thy baths shall ever tell;
> which I perhaps shall see no more, farewell!

MANCHESTER

We left Buxton in the early morning and reached this large and famous manufacturing city about noon. Dark with the smoke from the coal fires, it looks like a huge forge or workshop. Its people seem to be entirely concerned with work, profit and even greed. Everywhere the rattling of the looms of the cotton mills can be heard, and every man one encounters seems to be concerned with figures, nothing but figures.

The busy community inhabiting the city does not have much time to think of the joys or pleasures of life, even though some measures are taken to provide it. There is a theatre and an assembly room where during the winter subscribers meet for a game of cards and an occasional dance. And so that the good Lord should have his fair share, a modern temple-like church was recently built for Him – but it has turned out a rather clumsy piece of work.

On the whole, the spirit of conviviality is foreign to Manchester, as it is to other industrial cities. The men relax from their hard work with a bottle in the taverns while the women remain among themselves. Just how amusing a circle entirely composed of Englishwomen could be, we preferred to leave to the imagination rather than experience it ourselves.

The countryside around Manchester is not particularly inviting. The main public walk of the city resembles somewhat a botanical garden which would not be unpleasing, did it not pass all the time close to hospitals and lunatic asylums, with the result that one constantly hears the screaming and babbling of the poor mad folk. Far worse, from time to time one is treated to their being forcibly plunged into the water flowing past the asylum, possibly as part of their cure. While this is certainly not very pleasant, the citizens seem to have got used to these sights and do not allow such trifles to spoil their promenade.

We paid a visit to one of the largest cotton mills. A steam engine, placed in the basement, activated the many wheels and spindles in various storeys above. We felt quite dizzy in the vast halls, watching the movements of so many mechanical devices. In each room we saw women in readiness to re-fasten a thread on the constantly turning spindles on the rare occasion when it breaks. Children were busy winding the spun yarn onto reels. In another large place the unspun cotton was cleaned, spread out on tables in big square cotton-wool-like pieces, while a goodly number of women and girls armed with thin sticks in each hand, beat the stuff furiously. In yet another hall the

5 *New Jerusalem Church, Manchester*

cotton was driven through a machine, not unlike an immense comb. It now had the appearance of a very thin continuous tissue. Then in another room it was spun into a loose thread, some two fingers thick, and afterwards continued through many rooms, becoming thinner and thinner until it ended up as fine as a single hair.

All this was carried out with the greatest ease by the machines and every one of these seemed to be a miracle of industrial invention. We saw, for example, a special contrivance for the twisting and packing of the finished yarn. After being wound onto a bobbin the yarn was hung on another contraption, like a Roman balance, which showed by an indicator the number of degrees of fineness of the yarn. Every operation in the factory, down to the smallest detail, was performed with admirable precision, neatness and lightning speed. In the end it seemed to us as if the wheels were the living beings and the people working with them mere machines.

Stunned by all the wonders we had seen, we left the mill and got into the carriage which was to take us to another miracle, the aqueduct built by the Duke of Bridgewater. This gentleman did a great service to his homeland and particularly Manchester by constructing a network of canals facilitating the transport of goods around the area by water. Equally praiseworthy are the improvements in the workings of the nearby coal-mines which are the very heart of industrial life here. The sight of the aqueduct which is the Duke's greatest triumph, an enterprise worthy of comparison with Roman times, was truly marvellous to behold. Above us a coal-barge moved as if floating through the air, while down below it another travelled in the opposite direction. By great good luck this spectacle coincided with the moment of our arrival. A navigable river flows between high banks, while above it a canal runs transversely. Crossing the river in a straight line is a bridge resting on three immense arches. This bridge, made watertight God knows how, contains the canal in a bed which is deep enough to carry small and large craft. On both sides of this canal runs a footpath and strolling along it, unless one looks down, one appears to be on terra firma, not aloft on a bridge.

We then made our way to the nearby coal-mines. The waters, which usually gather in the mines and give much trouble to the miners, have here by the Duke's efforts been tamed into a navigable canal, extending for miles underground and deep enough for fairly large boats. The wide underground canal branches out in several directions and is at times broad enough for two boats to pass in opposite directions. The ceiling above the canal is not very high, being partly man-made and partly cut from the natural rock. When the water reaches the open air, it joins the other canals criss-crossing the country.

The entrance to this subterranean world is imposing: a large gate cut into a steep, vertical, majestically high rock. We stepped into a long narrow boat, normally used for transporting coal. Boards and cushions were used to provide reasonably comfortable seating for us. Candles in small holders had been placed on the edges and inside the boat, and supplied light as we sailed along the black, silent waters. Our guide was exceedingly talkative and we soon perceived that he had taken adequate liquid precaution against the cold subterranean air. But there was no need to feel any threat here. Holding forth without pause, he slowly propelled us along, from time to time using the vaulted roof to push himself forward. After quarter of an hour all trace of the golden daylight had disappeared and the world around us was cold, gloomy and dismal.

At the first mine we climbed out of the boat at a spot where vaulted walkways ran in several directions. They were so low that one could only crawl through them with difficulty, bent double. The coal was right at the surface here and was broken off with a pick by half-naked men, now kneeling, now lying on their backs. The work seemed extremely fatiguing to us and not without danger. Indeed many lose their lives in the mines, for poisonous vapours can arise suddenly and suffocate the miner, or these gases may ignite on coming into touch with his lantern. They could then burn him to death unless he lies with his face to the ground, the moment he becomes aware that the lantern flame is turning blue. A second's delay and it would be too late.

After each of us had cut a piece of coal to take with us as a souvenir, we felt no further desire to penetrate deeper into the earth. We returned quickly to our glowing boat and even more glowing guide, anxious to see again the light of the sun.

On the way back to Manchester we stopped at a pencil factory, standing on its own. The owners did not seem very happy to see us, but at the recommendation of our companion from Manchester, they allowed us to watch the whole manufacturing process. One man planed little pieces of cedarwood until they were smooth, another one then cut them into strips, the length of a pencil, and with a special instrument made a groove to take the lead which a third man then inserted. Before this they were immersed in some blackish liquid and after being put into the groove, they were trimmed to the correct length with a sharp knife. Finally the four-edged pencil was rounded on a machine, all this being done at lightning speed and very interesting to watch.

LEEDS

Next morning we continued our journey to Leeds in Yorkshire. The first half of the way was depressing as we drove through country where the steep rocks seemed to rise as high as heaven itself. How wrong people on the Continent are when they picture the whole of England as a beautiful, fertile, garden-like country. Everything around us was barren, uncultivated, without a trace of vegetation. Just as on Westphalia's bare heaths, which we know, the seasons here must pass almost unnoticed by the inhabitants, for they do not bring their changing gifts which so delight happier regions. As we proceeded we found no tree, no cornfield, no country garden, nothing but lead- and coal-mines everywhere, quarries, smelting furnaces, brickworks, and here and there a spinning mill or other factory.

The air was dark and thick with coal smoke. Wherever we went we saw the poor man working to make the rich man even richer, while he himself just laboured and scraped a bare living. It is a wonderful picture of human diligence but alas not seen from a very pleasing angle. How happy, on the other hand, is the sight of the hale and hearty countryman who, by the sweat of his brow, earns his daily bread from the good earth which he enhances by his labour. Sad is the sight of the pale and dirty miner who has to burrow like a mole deep into the earth, and then does not live beyond a few working years. A deep feeling of pity overcame us at the sight of it all, a feeling we experienced often and long on many occasions.

Near Wakefield the scene became more friendly and rural. We thought of the good Vicar, whom we all know from Goldsmith's homely novel, and we tried in vain to find his village and his hospitable house. Wakefield is a small town and full of factories.

Towards evening we reached Leeds, a fairly large city consisting mainly of textile works. Our arrival there found us witnessing a very sad and heart-breaking scene. To our amazement we beheld the man at the turnpike close to the city, crying bitterly. His wife stood beside him, showing signs of great distress, while two very small girls looked on silently, puzzled at their parents' behaviour. 'What's wrong with you, good people?' we asked, full of pity. 'Our only son has just been drowned', the man answered in a choking voice. Then, unable to contain her distress any longer, the distraught mother, wringing her hands, burst out: 'Oh, he was the most beautiful boy in the world; just fourteen years old, always obedient and diligent. At four o'clock today he came home from school, happy, with a good report, and now . . . ' We drove on, our hearts heavy and our eyes moist – helpless – for what stranger would dare to offer comfort in such dire sadness.

It is in fact remarkable that more children in England do not suffer accidents. Nowhere does the old pious belief, that each one of us has his guardian angel, count for more than here. Everywhere one finds children without any obvious super-vision: in towns and villages, even on the busiest streets, small babies, scarcely two years old, crawl about among the crowds, quite fearless, often almost under the horses and the carriage wheels, while the traveller, peering anxiously from his quickly moving vehicle, feels a sense of anger towards all those seemingly uncaring mothers.

Most of the citizens of Leeds are engaged in the textile industry. They have their own Trades Hall where everyone has his own place with his name on it and on market days he puts his wares out there for sale. This Hall is a large covered building, constructed round a spacious courtyard and is not unlike a stock exchange.

Leeds produces beautiful carpets on ordinary looms. It was most interesting to watch the richly-coloured flowers and patterns take shape so rapidly before our very eyes. To make the wider carpets for large rooms, two people work on a loom together, whereas the narrower ones for stairs and entrance halls are woven by a single person.

STUDLEY PARK, FOUNTAINS ABBEY AND HACKFALL

We set out from Leeds by a route which took us to Harewood House and the spa of Harrogate. The latter is composed of two small villages for the accommodation of visitors to the spa which, although small, is complete with a Master of Ceremonies and the usual entertainments to be found in such places.

We paused for a little in Ripon, a clean and friendly town, lying in a mountainous but pleasant region. It is a borough and has the right at every parliamentary election to vote for a member and send him to London. It so happens that every house in Ripon belongs to an immensely rich old lady of eighty, the owner of Studley Park, Hackfall, and several other estates in this fertile part of Yorkshire. She alone, as the only property owner in Ripon, elects the member and so her importance in the district, and indeed in the whole kingdom is great. After her death, which may well have occurred since our visit, a certain Miss Lawrence will inherit her wealth and privileges. This lady, though well past her first youth, is, as one might expect, surrounded by admirers and suitors, just as Penelope of old, but she resists them all and loudly declares that she will never marry any of them, as none courted her before she became a wealthy heiress on the recent and unexpected death of her brother. Miss Lawrence, by the way, was described to us as a very good lady and of pleasing appearance.

We drove to Studley Park nearby but the house did not seem to contain anything especially worth seeing, although its extensive walks are considered among the finest in England. The park has a rather stern appearance, perhaps because there are few open sunny spaces or green lawns. Its attraction lies in the shady walks beneath the very tall beech trees and oaks, the wooded gentle slopes and sweet-scented glades. We strolled here with great pleasure, quite unaware of the surprise in store for us. Our guide, a venerable grey-haired old gardener, suddenly opened a small door, hardly visible in a wall and before us, in the midst of a delightful vale, stood the most beautiful Gothic ruins we had ever seen. Rosy in the morning sun, they lay there in solemn splendour, the remains of Fountains Abbey, a monastery built in the twelfth century but in ruins for the last 250 years. The vast size of the building is still evident, although the roof has gone and most of the walls. What remains is a number of richly decorated columns, part of the former nave of the church, now looking like ghostly mourners at the burial of the glorious past. This glory is also reflected in the stout vaults and arched windows which still survive. A few old stone coffins lie there, exposed to the sun. The location of the former high altar can be clearly seen, also that of the cloisters, the refectory and the assembly room. Subterranean corridors and vaults have been preserved and the kitchen can easily be recognized by its smoke-blackened wall where the hearth had been.

The Abbey remains a graveyard of times past but nature lives on. Abundant ivy trails itself around the crumbling columns, clothing them in the green promise of new life. Flowers and shrubs stretch their stems and branches from high windows and the capitals of pillars. In the church itself one walks in the shadow of full-grown trees. Everywhere new life is springing up among the ruins, evidence of the transience of man's work, and indeed his life, while nature constantly creates and acknowledges no bounds.

These ruins form a wonderful ornament in the park, making all else seem paltry in comparison, even the endeavours of princes who would create artificially such wonders on their estates. It is true that the last owner of Studley Park bought the ruins for a considerable sum, but as a result he gave his property something grand and unique, at the same time saving those sacred remains if not from slow decay through the ravages of time, at least from the wanton destruction which threatens all things beautiful.

From Studley Park we proceeded to Hackfall. Up to now we had always found looking at parklands a very cheering pastime, each being an occasion we would remember with pleasure for years to come. Here, however, we were overcome by despair, the despair of the traveller who can only glimpse beauty fleetingly and then pass on, carrying the picture in his mind. We should have liked to stay here for ever. How lovely it would be to live permanently in this secret valley lying, green and flowering, amidst wooded cliffs. Walks abounded, now taking one to dizzy heights, now down into the gentle shade of the hills. Far below a crystal-clear river glittered, while rivulets gushed from the rocks around it, helping it merrily on its way. We mounted to the highest summit which is adorned by a pavilion, providing a perfect view across the fertile country-side. There at a distance was the hurly-burly of the world, here at our feet the valley and its serene peace. Most unwillingly we left this charming place in the evening, rolling over hill and dale in this beautiful part of Yorkshire, on to Catterick Bridge, a large and completely isolated inn.

ENGLISH INNS

On the Continent the pleasant amenities offered by the English inn are unknown. We shall therefore permit ourselves to dwell a little on the subject. In general, that is to say in the towns also, English inns are most praiseworthy: rooms, beds, service and cleanliness surpass anything one encounters in other countries. We might even assert that the good inns in the countryside surpass those in the towns to the same degree as English inns on the whole surpass their German counterparts.

Prices are not as high as one is inclined to think, once one has grown familiar with the customs of the country. For example, the fact that one does not ever eat by portion is certainly disagreeable. The stores of the house, meat, fish, vegetables, all that sort of thing, are displayed in a glass case in the hall, arranged with the greatest neatness and elegance. Here, one usually meets the hostess or her representative. Apart from some pastry and confectionery nothing is prepared in advance. The exception to this rule is at those inns where public conveyances stop at appointed hours. There the table is set at noon and in the evening, and the travellers arriving eat at a set price, and in company, should they wish. Otherwise the traveller must choose for himself from the store and state the manner in which he wishes his meal to be cooked. Then he must wait patiently until it is ready. Should he choose a roast of mutton or beef or any large joint, it will be brought to the table whole and he has to pay for the whole even if it goes out with only a small portion carved. This is certainly not satisfactory, but anyone acquainted with the country knows how to arrange matters and only orders simple, easily prepared dishes. Lodgings are not expensive. The room in which one eats and spends the day is usually not charged, even over longer periods unless, of course, one uses the room and eats elsewhere. In the bedroom one pays only for the bed which is seldom more than a shilling a night – and what a bed! There are the finest mattresses, the best sheets and blankets, with beautiful curtains round the bed, while in front of it lies a pretty little rug. A fine white nightcap and a pair of slippers are never missing and the English travellers, who carry very little luggage, use these without the slightest hesitation.

It has always struck us how this nation, with all its care for cleanliness, does not worry about a thousand little considerations which, to the German and even more to the Frenchman, have become second nature. For example, no Englishman, unless belonging to the highest rank, would refuse to drink with somebody from the same glass or porter jug, and should there be a shortage of accommodation, he will share a bed at the inn with an acquaintance or a complete stranger.

Even in the towns, the host appears at once to welcome the stranger the moment he steps from the coach. In the country one has the feeling that one has arrived on a long-expected visit. The innkeeper himself opens the carriage door and helps the traveller alight. His wife, standing in the doorway with the most friendly expression in the world, curtsies half a dozen times, seizes the lady travellers and takes them to a special room where she attends to their every comfort, while her husband does the honours to the gentlemen. Even if one only changes horses without stopping for a meal, the courtesy remains every bit the same. The innkeeper and his wife accompany the traveller to the coach, thank him for the honour of the visit and ask him to return soon. To be sure, in every case the innkeepers make some profit, for they service the traveller's coach.

The farther one travels towards the north of England and Scotland, the more the courtesy of the innkeeper seems to increase, showing a cordiality it is a pleasure to encounter. The host always carries the first course to the table, even though the inn may be large and handsome. He is followed by his wife and all the children old enough for the task. They walk in procession, according to their age, all bearing something. Often we saw a little cherub with a head of golden curls bringing up the rear, perhaps only three or four years old, busily tripping along, pepper-box in hand. All rooms have bells in good working order and the English traveller uses these to his heart's content.

As there are no more attentive innkeepers than in England, there are equally no more demanding guests. But somehow the running of an inn is handled like that of a factory: everyone has his department which makes for order and quick service. Horses are looked after by the groom, called an ostler, who must surely keep menials in the stable to do the actual work, as he himself looks far too elegant for manual tasks. Then there is the shoeblack. This lad, usually the most crafty and intelligent of the staff, called simply Boots, is a most important person in the establishment. He manages to attend to all external matters, carries out commissions, takes strangers round the town and has an answer for everything. High falsetto cries constantly echo through the house, shouting 'Boots' and always he is there at once.

On going to bed at night the chambermaid is called. She appears, wearing a fine cotton dress with a snow-white apron and a pretty little lace cap, in fact dressed in as neat and ladylike a manner as can be imagined. It is her duty to light a candle on the visitor's bedside table, and, irrespective of person or sex, she also escorts him to his bedroom and sees to his every comfort. This happens every night, even if one should spend a month in the place. On taking one's farewell, waiter, ostler and Boots appear and finally the chambermaid who, with a pretty curtsey, says: 'Don't forget the chambermaid.' One does not give these people very much, considering how expensive things are in their country, but one gives with pleasure for one has had good service.

After this digression, let us return to Catterick Bridge. Because of illness we had to stay there for several days, where we were nursed and tended as if among old friends. Our hostess, Mistress Fergusson, left the sickroom only when her business made it necessary. Her husband rode the 4 miles to the nearby little town of Richmond to fetch the apothecary, and the son of the house, a clergyman in the neighbourhood, carted half his library to supply entertainment for the sick and healthy alike. The apothecary was a sensible, good doctor and our ailments were soon cured by his remedies.

All over England apothecaries are the most sought-after doctors; in fact they are actually called 'doctor'. Except by the rich and the high-born, visits from proper doctors are only requested in cases of great danger. They are too expensive, as one cannot offer any of them less than a guinea for a single visit. This is put into their hand as they take leave. A consultation with the doctor in his own house costs half a guinea. The apothecaries here are paid about as much as doctors are in large German towns. Incidentally, nowhere will you find more quacks than in England. There is clear evidence of this in the newspapers where the greater part of the advertisements are inserted by such people.

RICHMOND

Completely recovered, we reached the small country town of Richmond. It is situated on a rocky slope, with the ruins of its ancient castle on the summit, high above the town. The present Dukes of Richmond take their name from the place but do not have as much as fifty pounds of income from it. The town is most picturesque and from the ruins of the wall of the town one enjoys wide and beautiful vistas. Woods, meadows, pretty country houses, gardens, villages and low fertile hills alternate in a most charming manner, while a stream with a single stone bridge further enriches the scene. One comes across some new beauty at every step. The wild rock on which the castle and the town are built forms a marvellous contrast to its pastoral surroundings. The ruins, though in completely different taste, and less magnificent than Fountains Abbey, still stand witness to one-time greatness and past glory. Alas, they are not well looked after and threaten to collapse at any moment, presenting a severe danger to the houses below. One single tower remains intact but the rest consists merely of high walls, luxuriantly ivy-clad. One can still see clearly its division into rooms, also the high-arched windows, but the roof has gone altogether, leaving all open to the wind and the rain.

AUCKLAND, DURHAM, SUNDERLAND AND NEWCASTLE

We travelled from Richmond to Auckland in a couple of hours. It is the seat of the Bishops of Durham and their residence, a large Gothic building, though pleasant, is very simply furnished, not showing any trace of clerical pomp. Indeed everything is as it should be in the house of a Man of God. The garden belonging to the house is not remarkable for the art lavished upon it, yet nature has given it a certain charm. Rocks and woods border a rushing river which tumbles along, now playfully, now boisterously, over boulders which try, unsuccessfully, to stem its way. Much beauty could be created here with money and taste yet, when one sees Nature thus unadorned, one spontaneously prays that things should remain as they are.

We drove on to Durham through the large and pleasant park. It is one of the oldest if not largest of towns in England, picturesquely situated in a delightful valley surrounded by cultivated hills. Next morning we continued via Sunderland to Newcastle.

Sunderland is remarkable for its iron bridge, the largest in

6 The Bridge over the Wear at Sunderland

England. A single enormous arch, 100 feet high, spans the water, high enough for a ship to pass under it without lowering its mast. Never before had we seen gracefulness and strength so well combined, for the bridge really does seem to be suspended in the air as if by magic. Only the arches on which it rests, and the railings, are made of iron, the rest being of stone. We were able to inspect the bridge's construction carefully from a vantage point below it. It is one span of 236 feet, consisting of six cast-iron ribs, laid lengthwise to form an arch. These ribs are joined by iron rods into a whole, and each rests on a number of thick iron rings, placed together vertically, and in turn resting on a lower series of girders. The superstructure is of wood, with a planked deck, and the abutments are of rubble masonry in lime mortar, with a dressed stone facing.

It is difficult to describe the sight of this work of art. What immediately becomes clear is the fact that a number of relatively weak component parts can combine to carry a heavy burden. Even if the ravages of time or wilful damage harmed these arches, there would still be enough strength left to save the whole. One might go so far as to say that it would never become derelict as any fault discovered could at once be easily rectified. A special guard lives next to the bridge and it is his task to see that it is kept in a state of good repair. There is a large engraving, also to be seen in Germany, which shows very clearly the features of this truly miraculous construction.

We next reached Newcastle where we found nothing of interest to do but rest and sleep. The town is fairly large and has, apart from many narrow and crooked streets, a few handsome ones. It is very important to the British economy because of its trade in coal. Alas, everything everywhere has the look and smell of this product, which makes the town less than inviting to someone who is travelling for pleasure only.

ALNWICK CASTLE AND BERWICK

A few hours after leaving Newcastle, we reached Alnwick, the ancient seat of the Dukes of Northumberland. From a distance the sight of the castle took us back to times long since past. We felt that what we beheld was a fortified castle of a time when the law of the strongest prevailed and every man had to protect himself against hostile neighbours. Above all, we were struck by the amazing state of preservation of this ancient building, showing no sign of crumbling or decay. This well-preserved castle has round corner towers and a wall surrounding the whole, complete with embrasures, parapets and everything invented in the old days for defence. In fact, it is a masterpiece of the architecture of the past, with several gates and drawbridges, leading across the moat. It all is very old yet looks as if it had been built only yesterday.

Life-size warriors, hewn out of stone, are placed in threatening positions on the battlements, walls and towers. They appeared to us from below to be very excellently carved. Above each gate was one in a crouched position, a stone held in both hands as if ready to crush anyone who dared to enter. This idea can certainly not be called a welcoming gesture but the whole decoration, strange and unique of its kind, is very effective. From a distance one could well believe that the spirits of the ancient warriors had returned. They seem set to bar the curious from entering their sanctum, and indeed they are not as harmless as one would like to think, for quite a few of these heroes, finding it too windy on their heights, have descended from their pedestals without invitation, causing damage and disruption below.

The interior of the castle is also in the spirit of a bygone age. There are high vaulted rooms with arched windows surmounted by pseudo-Gothic ornaments and scrolls, vast pillars and long galleries leading from one to another. The dark winding corridors would combine with this to make a frightening scene, were not the rooms painted so cheerfully in bright colours. Yet we are certain that if one were to read one of the English Gothic novels, alone here at midnight, it would not fail to make its proper effect.

We sped away into the friendly sunlight to the colourful modern garden which surrounds the castle, and to the well-constructed hothouses where, to our joy, we could provide ourselves with grapes and melons for the journey. The park seemed in no way distinguishable from any other, though we could only view it from the distance of the castle windows, not being permitted to drive through it. This was a difficulty we had not previously encountered. The road now took us along the coast, where we hardly ever lost sight of the sea, until we arrived at the ancient town of Berwick on the farthest tip of Northumberland.

In Northumberland and particularly in Berwick, the last English town, we were struck by the manner in which the people talked. The generally strange accent, particularly in the pronunciation of the letter 'R', combined with the many unknown provincial expressions they used, made it difficult for us to understand them. Immediately beyond Newcastle, English is pronounced in a very imperfect fashion, almost like Low German.

2 SCOTLAND

The drive from Berwick to Edinburgh – 54 miles, almost all of the time within view of the sea – would in itself be worth the journey. The countryside is of such unusual and extraordinary beauty that once again one finds it difficult to describe it with full justice.

The coast is cultivated, like a garden, right down close to the waves: cornfields, meadows with grazing flocks, orchards and vegetable gardens alternate in a splendour of luxuriance.

Perhaps because of the distance between these Scottish villages, they, surprisingly, look more picturesque to the traveller than the English ones. The countryside is neither very hilly nor very flat but rises and falls, wave-like in a gentle flow of hillock and glen. One passes country houses and ivy-clad ruins, witnesses to present and to past grandeur. And always there is the view of the sea, that eternally changing element which can enliven any scene, however desolate.

One passes small islands, each with its lighthouse and on the distant horizon sees blue rocks, jagged and wild. So many features combine to make this a wondrous scene. In sharp contrast to all this pastoral charm, one is suddenly arrested by the sight of warriors with their glittering arms and uniforms for there are two camps along the way, each with some 3000 men, guarding the coast. The appearance of these men and their tents seems alien to the scene.

Already, though still close to the English border, we were strongly aware of the difference between the English and the Scots. Their friendly, kind civility, their candour combined with great but cheerfully-borne poverty constantly reminded us of the inhabitants of the German mountain regions. Shoes and stockings, without which even a beggar would not be seen in England, are the height of luxury. Here the working class and most of the children, even of well-to-do parents, go barefoot in summer and in winter. Perhaps as often as not this is done from force of habit rather than poverty, but it does strike one forcibly on arrival from England where it would be unthinkable.

EDINBURGH

We could not find a room at any of the pleasant inns in which this city abounds as our arrival coincided with the last days of the annual horse-race week. Everywhere was crowded with visitors, some come to watch the noble sport and others for the festivities which accompany the event: the theatre, dances, concerts and a thousand other entertainments. However, we eventually found accommodation at the house of an engraver, one of the many Macintoshes, and we had much pleasure watching the populace enjoy itself in its own special way.

The city of Edinburgh is of considerable size and seems at one and the same time to be a most beautiful and a most ugly place. It might be compared, in that way, to Marseilles. The Old Town is a disagreeable collection of ancient, dirty houses in an advanced state of decay, built in narrow, crooked streets, apparently without any attempt at planning, just scattered about in a haphazard manner. The New Town, on the other hand, can stand comparison with Europe's finest cities, and Edinburgh's natural position is unique and of great romantic beauty.

The houses of the Old Town cling to the sides of a massive rock face, to which they stick like swallows' nests, one next to another and one above the other. Seen from one street, a few are ten storeys high, while from the other side they seem to rise to a lesser height, it being, in fact, possible to walk out into the street from the fourth or fifth floor. It is difficult to describe how crooked, narrow and winding most of these streets are. Some of them lead up and down steep hills in a most fatiguing manner. On the rock, high above the dwellings of the ordinary people, stands the Castle, the ancient residence of the Scottish

7 Old Town across Bridges, Edinburgh

kings. The deep canyon, from which this rock rises almost vertically, divides the Old Town from the plain below where the New Town has been constructed. Several beautiful stone bridges lead across it, joining the two towns. From these bridges one can see, down below, streets which appear to be Erebus, hardly ever reached by sun or moon. The roofs of the houses there do not reach anywhere near the foundations of the bridges and the people walking in the streets look like gnomes from above. It is hard to understand why, in view of the handsome new sections of the city, these miserable dwellings are still tolerated. Only part of this deep chasm has been built upon, the rest being used as grazing land or lying stony and barren.

The New Town is pleasantly and spaciously laid out, its streets well paved, with wide footpaths on each side. It measures up to Europe's finest cities and its handsome houses, full of character and built of natural stone, may even surpass their counterparts. Here, as in London, there are great squares surrounded by fine buildings, with pretty gardens or lawns in the centre, enclosed by iron railings. Nearly all the streets provide a view of the sea. It is a grand view, an ever changing, ever new scene made specially attractive by the many small islands in the estuary. In the blue distance, hills enclose one side of this glorious prospect while the other seems to stretch away into eternity.

We spent an unforgettable evening with friends in Princes Street. This street, a mile long, has very handsome houses on one side, while on the other an iron balustrade separates it from the canyon between the Old Town and the New. Here there are no buildings, just cows and goats grazing. Beyond this the bare rocks rise vertically, wild and jagged, of beautiful and varied shape. High above it all stands the Royal Castle and other ancient buildings, and farther off lies Arthur's Seat, shrouded in mists, an astonishingly shaped rock, almost like a throne. Many a gruesome tale concerning it makes the round among the people. Nearby are the ruins of another ancient castle, where the unhappy Mary Stuart was held prisoner by her own people before being sent to her death in England. Once again there is a distant view of the sea and we saw the setting sun make the tips of the rocks glow and, later, the moon turning the waves into pure silver. We left for home, convinced that it would not be easy to find another large, crowded city which could provide a similar spectacle.

The third part of Edinburgh is Leith. It is, in fact, a separate town, but as it almost adjoins the city, it can be considered as part of it. Leith lies at a lower level on marshy, rather unpleasant ground around the port. Here are to be found the wharfs, warehouses, offices and dwellings of all the people connected with the business of a seaport. There is a great deal of hustle and bustle in this area which, except that it is not hilly, is almost as ugly as Edinburgh's Old Town. The streets are very crowded and we were happy to make a quick escape.

Edinburgh's finest building is the Register Office, which serves many public purposes. There, in a rotunda, lit from a cupola above, we were shown a marble statue of King George III. Mrs Damer, a lady of quality in London, presented it to the city and, curiously, she had actually carved it herself. We must respect her good intention but, alas, it is a formless piece of work.

The Castle is worthy of note for its former use as a Royal residence, its age and its imposing position, high on the face of a rock. Holyrood House, on the other hand, the residence of the present King of Great Britain when he comes to Edinburgh, is a large, quite ordinary castle of no particular architectural merit, although it is certainly preferable to St James's in London. A number of private persons now reside there, with the permission of the King. It also housed, during his exile, the Comte d'Artois, who later became Charles X of France. Lodgings in this castle and around it have a special privilege in that debtors living there cannot be arrested, and so they are much sought after, especially, we were assured, by members of the Scottish nobility.

The Comte d'Artois lived in Holyrood, as far as possible in the style he had done at Versailles. Twice a week he dined by himself in public, as was demanded by etiquette. Three times a week he held a levee for a court of émigrés which he had gathered around him. We saw his rooms, which are of a very modest middle-class appearance and must often have made him reflect on how impermanent worldly things are. Only three things in the rooms seemed to us worthy of note: a portrait of the daughter of Louis XVI and one of her aunt, the Princess Elizabeth, together with a view of Malta which had been painted by this unfortunate lady in the Temple at Paris. One hopes it had given her that serene comfort which art offers, allowing her to forget, for a little, the agonies she endured.

In spite of its romantic splendour and beauty, Edinburgh does not lend itself to the promenade. There is little shade or rural charm close at hand, although this can be found by journeying an hour or two out from the city. For the first few days of our stay the races, which might be called the Carnival of the British, filled the whole city with an unusual animation. One entertainment followed another that week, but on the whole the people here live a more quiet and simple life than in London, more like the German family life. Children are not, as is the custom in England, educated in boarding school, but grow up at home under the eyes of their parents.

A formal piety and, especially, the observance of the Sunday are more apparent than in the south. One of our friends, who collected us on that day for a drive, carefully closed the blinds of his carriage while we drove through the city, as he feared people going to church might notice that he was driving for pleasure at that sacred hour. On a Sunday morning all musical instruments, all books not of a religious nature, all playing cards, needlework, even the most trifling, are carefully locked away out of sight so that these things should not be a tempation. Everyone goes to church as well as attending devotions at home, when all members of the household, even the most menial of the servants, have to be present. All diversions are prohibited, leaving the gentlemen only the bottle with which they remain rather longer than usual after a meal, while the ladies, of course, have their tea.

Courteous friendliness and a certain innate cheerfulness of manner distinguish the Scot quite noticeably from the Englishman. Foreigners are respected more highly here than in England. The population is better acquainted with their customs and manners, for poverty often forces the Scot to seek his livelihood abroad, and this he prefers to do in more distant places than England where his beloved country is looked upon with unwarranted contempt. The largest number of Britons settled in Germany, for example, are actually Scots.

Piety, honesty and diligence are in general the chief characteristics of the people. They have also a boundless love for their country and its native literature, so that anybody with the slightest claim to being educated is familiar with it, just as he is with the Classics. They have a great respect for anything which relates to their former and more successful days. Mary Stuart still has countless warm admirers here, and any relic which had a connection with her is sacred and carefully preserved.

The Fine Arts do not really thrive under the British sky but, as we found out, they do not always go a-begging. Proof of this was a truly excellent artist, of the name of Raeburn. We visited him in his elegantly built and furnished house where he lives in style with his wife and four children. All this he acquired by the work of his brush, as he was without a private fortune. He certainly chose a branch of art which could not earn its reward in any country better than in Great Britain. He paints horses outstandingly well, so faithfully that even a non-English eye cannot fail to be delighted by his work. He also succeeds with some felicity in portraiture, but it is the likenesses of the four-footed friends of many a rich milord that have been the basis of his fame and fortune. In a large room, which had been specially built for the purpose and was well-lit from above, we saw many of his paintings under perfect conditions and with real pleasure. Of especial beauty was the portrait of his eight-year-old son, painted life-size, facing the beholder. He sits on a charming little grey pony, loosely holding the reins. The whole is so well and faithfully depicted that we found it hard to tear ourselves away from it. Raeburn himself is a well-informed and charming man, something quite rare among artists. We spent some enjoyable hours in his company.

THE LEITH RACES

We simply had to go to the races, which had brought so many strangers to Edinburgh, and so we attended the last two most important ones. It is usual to hold such events on a piece of grassland which has been specially prepared for the purpose. Here, strangely, they chose the beach at Leith, a stretch of sand left by the sea at ebbtide. This naturally makes it necessary to fix the times of the races very carefully and the whole expedition appeared not without danger. Should old Poseidon prove capricious and decide to send his waves back a little too soon, the catastrophe of King Pharaoh in the Red Sea might well be repeated, wiping out in a flash the population of Edinburgh, for nobody stays at home during these important events. It all seemed a little odd to us.

On a stretch of wet sand, full of puddles, where it seemed inconceivable that horses could get a firm footing and which smelt like a fish market, a space is roped off, guarded by invalid veteran soldiers, who are there to keep order. The judges sit at one end of the area on a high platform decorated with bunting. They look as solemn as Rhadamanthus and his fellow judges in hell. The heroes of the day, the horses, stand next to them while a great crowd of people swarms over the whole place. Those on foot, anxious not to miss the sights, have found places on the roofs and at the windows of the nearby houses in Leith, standing on top of walls and on platforms specially erected for spectators, on the quays in the harbour, in short anywhere a space with a view is to be found. The spectacle of the crowd, seen from the course, is full of colour and merriment. Those who are fortunate enough to possess a carriage or a horse mill around, amusing themselves as the expectation mounts. Splendid carriages decorated with the coats of arms and coronets of the nobility, drawn by four proud horses, mingle with carts with just one weary old nag, while many other different conveyances and riders on a variety of mounts complete the colourful picture. Anything that luxury or the mere enthusiasm for driving or riding can invent is there, splashing around in the mud and wet sand without apparent aim or purpose.

During this time the judges carry out a very careful inspection to make sure that no sharp practice of any kind can happen during the races. The jockeys, who for some time have had to prepare for this great day by adhering to a strict diet, are weighed in with much care. None is allowed to be at all heavier than the next so that the lighter jockeys have lead put into their pockets to make up for their missing pounds.

In the meantime those of the spectators who are keen on gambling place their bets. Then the air is split by a roll of drums and everybody rushes to take up position at the sides of the course, all anxious to find the best vantage point. Many men alight from their carriages and climb on the roof while some ladies sit up on the high seat next to the coachmen. The air is tense with expectation. At the second roll of the drums the horses are off. Everyone holds his breath, eager to see the start as, for just a moment, they flash by like lightning, to be seen again shortly at the other side of the course. Then they approach again and rush past for a second time, hastening towards the finishing post. Twice, without stopping, the course is circuited and the horse who first completes it, wins the race.

The distance covered in these races measures exactly four English miles, the equivalent of five German ones. The time taken to complete the course is incredibly short. The moment the first race is over, everyone drives and rides about the place again, helter-skelter until another roll of the drums announces that the second race is due to begin, sending the spectators hurrying back to their places. Every morning during the week of the races, three such competitions are run. After the third, everyone returns home, well satisfied.

It is not very pleasant to see the horses arrive at the finish. Exhausted and covered in sweat, they are hardly able to breathe while blood streams from their sides where the flesh has been torn by the riders' spurs. The jockeys, too, almost collapse with exhaustion, the quick pace of the race having taken their breath away, to such an extent that they have to use one hand constantly to fan the air in front of their faces to escape suffocation.

The remainder of the day, apart from dressing and enjoying

the pleasure of the table, is spent in many different ways. There
are plenty of diversions available: wax-figure cabinets, tight-
rope walkers, 'invisible maidens', and a very interesting
panorama of Constantinople. The evenings bring balls, concerts
and assemblies in handsome rooms kept specially for the
purpose. There is also a small version of the Vauxhall Gardens,
well arranged but in no way comparing with the famous
London ones which are surely unique.

The theatre is well frequented, with a noisy and boisterous
audience ruling supreme, just as in London. The actual
building is not big but very prettily decorated and well-lit and
equipped. Unfortunately the actors do not distinguish themselves in any way; none of them rises above the mediocre and
the actresses are considerably worse.

The presence of a very excellent comic actor from a London
theatre, a Mr Bannister, engaged to play special parts during
this festive week, made this even more apparent. Compared to
him, all the other actors seemed puppets, only there to follow
their cues. The public showed their appreciation of his playing
by applauding loudly. And when during the entr'actes he sang
a few amusing songs, with allusions to topical politics and the
follies of fashion, cheerful enthusiasm simply knew no bounds.
Nearly every song had to be repeated three times and it seemed
as if the walls would fall in with cheerful noise and laughter.

We listened to a typically Scottish concert in a pleasant hall,
performed before a brilliant audience. It was announced as a
vocal concert and consisted of three singers accompanied on the
piano. They devoted the evening to light romantic songs,
lieder, canons for three voices, called glees here. This kind of
music is very popular in England and even more so in
Scotland. Both the music and the texts were very Scottish,
with the latter often taken from Ossian whilst the music was
soft, in a minor key, with an air of melancholy throughout it.
We heard many an ancient tune, all received with exultant
patriotism. The whole evening would have been most
agreeable for an hour or so, but it suffered from that mistake to
be found in all entertainments in Great Britain: it lasted far too
long. Nevertheless the audience remained attentive to the very
end with only a few elderly gentlemen, who at table had

perhaps taken the welfare of the nation a little too much to their hearts and now fell into a sweet slumber, snoring over-loudly and providing a ground bass to the somewhat pallid accompaniment of the piano. The singers had good voices and rendered these simple melodies as they should be sung – in an artless manner, yet conveying their true meaning.

Eventually the busy week was over, the entertainments packed away, the Assembly Rooms closed, the visitors gone away and any of the local populace retired to their country houses. Everything returned to its accustomed order and quietude.

We stayed on for a little in order to see and enjoy Edinburgh's normal quiet life until, at last, the day appointed for our departure arrived. When we stepped from our lodgings to the coach, we encountered a scene quite unknown in England: a crowd of beggars surrounded the carriage and we had to buy our passage by payment to these sons and daughters of misery. Finally, as the morning sun steeped the castle, King Arthur's Seat and the ruins of Mary's prison in a rosy glow, we trundled off. Looking back we had one last glimpse of the city with the bright shining sea beyond, and we sped onwards, filled with expectation, towards the Highlands.

CARRON AND STIRLING

We proceeded quickly along level roads through cultivated not very hilly country. Soon we saw at a distance many large buildings with strange high chimneys. Black smoke rose from them, rolling across the smiling scene and making everything suddenly seem gloomy as the great flames leapt into the air. We were approaching the famous Carron Iron Works, perhaps the biggest in the world. Cannons are made here and mortars, large boilers and every conceivable thing of cast iron. For the last few years strangers have not been allowed to enter this abode of the Cyclops. We, too, were refused admittance and confess we were not particularly disappointed. It is a fact that while travelling one tends to look at things just because they happen to be there, without real pleasure or inclination. One is inspired merely by some sense of duty, and often wishes afterwards that one had not taken the trouble. The whole area here, in spite of its great size, is very uninviting. The smell of coal-gas took our breath away and combined with the deafening bangs and hammerings from within the buildings, all drenched in an eternal twilight of clouds and steam, was overpowering. Around the works is a wide area of trees and plants, covered with ash and soot, dressed, as it were, in mourning.

Not far from Carron we saw a big canal which connects the two rivers, the Forth and the Clyde, and is of great benefit to home trade. We reached Stirling towards evening. It is a fairly large and lively town, considered as belonging to the Highlands. It was full of soldiers which made the streets and houses look more cheerful. The town's position at the base of a steep rock is very beautiful. Several streets lead right up the rock at the highest summit of which stands a castle, now serving as army barracks and living quarters for the officers.

We had a superb view from the terrace in front of the castle. Before us lay a broad, fertile valley, displaying good cultivation, scattered houses, villages and splendid trees. The River Forth winds its way in many curves through the countryside. Now it runs straight, then turns again for long stretches, then, somewhat hesitatingly it runs on again, almost as if it were unwilling to leave this earthly paradise. Carron's smoky clouds can be seen in the distance as if they were rising from a volcano. On the blue horizon hills enclose the perspective and straight ahead the scene stretches into eternity.

Stirling has many factories: fine carpets of all kinds are made here, also the multi-coloured woollen-cloth, used for the Highlander's clothing. We looked at one of these factories and were forced, once again, to admire the inventive spirit which simplifies and eases work in this country. We saw a machine we had never seen before, which enables one girl to reel off more than fifty bobbins at the same time. The bobbins are fixed next to one another in a large circle, and the thread of each is attached to an enormous windlass above. With the help of a wheel, the girl is able to put the very simple machine into action, easily and expediently.

Dogs, too, are conscripted into industry here. We saw a handsome large dog, treading a wheel like a squirrel to set a mill for grinding colours into motion. We recall that this work did not seem to amuse the dog particularly, for he seized the chance to escape with incredible agility, at the very moment he was to display his skill to us. Young and old pursued him with much shouting, but happily he managed to escape from his pursuers, to our great delight and the distress of his master.

The national costume of the Highlanders is seen less in Edinburgh than here in Stirling where, in fact, it is much in evidence. The men wear blue bonnets with a red pompom, sometimes decorated with a feather and with facings of red-and-white checked material. Their jackets are fairly long over a closely pleated skirt or kilt of the popular checked cloth. The kilt, not quite covering the knees, his held up by a belt into which is stuck a kind of dagger, and from the belt hangs a leather pouch decorated with tassels, in which the Scots carry money and tobacco. They wear red-and-white checked stockings which only cover half of the calf, while the rest of the leg is bare. This gives the Scots a very strange appearance, rather like Roman soldiers in an opera, while the red stripes in the stockings seem like ribbons attached to them.

The main piece of their clothing, we might say their *pièce de résistance*, is the plaid. It is a long broad piece of material, again the checked Scottish variety, almost the size of a large shawl. In good weather they carry it slung carelessly over their shoulder, hanging down right to the hip. Sometimes the plaid is fastened across the shoulder by a large silver pin and this way of holding it looks very well. In rainy or cold weather the men pull it over their heads so that they are completely covered by it. When travelling it serves as a shelter and bed. In their homes, too, the men usually sleep on the floor or wherever they can find a place, wrapped in their plaids.

The women's costume is not very special. They, too, use the traditional Scottish cloth, but, on the whole, they appear rather shabby, even dirty, with bare feet and their short-cut hair, often without bonnet or hat. In beauty Scotswomen are not inferior to their English sisters. Indeed they may well surpass them. Yet, in the way they dress, particularly the lower classes, the maidservants and village women, they are very different. No long dresses, no straw hats, which we saw everywhere in

England, nothing but bare feet, poor cotton skirts, shapeless jackets right down to the knees, sometimes held by a belt at the waist, more often hanging loose. Their white bonnets cover the entire head and have a frill round the face down to the shoulders. This is the costume worn by the poorer Scotswoman in the towns and there is little difference in the country and the Highlands.

Houses in the villages, and cottages we passed, looked very poor. They often seemed thrown together with nothing but rough stones and lime, hardly resembling human habitations at all. It is difficult to reconcile this apparent great poverty with the fertility and high cultivation of the countryside and the educational standard of the people who live here.

PERTH

A day's journey from Stirling took us to Perth, a fair-sized town, with pleasant large houses and fine broad streets, full of life. Everything looked prosperous, for here, too, commerce and manufacturing flourish, the bleach works at Perth being particularly famous.

Leaving Stirling, we at first enjoyed many splendid views but then gradually the charm began to fade, and beyond the rather dull landscape we could discern the gloomy, rocky chain of mountains, the Highlands, in the blue distance. Our coach laboured up the increasingly steep hills until suddenly we began to descend again and found before us the charming valley along the river Tay, on whose banks the town of Perth is built.

From Perth we took a short excursion to Scone Palace, once the residence of the kings of Scotland and where their parliament used to assemble. Today it is little more than a decaying rabbit warren, more like a barn than a palace. It now belongs to Lord Mansfield, to whose family it had been given by King James II. The owner still lives there from time to time, even though the condition of the house is so poor that a small shopkeeper would hardly care to have it for his summer holiday. A new dwelling is in the process of being erected beside it, but the old building is being carefully preserved, unchanged, as its venerable age and ancient usage deserve.

We were shown some of the rooms in the palace, faded reminders of one-time Royal splendour. We saw the bed used by Mary Stuart during her imprisonment in the now ruined castle in Edinburgh, in which she may often have tried in vain to find rest and forget her sorrows. It is kept here as a sacred relic. There is also a piece of embroidery on which the Queen, as a prisoner, had worked meticulously. With silks and a silver thread, she had embroidered a violet velvet curtain with a scattering of little flowers and although the design is stiff, worked in a kind of chain stitch, it is tidily and attractively executed.

The Assembly room, serving the Scottish Parliament, is no more than a long, narrow and dark gallery and, looking at it, it is hard to imagine its former grandeur. On the barrel-vaulted ceiling, covered in wood, there are traces of paintings which, even in their prime condition, must have been pretty ordinary. Lost in the gardens, there is an old disused chapel, once the scene of the crowning of the Kings of Scotland, now used as the burial place of the Mansfield family.

The countryside between Perth and Scone Palace is pleasant and fertile. On our return journey we stopped at one of the bleach works, of which there are so many, and the owner was delighted to take us round. In the building there is a spinning mill and an area where the stamping and calendering of the linen are carried out, all by the power of water, for no steam power is required in the works. The final processing, particularly of the table linen, seemed to us remarkable. The cloth must acquire a gloss superior even to the most shiny satin. This is achieved by rolling a piece of linen from one large wooden cylinder to another. Set between them is a small cylinder and the three are closely held together, so that the linen can only just pass between them. It is apparently the friction thus caused which produces the excellent gloss.

We were determined to visit the real Highlands for which Perth was an excellent place to set out. The roads, if not as good as in the rest of the Kingdom, are nevertheless to a large extent passable due to the construction, not so long ago, of the so-called military roads. Staging-posts had not yet been established, with the result that it was rare to come across a change of horses. We decided therefore to hire them in Perth for the whole journey, and then set off into the mountains, towards Dunkeld, where we were fortunate in finding a good inn.

At Dunkeld is the seat of the Duke of Atholl but, as he was in residence, we were unfortunately able to see it only from the outside. It seemed a substantial, if plain, building, with little ornamentation, surrounded by lawns and flower gardens with a bridge leading over a deep ravine to the park, Opposite the house is the family burial ground and close to it the ruin of a large church, overgrown with moss. As in so many other places, here again the blind zeal of the Reformation had destroyed what must have been a fine building.

Our guide, a sensible old gardener, led us to an excellent viewpoint where we could sit and rest with the woodlands spread before us and the murmur of the river not far away. On the back of the little pavilion in which we sat was a picture of the bard, Ossian, someone who seemed to us to be present everywhere in the Highlands.

We saw a small button, which we pressed, causing the picture suddenly to disappear so that we found ourselves facing another pavilion, fantastically decorated with mirrors. To come upon such artifice here in the midst of nature was an unforgettable experience and we found it hard to tear ourselves away. When dusk came, we crossed the river again by the gentle light of the moon and returned to the inn.

KENMORE

Next morning we set off for Kenmore, and after travelling through a fairly flat region, we came to a fertile valley, flanked on both sides by high, wild-looking rocks. The road wound round the foot of them and alongside the broad River Tay flowed through the cornfields and orchards. Deep in a hollow, as if hiding itself from us among the rocks, we espied a small village. A throng of merry children played around noisily, while their mothers sat spinning in the doorways. The men, in their romantic costume, worked busily in the gardens and fields. The whole scene looked to us very foreign, yet we found in it peace and happiness.

Continuing along the shores of the Tay, we took the road towards Kenmore, travelling close to precipices which made us shudder, sometimes close to the banks of the river, at others only seeing it from our heights or losing it altogether. All the time we felt a sense of restfulness in this quiet remote place, as we watched the lively, clear waters of the Tay gurgle and tumble through the valley between those towering mountains. They did not stare down at us, gaunt and bare, as the Derbyshire hills had done, but were instead covered almost to the highest summit with trees. The sight of the miserable cottages along the way might well have distressed us had the people seemed less satisfied with their wretched conditions. We saw much poverty but no actual misery. Every cottage had its own small potato patch which fed the family. They kept goats, and sheep of a special small breed – not unlike the *Heideschnucken* of north-west Germany – which provided them with milk and cheese as well as wool for clothing.

Houses in the Scottish Highlands are perhaps the most wretched human habitations in civilized Europe. They are so small that it is difficult to see how a family can find sufficient room in them. They are built of natural stone, simply laid together, often without mortar, the joints filled with moss and loam. The windows are tiny, usually not even glazed, and the doors made of boards, roughly put together, having no lock of bolt (but then, who could possibly fear thieves here?). The low roofs are thatched with reeds, moss or sometimes just grass; only occasionally are they of wood or slate. In place of a chimney there is simply a hole through which the smoke escapes. The interior corresponds to the exterior. Men and beasts live under the same roof peacefully, separated only by a wooden partition. The single room of the house, with its almost total lack of any domestic equipment, illustrates only too clearly how little man really needs for his existence. The floor is made of trodden soil, the large hearth is not raised but on ground level, and is used for heating as well as cooking. A kettle on a chain above the fire, a few wooden stools, a roughly-made table in the corner, a place to rest of moss and straw: that is all these hardy people have for their daily comfort.

The appearance of the men is wild and no doubt their strange attire, so different from any other in Europe, is partly the reason for this. On closer inspection, after the initial shock wears off, one's impression changes, for their faces, weathered by the open air and hard work, are very expressive with agreeable, regular features. A serious serenity, amounting almost to melancholy, seems to be the fundamental quality of their nature. They can, all the same, be merry too. They are much better educated than one might expect, and know all about the history of their forefathers, and about their Bardic poetry. In practically every cottage we visited, we saw a Bible, a Prayer Book and some old chronicle from which, on Sundays, the head of the house reads for the edification of the family. During the winter, when the state of the roads often makes a visit to church difficult, only very harsh conditions prevent the devout Highlander attending service, although for most of them this means travelling a considerable distance. When asked what they did in winter when the snow and the cold kept them in their cottages, the beautiful girl said in reply to our question: 'We pray and we spin.'

In almost every house you will see the genealogical tree of the family, something in which they take great pride. Usually a knight in armour is portrayed on them, lying prostrate, with a tree sprouting from the chest and spreading into innumerable branches. He is given the name of some ancient, perhaps legendary king. In Scotland there are basically only a few families, but these are very prolific, with their members all bearing the same names or slight variations on them. They are spread all over Britain, over the whole world in fact, and they feel united by some sacred bond. They acknowledge this enthusiastically wherever they meet, even if they are complete strangers.

Kenmore is a village of some twenty cottages, poor and small like the others here, but another good inn welcomed us. This was the entire village but we were to learn that in Scotland it was usual for many of the cottages to be scattered over a large area, often miles from each other.

KILLIN

Killin is a short day's journey from Kenmore and on the way we passed Taymouth and the seat of the Breadalbane family, one of the biggest landowners in the area. There had previously been an old, unimpressive house here but this had been pulled down and a new building in the popular modern Gothic style erected. As we continued on our way the cliffs grew higher and wilder, but we were never out of sight of the river until it broadened out into Loch Tay. As we rounded the lake, the high rocks rose threateningly, directly above us. Round their summits, strangely-shaped clouds scudded past in the wind, making everything awe-inspiring, grand and lonely. Guided by a local man, we climbed a mountain which he called Ben Lawers, from the top of which we faced one of the most desolate views we had ever seen, just bare, harsh rocks and dark, lonely valleys. Ben Mohr, the highest mountain in Scotland, loomed in the distance, its summit shrouded in mist. In the whole scene, the only sign of life were some flocks of small sheep, tended by a solitary shepherd boy.

We descended to Loch Tay and soon reached Killin where we found lodgings in a remote but quite handsome house, built at the edge of the lake with a few cottages around it. The rivers Dochart and Lochy flow into the lake here. The surrounding country is very green, with trees and shrubs growing in abundance, something we would not have expected in this northerly corner of the world. There is much cultivation with cornfields and potato patches protected by stone walls from wild animals and the sheep which graze everywhere. This charming place is surrounded by high rocks which seem to be trying to hide it from prying eyes, keeping its beauty as a treasured secret. We spent much time at the bay window of the inn, for the view is greatly renowned, something borne out by the many inscriptions, in prose and rhyme, near the window in praise of it.

Just in front of the house the lake forms a little bay where a lone rowing boat cut the water's silver surface. The trees and the clouds were reflected in the clear water and the high rocks

8 Glencoe

behind glowed in the light of the setting sun, their summits turning to purple and gold as they disappeared in the swirling mist. From the boat the plaintive notes of a Scottish folk song came through the solemn stillness of the gathering night.

While we remained at the window, filled with peace and joy, our friendly hosts saw to all our needs. Soon a delicious salmon trout stood, steaming hot, on the table, caught by that same fisherman to whose simple song we had just listened. This fish, a native of the Scottish waters, is a very special variety indeed and, for its sake alone, a pilgrimage to Scotland by our modern gastronomes is essential. Even the most famous trout of Switzerland cannot surpass it.

Next morning, on the way to Tyndrum, we passed a waterfall cascading into Loch Tay from a considerable height, gushing wildly and casting its foam over the rocks. For centuries these drops of water have fallen like tears on the moss-covered stone of a nearby ancient tomb. The sound of the water seemed like the echo of the Bardic songs, once upon a time sung here in praise of the deeds of the departed heroes and guiding their souls towards the heavenly mansions.

We proceeded onwards, the road becoming steeper and steeper as we mounted higher into this desolate, lonely country. As the torrents gushed into the valleys below and the swirling clouds rolled round the summits, with wisps being driven by the wind through the valleys below like ghostly figures, we thought it might have been a scene from Ossian. From time to time flashes of sunlight illuminated the vista before us. Only the occasional patch of corn or humble cottage in this wilderness served to remind us that people actually inhabited such remote regions.

Nature here is exactly as Ossian described it: torrents, rocks, solitary oak trees of great age. The wind howls across the heath, the thistle waves its head in the storm over the grave of some ancient warrior. Four grey, moss-covered stones stand watch over the hill of the heroes, silently reminding the traveller of mankind's past history. We saw a number of these old monuments, reverently tended by the descendants of those heroes whose ashes rest in the tombs. According to legend, King Fingal sleeps in this valley in his deep, dark bed, and the local people firmly believe they know the sacred spot. His son Ossian's name and songs still linger among the rocks and the spirits of the departed can still enjoy his ancient, well-loved melodies as they look down from their seats in the clouds.

At Tyndrum there stands in the stark wilderness, a lonely inn, at, some say, the highest inhabited point in the Scottish Highlands. By now it was raining heavily and we watched the clouds rolling along the mountainside, sudden flashes of sunlight lighting a distant bare height, while the wind whipped up the rain. Towards evening the weather cleared and we had the magical experience of the changing light. Mountain tops still lay shrouded in rain, while lower down wisps of cloud rushed through the valley at great speed, forming strange and wonderful shapes. It was an endless battle between sunlight and storm.

DALMALLY

Although it was still passable, the road from Tyndrum was, at this point, the worst we had encountered so far on our travels. The wilderness had become even more grim and desolate and the only sound in the uncanny stillness was that of the torrents rushing down the mountainside. Here and there a few sheep roamed the hills and from time to time a young shepherd would look down curiously from above at our coach, which must have been a rare sight to him. There was no other sign of life although many an old gravestone showed that at one time there must have been more life here.

Dalmally is a small village, much like any other, comprising a handful of cottages. Once again we found an inn which was, considering the remoteness of the area, very good. Here we saw our first church in the Highlands, barely distinguishable from the rest of the houses in the village. It only came to our attention because of the cemetery surrounding it, just a few graves in a small enclosure.

It appears that death is rare in these parts. These simple people live to a happy old age and at sixty do not consider themselves old at all. They travel cheerfully towards the goal set them by nature, and only with the last drop of oil, is the light of their life extinguished, peacefully, almost unnoticed. In the village we met a man who was 103 years old; in fact his neighbours even calculated he was 111 years old and that he was pretending to be younger than he really was. In our more sophisticated countries one would have taken him for sixty at the most. A fortnight ago he had married a woman of forty and on that very special day had danced a little jig and played three songs on his bagpipes. He was still considered one of the finest virtuosi on this favourite Scottish instrument.

We had first eaten oatcakes, the staple food of the Highlanders, at Tyndrum. Here we found nothing else, although up to this point we had always been able to obtain wheaten bread at the inns. An oatcake is a thin cake like a German egg pancake, baked on both sides as hard as a crust and dusted with flour. The taste is slightly bitter, a little like groats, but they are praised as wholesome and nourishing and in time one might grow to like them.

This village again brought strong visions of Ossian. An aged man, wearing the traditional dress, sat on a stone near the cemetery, his long snow-white beard flowing in the wind. His looks were wild and his dark eyes glowed beneath a high receding hair-line. His plaid was draped in a fantastic manner, drooping from the shoulders like a coat. He held a small harp between his knees, from which he produced a series of chords with great vigour, while in a strong deep voice he accompanied the music with ancient songs, monotonously rendered like a recitative. The whole village, including the centenarian, had gathered round him, listening with keen attention. Our arrival did not disturb the singer nor the audience in the least; they simply made room for us in their circle with great natural courtesy. We were told that the old man was a singer, travelling the country with his harp, having no real home but being a welcome guest everywhere, as had been the Bardic singers long ago. Alas, we could not speak to him as he did not understand English. In fact, for the last few days, except at the inns, we had seldom met anybody speaking English or even understanding it.

INVERARY

We journeyed on through the steep and inhospitable mountains, until, suddenly, the road descended, to reveal a great silvery lake stretching before our astonished eyes: it was Loch Awe. The abrupt change to this watery expanse, with its green fields, its little cottages with their gardens, took us completely by surprise.

For 24 miles the lake winds itself across the green valley, with many small rocky islets rising from its waters. One of them distinguished itself from the others through its fantastic shape, from a distance looking like the ruins of ancient walls and, even as we drew closer, leaving us uncertain whether we beheld rocks or ruins. There was no boat to take us across, and anyway the shores seemed too steep to make a landing. The countryfolk to whom we spoke could not understand us and so, disappointed, we continued our journey. The view of the lake and its shores gave us the greatest pleasure after many days of seeing nature in its most raw grandeur. Later, however, in the inn at Inverary, we learnt that those rocks were, in fact, the remains of an ancient stronghold, part of the property of Lord Breadalbane. Only when the water is very high, as it is at present, does the rock on which these remains stand, appear to be an island: it is actually part of the mainland. All too soon we left the lake, the road taking us over even steeper and more rocky ground than before, until, an hour or two later, we were again welcomed into the shade of green woodlands. A beautiful English park came into view, with deer gazing at us from the roadside, and in its centre, the neo-Gothic castle with a tower at each of its four corners.

This was again truly paradise. The beautiful castle of Inverary, the seat of the Duke of Argyll, stood amidst fine trees and shrubs, gardens full of flowers around it, while the roedeer, full of curiosity, came right up to the fence surrounding the rose garden. A steep rock of strange formation was crowned by a pavilion, easily reached by a path. The view from the top was astonishing. From the castle, green fields stretched right down to Loch Fyne, an inlet from the sea which

9 *Inverary*

cuts deep into the country. Where the river enters into it, there was a handsome arched stone bridge. On both shores the rocks rose, and beyond them the mountains. The end of Loch Fyne was out of sight, the far-off sea forming its natural boundary. Its surface, as green as the sea, sparkled in the sun and little white-tipped waves rocked the fishermen's boats on its surface.

Near the castle, over the bridge, lies the little town of Inverary, round a pretty harbour, full of craft of many kinds. It is of seemly and agreeable appearance, with its orderly streets and pretty white houses, amongst which the inn takes pride of place. Everything looks as though it had been built only yesterday. And that is almost true. At one time it lay opposite the castle but the Duke, who felt that its position marred his view, had it pulled down and rebuilt in its present place. This is something which only seems credible in Great Britain.

The castle itself is noble and spacious, furnished with great taste. A large central hall, lit by a cupola, is surrounded by open galleries which give access to the rooms. In the centre of the hall stands an organ, a favourite musical instrument of the British, and a number of statues by Werth. The fine fireplaces are made of local marble, both coloured and black, and there is also a splendid one of Carrara marble. In one of the rooms, two French painters had been employed to decorate the walls with pretty arabesques, and they had painted the ceilings and the areas above the doors grey, imitating sculpted stone most successfully.

Some rooms are hung with rich silk material from Lyons, others contain family portraits and some very beautiful Italian paintings. To us, all this splendour, set amid so much natural beauty, appeared to have a magic glow, after the wild, almost barbaric scenery we had been through during the last few days. We had, now and again, to remember the Highlanders' wretched cottages, but, on reflection, were comforted by the feeling that they, too, seemed to be happy within their modest limitations.

ARROCHAR

We drove 9 miles on a fine level road from Inverary along the banks of Loch Fyne to Cairndow. We could at first have believed that we had lost our way, had that been possible here where there is only one passable road through the mountains, for the steward at Inverary Castle had described the road we were to take as the most terrible in the whole land. We had, he assured us, never seen deeper ravines or more desolate rocky mountains and he spoke much about an especially high mountain which he called 'Rest and be Thankful'.

Immediately after Cairndow, however, we realized that we were indeed on this very road. As we began to climb, the lake, the pretty valley and all the countryside's charm disappeared from our view. For several hours we rose higher and higher across bare rocky ground, through dark, narrow hollows and sometimes gloomy valleys, then again ascending into the mountains. The rocks were covered only with lichen, no other vegetation to be seen nor any sign of life. All around there was a deadly silence, a desperate loneliness. Not a sound was to be heard in this wilderness apart from the roaring of the torrents, tumbling from the mountainside. No trace of human life was seen except here and there one of those miserable cottages next to a foaming stream, nestling between rocks, lonely and lost. These sad dwellings make the loneliness even more over-whelming. In winter the inhabitants must surely have no chance of seeing other people and their life be like that on a desert island, possibly seeming more deserted in a country where even in summer the sun only rarely shines. All the same, they seem to have no desire to change their home, and in spite of all the desolation the countryside has a lofty grandeur, with mighty rocks rising all around like giants kneeling in strange silence. The bloom of the heather covers their colossal outlines in a mantle of purple, without hiding them from sight, while their heads are plunged in eternal mists which the rays of the sun turn into haloes.

At long last we reached the highest point, and there we saw 'Rest and be Thankful' carved on a stone, next to the names of the regiments who had built this road. At this point we met the only pedestrian on the whole journey through this veritable desert, a young, nimble Highlander, wrapped in his plaid. He spoke a little English and most obligingly helped us to climb a nearby hill from where we enjoyed a distant view. We saw before us imposing masses of rock, the black, jagged crowns of inumerable bare mountains. The torrents which tumble from their heights disappear in the dark depths below, so deep that we could not hear their noise from the height on which we were standing. Wedged between these rocks lies the gloomy valley of Glencoe whose inhabitants, at the end of the fifteenth century, fell prey in one night to the swords of English assassins, thirsting for revenge on the Highlanders who were loyal to a king they recognized as the only legitimate heir to the Scottish throne.

From our height the few small cottages looked like birds' nests, while the dark gloomy valleys were no more than gaps in the rocks which afforded them only a few hours of daylight. Now and again we saw in the distance, flocks of small sheep, miserably gnawing the tops of the heather. At one point a greenish-blue stretch of water came into view. It was Loch Long on whose shores lies Arrochar, destination of our day's journey. We now descended steeply across rocky ground and through dark, narrow glens until we reached the Loch which winds its way like a river through the valley. It is in fact an arm of the Atlantic Ocean which cuts deep into the land. Rocks rise vertically from its salty floods, casting dark shadows on everything around, while torrents, glittering in the sun, cascade into the Loch on all sides. Arrochar, with a good inn, surrounded only by a few cottages, lies close to the lake shore. The house had earlier been the residence of a noble family and its architecture still shows traces of its former glory.

LOCH LOMOND

A few miles from Arrochar we proceeded through narrow gorges to the banks of Loch Lomond, the most beautiful and biggest lake of the Highlands. Pastoral charm and sublime grandeur alternate in its surroundings. At one moment pleasant, mostly wooded hills come down close to the lake as if they wished to have their beauty reflected in the clear waters, then they give way to grassland and fields.

We began our journey through fresh, green woods, enjoying the silver glitter of the lake and the reflections in the water. Then a mountain, one of the highest we had encountered so far, seemed to bar our way, but we were able to reach the summit, and as the road descended again, there before us, in all its glory, lay the vast stretch of this beautiful lake. It was studded with green islets of varying size and fishermen's boats moved between them, breaking the silvery surface in white ripples. On the other side of the lake mighty Ben Lomond rose vertically to the clouds which hid the summit. The whole area is of such wonderful beauty that we shall never forget the day we spent in these parts.

In contrast, our lodgings in Luss, a village built close to the banks of the lake and our last stop in the Highlands, were not at all pleasant. A party of drunken Highlanders had taken up residence in one of the rooms on the ground floor where they happily danced to the music of an out-of-tune violin and the bagpipes, just among themselves, without women. The girls had understandably not wanted to take part, but this by no means prevented the men from dancing their national dances and enjoying themselves. The horse-like stamping, the shrieks of joy when some leap had succeeded particularly well, would have driven us out into the open air, had not the charms of the countryside lured us anyway. Our only fear was of the night and we had good reason, for after we had retired, our host who was also drunk, and with it extremely convivial, had to be politely ushered out of our room every few minutes. We found his daughter, a very pretty girl, most interesting. She took great pains to calm her father, yet always showing much tender forbearance, anxious to maintain the proper father-daughter relationship. She was at the same time ashamed that we, strangers who had come a long way to see her beloved Highlands, should meet him in that deplorable state and be inconvenienced by it.

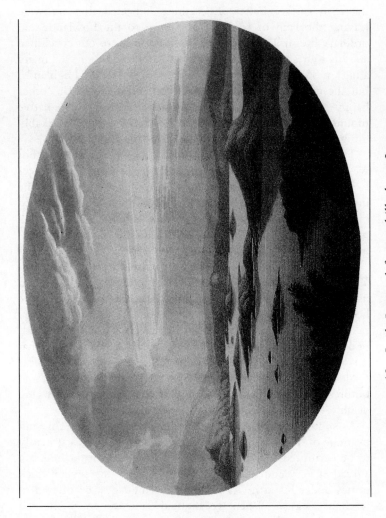

10   Loch Lomond from a hill above Luss

GLASGOW

Beyond Luss the countryside gradually became more level and the road surface better. Everything indicated that we were leaving the land of romance to return to the Lowlands and ordinary life. In Dumbarton we said goodbye to our coachman and his four stalwart horses who had conveyed us across many a high mountain and peaceful valley. So we left the Highlands, but the memory will remain with us always, to add to other happy recollections of Switzerland and our own native mountains, although those we had just seen are remarkably different.

The country around Dumbarton is famed for its beauty, but we confess that we were still too full of our recent experiences to pay much attention to the new scene. The situation of the little town is attractive, crowned with a picturesque, fortified castle on the rock above it, water before and the dark mountains behind it, the very ones we had just left. With posthorses we managed to reach Glasgow that evening.

This is a fairly large city with fine broad streets and squares. The houses, built of natural stone, are excellent and reminded us of Edinburgh. In both cities we discovered that all the houses had wide staircases made of stone with wrought-iron railings, an amenity of which the inhabitants are very proud, praising it at every opportunity. They delight in stressing that it is much superior to London where, they say, it is impossible to sleep soundly at night in the upper storeys of a house, as an outbreak of fire would almost certainly mean a horrifying death.

As soon as we entered the inn, we encountered an amusing example of 'local enterprise'. A gentleman asked most urgently to be permitted to visit us in our room. When, in the end, we agreed, a very courteous man appeared, carrying several thick tomes under his arm. As a master of languages, he offered to teach us English. When we alighted from the coach, he had chanced to overhear us speaking French and believed us to be French émigrés to whom he wished to offer his help.

Glasgow is certainly more lively than Edinburgh and is the

11 *St Vincent Street, Glasgow*

centre of much industry and business. However, despite our inquiries, nobody could tell us about any building or object of note which, to a non-commercial mind, would be worthy of closer investigation. So, in the true sense of the word, we rested for the few days we spent there. We had an offer to see round some factories but that would just have been a repetition of what we had already done. Also, it rained mercilessly all the time, a fact which pleased us as we gave thanks to the Lord that he had not sent this Flood upon us while we were in the Highlands.

We felt happy among the citizens of Glasgow, whom we found to be hospitable, decent, liberal and well-educated: in fact they combined all the good qualities which we have already praised in their countrymen, with the addition of an affluence and sense of luxury which a flourishing trade allows.

These helpful people gave us much useful information for our onward journey, and when eventually the weather improved, we set off towards Hamilton. Hamilton Palace, the seat of the Dukes of that name, is impressive and contains an interesting collection of paintings, including a Madonna by Titian, works by Caravaggio and many by the Dutch masters, not to mention the usual series of family portraits by van Dyck.

THE FALLS OF THE RIVER CLYDE AND GRETNA GREEN

We continued on our way through one of the most pleasant parts of Scotland, towards Lanark, to see the famous falls of the River Clyde. Passing woodlands, cornfields and country houses, we reached the dense thicket which hides the roaring river from the road. Leaving our coach, we took a steep and slippery footpath down to the water's edge. The river tumbled noisily from a considerable height across large slabs of rock, forming masses of foam and then appearing to rush off angrily through a deep valley. We were delighted by everything, the cascading waters, the surrounding trees, wreathed in tendrils of ivy, covered with millions of drops of water, sparkling like diamonds in the evening light. One cannot really paint waterfalls, either by brush or pen, a truth which becomes very obvious when one tries. We reached Lanark rather late and the next morning went on to Douglasmill and the other two great falls on the river. After moving across hill and dale for a few miles, our coach laboriously ascended a steep incline with high rocks towering above. At the top the view was breath-taking but awesome at the same time. It was impossible not to look down on it, yet it made us quite dizzy for we were travelling on the very edge of a precipice, not a hair's breadth, it appeared, from perishing in a horrible manner. One false step by the horses, or the smallest mishap to the coach, would have meant instant death. It was impossible to stop and equally impossible to get out of the coach at the other side as it was almost touching the rock-face. We were trapped and simply had to forget the danger and admire the sight of the valley in its morning splendour, with the Clyde winding its way leisurely between gardens and fields. A small town lay in the middle of the valley and we saw two or three spinning mills which, as in Perth, were driven by water. We could see the wheels turning rapidly and the little cascades of water, caused by their motion, glinted like silver in the sun. Yet, they were so far below us we could hear no sound.

Later, to our relief, the road descended again, and we heard once more the river thundering along. We entered a small garden and from a hillock saw the water crashing down from a great height onto the rocks in a manner even more impressive than yesterday. The river falls from such a height, forming a great arch, so that if one dared or was able to, one could walk between the rock-face and the torrent of the waterfall. Down there, one could imagine that one was in the abode of a water-sprite. It must be deafening to stand there with the roar of the foaming, surging water above one's head, to look at it and to be surrounded by it on all sides. It is seldom, however, that anyone dares to go down, for the mere sight from a distance is frightening enough. As we left the garden, we passed a country house to which it seemed to belong, and we trusted that the owner had the sense to be grateful for his good fortune in his surroundings.

Douglasmill is a dreary, small desolate place, and Elvanfoot even more miserable, so, as we proceeded towards Moffat, we had nothing to distract our thoughts from the beauty of what we had just seen. In Moffat we found a friendly woman host at the excellent inn, where we rested after the joys and inconveniences of the day. The town is a small spa, much visited by the Scots. The health-giving springs are considered most efficacious, but we could not find out what ills they were supposed to cure. Certainly not boredom, as so many spas do. The situation of the place is pleasant and it is friendly enough in itself, but we noticed no sign of arrangements for those entertainments one has come to expect in a spa: assemblies, balls or the theatre. We took it therefore that only those who are truly ailing come here, since there seem to be no diversions for the healthy.

Next day we travelled by Lockerbie, to the small village of Gretna Green, the last on the Scottish borders. While it may look insignificant, it is a place of great importance. There are those who rue for the rest of their lives the fact that they ventured here rashly once. Gretna Green is the nightmare of all parents, guardians, uncles and aunts in England who find themselves in charge of rich or beautiful maidens. On the other hand, it is the comfort and hope of all those misses who have, at finishing school, filled their heads and hearts with romantic novels, and in equal part, also the safe haven towards which all fortune hunters travel, many from Ireland, arriving with empty pockets and open hearts at Bristol, Bath, or perhaps London. With the help of the little blind god, these gentlemen hope to be able to settle themselves comfortably for life.

For in Gretna Green lives the famous old blacksmith who forges that most permanent of bonds. In his village he is a Justice of the Peace and this function gives him an important status. In Scotland marriages need no legal notice, no consent of parents and no clergyman. The loving couple simply goes to a Justice of the Peace where they declare that they are free, single and not forbidden to marry. They can then be joined in marriage without further ado. This marriage is as valid and insoluble in all British courts as one blest by the highest cleric in the land. Whosoever, then, in England – with its different laws – has a sweetheart guarded by some bothersome Argus, will take the first opportunity of packing the girl into a chaise with four quick horses and driving her at the gallop to Gretna Green. At this village on the Scottish Borders, the afore-mentioned blacksmith is ready day and night to officiate for a reasonable fee.

At the inn where we lodged, the woman innkeeper preferred not to talk about these things. She just showed us the blacksmith's house from a distance. She would have liked to deny the stories, but the walls and windows of her inn clearly betrayed all the secrets. They were covered with inscriptions and the names of happy couples who had given vent to the feelings of their overflowing hearts and entrusted to the walls the record of their sweet and joyful sentiments in this way.

We found it impossible to make the blacksmith talk, for he obviously realized that we were not a paying proposition. However, we heard from other locals that the forge is much frequented and that often several couples arrive on the same day.

During the first day's journey from Gretna Green on English soil, we were surprised to find that nobody stopped us to ask for tolls. Indeed all the turnpikes flew open at once. Only later did the obliging customs officers come to the inn where we changed horses, in order to collect their dues. It all seemed to be a silent conspiracy in this part of the world to extend to the fugitive couples a helping hand.

3 RETURN TO ENGLAND

THE LAKE DISTRICT

On our visit to the lakes of Cumberland and Westmorland, one of the most celebrated regions of England, we travelled by way of Carlisle, the first town back on English soil again, and from there proceeded to Wigton. For the last twenty years or so, it has become the fashion in London to make pilgrimages to this region and return enchanted by its natural beauty. London people call it the English Highlands, just as in Germany the country near Schandau is called Saxon Switzerland, and with as much justification.

From Wigton we travelled through rough, bare country until we were near Keswick. At this point a pleasant cultivated valley opened up before us, with a small lake, Bassenthwaitewater, lending it charm. While the scene beyond was mountainous, the cliffs had neither the interesting shape nor the imposing size of those we had seen in Scotland. Keswick is a friendly little place with very agreeable surroundings, by which we would have been undoubtedly delighted, had we not just come from Scotland. These bare rocky hills make little impact compared with the giants of the north, towering one higher than the other; these lakes shrink to mere fishponds, when one recalls Loch Lomond. One should not make such comparisons, but we felt forced to do so by the feelings of the local inhabitants and the name 'The English Highlands'.

After Keswick the scene became more romantic and the rocks grew higher, but what we missed were the woods, in their ever-changing shades of green, which cover the lower slopes of the hillsides in Scotland. We soon reached another

[90]

lake, winding irregularly through a valley, wide at times then narrowing and looking almost like a river. It was called Derwentwater and we were pleased to renew again our acquaintance with that pretty nymph who washes Matlock's rocks. Several fine country houses were situated on the shores of the lake, set in a variety of trees and fields. We left the lake and entered a narrow pass bounded by rocks, following the lively stream which turns into the small lake of Thirlemere. A bridge here and there adds a picturesque touch. We were vividly reminded of the Plauische Grund, near Dresden; it was like seeing a miniature painting of those famous regions. Near Ambleside, wide vistas proved a welcome change after the narrow valleys we had been through. Several small lakes glinted in the distance, surrounded by rich vegetation. The town is situated high, with fine views, but it was on the far side of this friendly little place that the real spectacle lay. Between the hills and the woods a large crystal-clear lake came slowly into view. Ten tree-clad islets of varying size seemed to float on its surface. On the largest of them stood the villa of a wealthy landowner, surrounded by gardens. It is called Curwen's Island, after the owner, and around it graceful gondolas bobbed up and down on the clear ripples; everything breathed calm and delight.

The shores of the lake have a great variety of beauty to display: rough, jagged rocks, green hills, some cultivated, some wooded, single trees of majestic size, cornfields and rural dwellings spread before us with the hills of Keswick forming a distant blue backdrop. We lodged at Low Wood, an excellent, secluded inn on the lake's shore. We were, of course, at Lake Windermere, one of the largest areas of water in England, which it would take several hours to circumnavigate.

LANCASTER

After we had seen Lake Windermere, the jewel of this famous region, we considered it unnecessary to visit the remaining number of smaller lakes, and so we continued on our way to Lancaster. The countryside here is cultivated like a garden

12 *Windermere Lake*

although the town itself is neither large, lively nor attractive. Many Quaker families live here. These good people are nowa-ays closer in appearance to the rest of God's children. Seldom does one hear the old, simple 'thou' from their lips, while the grave stiffness of their movements and clothes is less noticeable although remaining enough to make them conspicuous.

The girls and women of Lancashire, known as the 'Lancaster Witches', are renowned for being the most beautiful in all England, and at practically every step in Lancaster we met proof of their well-deserved fame. There is nothing more charming than the young Quaker women, wearing their unassuming, modest dress, whose dark colours, apron, large kerchief of finest muslin and little black silk hat, all without any ornament, all enhance the loveliness of their youthful faces. There is something nun-like in their appearance, yet as they walk about, free and easy, in God's fresh air, they do not induce the concern one feels for a nun. Also their simple, clean dress is more agreeable to the eye than that disfiguring Gothic garb.

The prison in Lancaster owes its excellent arrangements to the noble philanthropist, John Howard. It is a large building, a little Bastille-like from the outside, surrounded by high walls with four corner towers which serve as dormitories for the prisoners. Inside are a number of small courtyards, separated by walls, which are constantly guarded. Prisoners spend their day in these courts, able to enjoy the sunlight and fresh air, eat in a room adjoining the yard in which they can also employ themselves as they wish during the day, and at night are taken back to their dormitories.

The whole institution seemed to us well suited to its purpose, while at the same time being as humane as possible. Even his work in the prison had not extinguished the jailer's sense of pity. We noticed with pleasure that whenever he spoke of the unfortunate inmates and the reasons for their imprison-ment, he always did so in a low voice. The prisoners are separated in the yards in accordance with the type and severity of their crime. In the first and largest courtyard, at the entrance, were the debtors, a great number of them, many quite cheerful, some playing a game with a ball. Others just stood around, lost in their misery, their misfortune obviously resting heavily on their minds.

In spite of the fact that the blue sky and the bright light were able to penetrate this abode of suffering, we could not help finding the high walls, the narrow, low doors and the constant rattling of the bolts depressing. The building also contained two large courtrooms, well-furnished, the one for public hearings, in a rotunda, having seating arranged in the manner of a Roman amphitheatre. It must be an imposing sight when crowded with spectators.

We drove by the pretty and friendly little manufacturing town of Preston towards Liverpool. Immediately after Preston we felt transported, as if by magic, to Holland. The countryside is as flat as can be, stretching as far as the eye can see, crossed by canals, with ditches full of water on either side of the roads, which are paved with stone. Everything is exactly as it is in Holland, with only the spruce and tidy appearance of the Dutch houses missing. In England the outside of a house is not painted or plastered, with the result that the brick of which most of them are built acquires an old and smoky look within a few years, displeasing to the unaccustomed eye. In comparison, nothing is prettier and more friendly than the houses in Holland's countryside. The woodwork there is painted regularly every year with oil paint, the bricks being coloured red and the joints white. Thus everything always looks fresh, with a cheerful and prosperous aspect.

LIVERPOOL

The City of Liverpool, next to London the biggest in England, is however in size and beauty much inferior to Edinburgh. Nevertheless, as commerce and industry have emptied their horn of plenty over it, the stranger is struck by the wealth and luxury to be found everywhere.

The prosperous merchants spend their riches in a very commendable way, by improving their basically not very beautiful city with the construction of new and splendid buildings. Many palace-like coffee-houses, here called Newshouses, have been built recently by subscription. A beautiful theatre, a concert hall, a large inn and many charitable institutions all owe their existence to the efforts of the city's praiseworthy wealthy patrons. Of all their united enterprise, however, the most magnificent and valuable achievement is the docks. In this 'artificial' port, ships are harboured safe and sound almost in the centre of the city. They are even built there, repaired, loaded and unloaded and, most important, their cargoes are secure from thieves. The construction of docks is an enormous undertaking but one of the greatest value to the trade of a port.

We did not find our walk along the dockside pleasant. The crowds, the noise and the general bustle were stupefying, and the smell of the sea disagreeable. Yet the view of the open sea beyond the docks made amends for it all. Those born by the sea have feelings about it as do people born in the mountains for their heights. We long for what we are used to, miss it and, seeing it again, we delight in it as though we were meeting an old friend. The sea embellishes every scene and even the most desolate waste gains from it an indescribable sense of charm. The beating of the waves sounds like familiar voices from the days of our youth and we surrender ourselves to hearing it with a tender nostalgia.

As we have already said, Liverpool is not really a beautiful city and its surroundings have nothing to distinguish them. We must however mention the establishments of some of the wealthy merchants, which are situated on a gentle slope, apart from but still quite close to the city. Very elegantly furnished, they combine the advantages of town and country life in a most agreeable way. Alas, this advantage is not destined to last for much longer, as day by day the city grows bigger, and one can already calculate that in the course of a few years these houses will be engulfed in its tumult.

The mood of Liverpool society is perhaps a little more relaxed than in London, but here, as there, a kind of general interest is lacking in conversation, the interest which would make a stranger feel at home. Once the ordinary politenesses, called for by etiquette in this country, have been exchanged, and one has said all there is to be said about the weather and one another's well-being, one usually finds oneself at a loss as to what to say if one does not know anything about trade and politics.

The men of this city have nearly all visited the Continent. They are acquainted with foreign manners and customs, which makes them tolerant of strangers. The women, however, are Englishwomen in the truest sense of the word. In general, they lack the higher education which is more easy to come by in a big city like London than in the provinces. To make up for this, they boast a thousand little acquisitions and affectations which are intended to show off their wealth and their *savoir-faire*. This behaviour grows very irksome to anyone not accustomed to it.

The people of Liverpool possess to a high degree the virtue of hospitality, not particularly a characteristic of the English town-dwellers, nor suited to their domestic arrangements. It has to be admitted that at their richly-appointed tables boredom again presides. At any rate, this is certainly the case until the ladies have withdrawn and the men are free to discuss politics and kindred subjects over their wine.

In Liverpool, as in the whole of Lancashire, there are many Quaker families. While in some ways they have rather degenerated here and seem ashamed of their ancient, simple customs, modern fashionable ways are still strange to them and the young men, especially those aspiring to be dandies, seem very awkward. They, whose fathers would not lift their hats to the king, now, for example, greet practically everyone in the street, just to show how free from prejudice they are. They behave like fashionable Jews who, to demonstrate how free their education has made them, acquire digestive troubles by eating ham in public places. In some shops we came across Quaker women still wearing the simple clean dress their religion prescribes. In their mouths the use of 'thou' sounded so courteous and modest that our 'you' seemed quite ridiculous by comparison. They are excellent to deal with and their goods are always of first-rate quality. They never overcharge nor is there any haggling or bargaining, as they would simply find this offensive.

The theatre is not large but is most elegant and comfortably furnished. One can hear well in all parts of the house and the stage and the lighting leaves nothing to be desired. We saw presentations of several recent plays which we had already visited in London and on the whole we were satisfied, at least with the actors, although we must admit that the actresses seemed to have come to an agreement among themselves not to aspire above a very mediocre standard. The audience was much less noisy than in London. We beheld, however, in the pit, the two most drunken individuals we had ever seen. Both were quite elegantly dressed and sat there, deadly pale, as stiff as corpses, their glassy eyes wide open. Suddenly one of them dropped like a stone from his seat, while the other sat quite rigid, as though unaware that anything had happened. They were carried out by some of the spectators with so much forbearance and sympathy that they must have thought to themselves quietly: 'You today, I tomorrow.'

We have mentioned before the many philanthropic institutions in the city which owe their existence to the charity and wealth of the local people. We visited one of them, for the blind, with a mixture of joy and emotion. Its funds are not yet sufficient to build a house big enough to take all these unfortunate people and so many are lodged in private houses in the city, meeting every day in a building specially furnished for them, called an asylum. There they take their meals together, receive tuition in music and those handicrafts at which they are able to work in their sad state, spending the rest of the day in any way they wish. In two rooms there are good pianos for their use and in a third an organ. When we entered that room, a young man sat at the organ, accompanying three young girls, his fellows in misfortune. They sang together a touching lament, made bearable only by their quiet resignation and hope for the day when their long dark night will be illuminated. Their voices were agreeable and pure and, as they did not notice our entering the room, they continued singing undisturbed. We stood at the entrance to the room, quite moved, keeping very quiet, anxious not to interrupt them.

On the whole these blind people, like almost all their fellow sufferers, are always bright, cheerful and talkative. In the lower room we found a group of women and girls spinning, wheels and tongues vying with each other, buzzing away merrily. In another room where men and boys were busy making baskets, the mood was equally happy. We admired the fine workmanship of the baskets and their pretty shapes. They even wove patterns of green and red willows into them and knew how to distinguish the colours carefully from the white ones, merely by touch.

The blind also make a number of other useful things which are sold in a downstairs shop to benefit the institution. They weave and make ropes, and there are even shoemakers among them. This particular institution seems to be one of the most useful and beneficent of its kind. Far from making any pretences, its sole aim is to provide real help to these unfortunate people, turning them as far as possible into useful members of society and through work and music, cheering their lonely, dark lives. In this place, their misfortune, which should be one of mankind's most sacred concerns, is not, as in other similar institutions, exploited for the amusement of an idly gaping crowd, titillated by the spectacle of something out of the ordinary.

The day before we left Liverpool a deafening peal of bells suddenly rang out from all the churches. It lasted, uninterrupted, for a whole hour. The bells rang merrily, running up an octave, then down, now in major thirds, now fifths, through the whole scale according to the whims of the sextons. Each of these gentlemen rang to his heart's content without paying the slightest attention to his colleagues. We thought that news of a battle had been received, that the birthday of a member of the Royal Family was being celebrated or that, at least, there was a grand fashionable wedding in the city, for we knew that even on a happy, private domestic occasion any Englishman is allowed have all the bells rung, as long as he is prepared to pay for it. However, there was nothing like that. It appeared simply that an old spinster who had died more than a hundred years ago was responsible for all the noise. In her will she bequeathed a leg of lamb to be served with a cucumber salad and a glass of porter every Thursday night of the year to every Liverpool sexton for all eternity. They partake of this meal together, but before they can eat they must make this terrible noise with their bells, driving those living close to the churches to despair. All this is done in memory of the benefactress and it is questionable whether this way of gaining immortality is not as good or even better than many another.

On leaving Liverpool we found the countryside just as Dutch as that which we had passed through on our way there. It is as flat as possible and very highly cultivated, criss-crossed by navigable canals. We reached Manchester for the second time by way of Warrington, a very friendly little town, famous for its glassware of all kinds and from there we proceeded to Disley over very rough, stony roads. English roads are, on the whole, rightly praised as excellent, but close to the large manufacturing towns, where heavily laden carts and wagons ply back and forth all day, they are much less so and certainly inferior to the main roads around Dresden, the Dessau region, Austria and in other parts of Germany.

One inconvenience for the stranger travelling in England is the difficulty of setting forth early in the morning. The host and his servants sleep on well into the day. Only the Boots is ready at any time, but his authority goes no further than perhaps getting the horses ready. This is a hardship felt only by the foreigner, particularly the German, as on the whole the English are used to breakfasting only a few hours after rising and usually travel one or two stages before they ask for their tea and toast. We thought we would follow this English custom in Disley but the house there was so dirty and in such disarray that we found it impossible even to leave the coach.

It so happened that our journey took place at a time of general rearmament of the nation against the landing of the dreaded *bateaux plats*. Old and young played at being soldiers: offices, factories and shops were empty for half of the week. Every young man tried to show his courage in front of the ladies by wearing a handsome uniform and, if the weather was fine, drilling. In rainy weather, however, they went, like the Papal Guard, with umbrellas to parade. Once the drill was over, their patriotic exertion was assuaged by generous communal feasts in the inns, well supplied with bottles, while the rest of the night was spent in dancing and gambling. This way of life was then common all over England and the heads of offices and factories were really in despair over this great patriotism being shown by the young heroes.

In Disley such a patriotic feast had taken place the previous night. Traces of it were apparent everywhere, particularly obnoxious to the incomer. After leaving Disley, at first the countryside seemed very pretty, being very English, very green everywhere. But soon we again found ourselves among high bare cliffs, sparsely covered with heather: we had all the discomforts of a journey in the mountains without any compensation of lofty beauty. Just before reaching Middleton we entered a narrow gorge which wound between rocks of a more beautiful shape but then continued across higher and equally unpleasant rocky country to Sheffield.

This is a large but not friendly manufacturing town. The air is full of coal smoke and there is everywhere the indescribable dirt of a blacksmith's shop. The streets resound with wild and deafening shouting and hammering, and everything has the look of a coarse and unpleasant trade. Yet many very beautiful steel and plated goods are made in Sheffield. However we did not find it at all attractive and after a brief stay, we hurried on our way and soon rejoiced in breathing fresh air again in nearby Wentworth House, the country residence of Lord Fitzwilliam.

WENTWORTH HOUSE AND ROTHERHAM

We were allowed to drive through the park at Wentworth but, although it is large and pleasant, we found that it had nothing to distinguish it from any other, which is true also of the gardens and pleasure grounds. It is the splendid stables which are the remarkable thing here, more like a palace than a home for horses. They are built around a large quadrangle and one wing of this architecturally elegant building is equipped as a riding school. In the three remaining stables we saw the most beautiful horses, among them many hunters, mostly of Arab descent, as well as several racehorses who had gained fame at the courses. The air in these stables was much purer than that in Sheffield. All the horses stood on stone slabs into which holes had been bored here and there to allow the moisture to drain off, thus doing away with unpleasant smells. Above the boxes of most noble horses, the hunters and the racehorses, were their names, beautifully inscribed, those of their illustrious parents and in some cases a much longer genealogical tree. Some brood mares had large mirrors in front of them, no doubt in the hope that their descendants might match them in beauty. In a separate part of the yard a very pretty little Arab horse ran about. We were told that it was more than twenty years old. It was as tame as a dog and not much bigger, a graceful little animal. It answered every call by jumping up in a friendly and affectionate manner.

Tired out by our keen observation, for we had also toured the house, which is in keeping with the stables, if perhaps a little overloaded with ornamentation, and had admired Lord Fitzwilliam's fine collection of paintings, we continued on our way to Rotherham where remarkable things of a differeing kind awaited us. Once again we were in the abode of Vulcan, but on this occasion we fared better than we had at Carron for we were allowed to enter the works where we had a friendly reception. This iron foundry, in size and importance next to Carron, belongs to a Mr Walker. Although here, too, strangers are not admitted without a special recommendation, and we had none to offer Mr Walker, he was satisfied after glancing at some open letters of introduction which we had brought from London for other places in England, and gave orders for us to be conducted round everything. A vast quantity of sheet metal is made here, cleaned, cut, tinned, then packed in crates and sent all over the world where it is used in a thousand different ways. The raw material has all come from Russia, partly in its crude state, partly as long bars.

These works were of great interest to us. The high flickering flames and sparks were a terrible yet beautiful sight, as were the red, sizzling streams of fire which slowly and glowingly ran along until they flowed into the mould, as into a grave, congealing there for ever. The enormous black men working among all this increased our fascination. The large iron bridge which we had admired near Sunderland was made here and another even larger one was recently sent to Jamaica. The iron is moulded into many different shapes, from colossal bridges right down to the humble domestic flatiron. They make the most attractive railing work, mostly based on antique designs, which is used extensively for the decoration of balconies, windows, garden gates and stairs, and looks rich and elegant. Through the invention of casting, instead of beating out the metal, the use of such ironwork has greatly increased. Of course the beaten iron lasts longer than the cast, but the latter costs only half as much and as it is still iron, it lasts well enough.

We had the great good fortune to see a 24-pound cannon being cast. The liquid metal flowed from two furnaces into two channels, banked up with sand and earth. They soon joined into a single channel from which the steady flow of molten metal filled a deep-set mould. At this sight Dante's hell and the fiery Phlegethon came vividly to mind. The cannon takes three days to cool after which the mould is broken and the part-finished article extracted. We were also permitted to watch a cannon being bored, for they are of course cast solid. This used to be a secret operation but it was shown to us without any objection when we expressed the desire to see it. The machinery used for this process is driven by water. A long iron rod, the thickness of the required muzzle of the cannon, is placed in a horizontal position. On the end of the rod is a flat, thin piece of steel with sharp ends, shaped like tongues. The cannon, driven by water with incredible power, is forced to rotate, winding itself round the rod as an axle. These tongues cut the metal from the opening, allowing the rod to polish the inside of the bore smoothly and evenly. It is impossible to contemplate this power in action without amazement, a force which treats hard metal as if it were soft wood. How little can man do with his strength alone and how many astonishing things does he accomplish with the help of the elements when he harnesses them to serve him. But these same elements may often take cruel revenge on their powerless master when they break the shackles he cunningly invented. Then they rage in unbounded freedom, destroying whole generations in a mere moment.

FROM NOTTINGHAM TO
STRATFORD ON AVON

The area near Rotherham abounded in grand houses. We paid brief visits to Worksop, Welbeck and Clumber, the seats of the noble Dukes of Norfolk, Portland and Newcastle. They were all splendid mansions with collections of paintings and libraries to match. We finally passed through the pretty little town of Mansfield and reached Nottingham, a handsome manufacturing city with many large factories, mainly employed in the making of hosiery, for which it is renowned. From there we went to Derby, through pleasant countryside, across parklands, past friendly rural dwellings, some beautiful, some stately, some the great houses of the aristocracy. At one point our postilion fell off his horse and the horses bolted. On these good and busy roads such an incident is of little import, even though in English novels it is often used as an important motif. Our runaway horses were soon stopped and we reached Derby, admittedly a little shaken, but safe and sound. Alas, the races to which we had looked forward had just finished, and, as we had already admired the sights of the town when we previously passed through, we continued on our journey towards Warwick. This town is situated on the banks of the Avon and is notable for its ancient, imposing castle, a good example of the architecture of its time, but with an interior which proves disappointing due to the mixture in the styles of decoration.

From Warwick we reached Stratford on Avon, a small place, poor and insignificant, but wearing a glorious halo. For it is here that Shakespeare came into the world, the place to which he returned at the end of his life, and where his mortal remains were laid to rest. Nobody is quite sure of that exact spot but in Westminster Abbey, the resting place of kings, there is a splendid memorial to him, erected by the nation whose pride he is.

We were taken to the cottage where his father, a wealthy glover and wool merchant, lived and where the great spirit, still unaware of itself, felt restive and oppressed in these narrow confines. Until into his sixteenth year, Shakespeare was in

[103]

constant conflict with his limiting surroundings, kicking against the ties which restricted his freedom. At last, after many wild escapades into which his youthful spirits and energy drew him, he fled from the narrow constraints of rural life, free at last to follow the call of his genius.

One felt that the rude mud walls of the house can scarcely have withstood the passing of two hundred years or more, but the local people insist that this is so. In the partition wall near the fireplace an old wooden easy chair has been placed in a recess. The fireplace itself looks very old, with a large stone slab in front of it and it seems certain that this is where Shakespeare's father must have sat, worrying about his son's youthful pranks. Although close in ties of flesh and blood, the father was a stranger to him in nature and would remain so for ever.

In one of the upstairs rooms we were shown a large old bedstead where Shakespeare's mother gave birth to him. His family tree also hangs there. The house is at present occupied by a butcher, who appears very poor but watches very carefully over this sacred place, knowing that the visits of strangers provide a very welcome support to his meagre income.

TEWKESBURY AND CHELTENHAM

In the friendly little country town of Tewkesbury we heard that big races were to take place there in a few days' time. Among wolves one learns to howl, as the proverb goes, so among the English one finds oneself becoming eventually a kind of John Bull. We decided therefore to spend the time until the races in the nearby spa of Cheltenham and return to Tewkesbury on the actual day. So we departed for Cheltenham.

This famous spa is a pretty little town, situated in a pleasant broad valley, surrounded by hills. Everything in it looks new and, indeed, the greater part of the town has been built during the last fifty years. It was about that time that the local spring, which made the town famous, was discovered.

Cheltenham consists of a single street, at least a mile long. On either side small streets branch off and sometimes there is just a single building in them. On the main street there are elegant houses, handsome shops, lending libraries and coffee shops, and here the beau monde strolls slowly up and down seeming, as it appeared to us, rather bored. In twos and threes the ladies, with many a yawn, wander slowly from one shop to another while the gentlemen try to while away valuable time in their own way by riding, drinking and reading the newspapers.

The spirit of social enjoyment is as little native to this place as it is to the rest of England. Everything is done seriously, and in that way pleasure becomes work. When the morning has been endured, balls, assemblies, concerts and the theatre, whatever happens to be on, help to pass the remaining hours of the day. In Cheltenham all these entertainments are certainly available, even if on a somewhat reduced scale. During the season a Master of Ceremonies from Bath presides here, as in the summer he has time to spare. Of this appointment at English spas and the general mode of life there, we propose to talk in detail later on when describing Bath, the queen of all English spas.

The promenade which leads to the spring at Cheltenham is considered one of the finest in England. Possibly it acquired this fame through being in a country where avenues planted with tall trees are very rare. Here tall, shady elms are planted on both sides of a broad, dead straight walk, some 900 feet long. The spring is at its centre, enclosed by a temple of slightly clumsy design. Next to it is a pretty hall for the use of the spa guests in bad weather. Inside a book for subscriptions is laid out, these to cover the maintenance of the promenade, the hall, etc. . . . Every well-bred spa guest signs this book with his full name and rank. Should he neglect to do so, he is taken for a Nobody and ignored – and rightly so. At the far end of the promenade is an ordinary English garden where another pretty building, also for the use of visitors, closes the avenue. At its other end a pointed church spire completes a fine vista.

It is a pleasant sight in the mornings, between eight and ten o'clock, the usual hour for taking the waters, to see the world stroll slowly under the noble trees. The special charm of English women in their morning outfits is well known, and here in the green half-light the nymph-like figures in white are shown off to great advantage. This avenue does not bear comparison with that of Pyrmont but the English are proud of it and believe it to be the most beautiful in the world. While one takes the waters and wanders up and down in what is characteristically called the morning parade, a band of musicians plays away to its heart's content, as well they know how to, loudly intoning 'God Save The King' and 'Rule Britannia'.

It is a strange arrangement that the only access to the promenade is by way of the cemetery. It happens to be quite a pretty one with tall lime trees, but one feels that the tombstones may well awaken ideas in some of the sick who have made the pilgrimage to the spring, and, consequently, diminish its healing powers.

The waters of Cheltenham are mainly used against skin ailments, scurvy and such complaints. George III made the spring fashionable by visiting it several times. Alas, however, he suffered for it. He was seeking a cure for a deep-rooted skin disease with which he was possibly born. He succeeded. The skin trouble disappeared, but good George fell into a deeply depressed state of mind, in which he remains.

At last the great day which was to draw us to Tewkesbury arrived; the whole of Cheltenham seemed to emigrate with us, a long and colourful procession of carriages and people on horseback. When we arrived there, the town was full of life and bustle, with everybody dressed in his Sunday best. Pretty girls in white dresses and yellow nankeen shoes ran about cheerfully. A band of tightrope-walkers and two troupes of strolling players had set up Thalia's and Terpsichore's temple for the night, and there was also a ball and an Assembly. Just think what excitement this would generate in that little town of Tewkesbury and how young hearts, unaccustomed to all this splendour, would beat faster, merely at the thought of it all. And to top everything there were those elegant ladies and gentlemen from Cheltenham, the carriages, the beautiful horses, the servants and the rest of the hangers-on – a sheer delight. Fortunate was he who, like ourselves, had taken the precaution to secure lodgings and lunch beforehand, for otherwise it would have been difficult to find any place in the midst of all the commotion.

At twelve o'clock every man, horse and carriage went to the racecourse. The town forms a semi-circle around a fine green meadow which had been specially prepared for the event, while the distant blue hills provide a suitable backcloth. The locality, very pretty in itself, was now animated by several thousands of happy people of every rank, presenting a lively spectacle. In the centre of the meadow the tightrope-walkers had erected their platform, colourfully decorated with a lot of bunting, where they would perform in the evening. These artistes in their light fantastic costumes, running about among the crowd or grouping themselves on their platform, together with the Turkish music being played to attract people's curiosity, all combined to enhance the liveliness of the scene. The rival groups of entertainers strove to attract attention and to get the better of each other. Untiringly they distributed leaflets extolling the merits of their companies, showering them through the carriage doors. No sooner was a handful thrown through one door than a rival would thrust more through the other. In the midst of all this happy confusion the only serious note was struck by those placing bets on the races, identifiable by the zeal in their faces and the contempt with which they regarded the happy crowd.

At last the signal was given for the races to begin. The horses ran splendidly, and among them were a few famous racehorses. We found the whole event a lot more pleasant than in Edinburgh, in fact so much so that, like the greater part of the company, we returned for the second races after lunch. But by now the novelty had worn off and, in order not to spoil what had been a very pleasant day, we decided to give a miss to the balls, the Assembly, the equestrians – in fact we did not even wait for a decision as to whether Jenny Spinster had passed the winning-post a quarter of a minute before Edgar, or whether both had arrived at the same time.

We wished the good people of Tewkesbury, whom Shakespeare immortalised in one of his masterpieces by calling them makers of good mustard, much joy for the evening and the day to follow when new pleasures awaited them. We found time, however, to admire the Gothic church, one of the finest and largest in the country, and then departed in a merry mood for Gloucester. In passing through this town, we were delighted with its pretty houses and broad streets but, as far as we could make out, it offered nothing to merit our closer attention.

BRISTOL

The journey from Gloucester to Bristol is most pleasant and interesting as it takes one through a region where the character of the countryside differs from the rest of England. It is softer and more varied and, although the vegetation is splendid, green is not always the dominating colour. The trees seem taller, planted in large compact groups, but in addition there are the many orchards of fruit trees, enclosed by walls instead of hedges, and these are the finest to be found in Britain. Among the light green foliage glows the pippin, England's pride, crushed under the press in autumn when it is made into cider to give joy to the hearts of the middle classes who cannot afford expensive French and Portuguese wines. Here the pear ripens on stately trees, providing the Perry which is often sold at high prices by wine merchants under the disguise of sparkling champagne.

The beautiful River Avon enlivens the scene, with small boats floating on its silvery surface. Near Bristol this river becomes deep enough for large ships of forty or fifty cannons. Eight miles further on it flows into the Severn, which in this place is actually an arm of the sea which cuts deep into the country. Without doubt Bristol's surroundings are the finest in England, for everything comes together to make a perfect whole: the sea, the navigable river, the hills and the dales, the fields and the woods, above all the great abundance from the land, the result of good soil and hard work.

The town seemed to us bigger than Edinburgh. The streets and squares are broad and well-paved, filled with bustling crowds, full of beautiful private houses, public buildings and churches, among them the particularly renowned venerable Gothic cathedral and St Mary Redcliffe. The theatre, with its façade of Corinthian columns, is spacious and elegant and, during the season, Assemblies and balls are held here under a Master of Ceremonies.

Bristol is often compared to Rome, for, like that queen of cities, it is also built on seven hills, though, alas, the roads leading up to the summits are mostly very steep. Apart from the navigable Avon, a smaller river, the Frome, flows through the town, and both are crossed by a series of pretty bridges. The quayside by the port is splendid, a masterpiece of its kind, but we turned away from it, shuddering, for this is the place where human greed furnished the ships for the slave trade which made Bristol's citizens wealthy. These stones must have witnessed the suffering of many a slave and, pondering on all this, we were unable to take pleasure in the sight of these handsome docks, which, like those in Liverpool, safely harbour ships from all parts of the world.

One of the finest houses in the Bristol area is King's Weston, the country residence of Lord Clifford. The façade of the house is broad and stately, if a little clumsy and overdecorated. We felt no desire to pause for closer inspection and moved quickly through the pretty gardens, seeking the simplicity of nature beyond to soothe our senses which had been distracted by such artificiality. King's Weston lies at a considerable height and looking down on one side one beholds a charming valley, seemingly cut off from the world by gentle hills, full of the rich vegetation which makes England one of the most beautiful countries in Europe, while on the other side the mighty Avon winds its majestic way through an equally verdant paradise. Small craft skim on its surface, catching the eye as it lingers on the river's course, watching it grow mightier and broader as it proceeds into the blue distance, there to be united forever with the sea. For a long time we were lost in this enchanting spectacle until, at last, we made our way back through the fine old trees of Lord Clifford's park to a still higher hill, called Penpole Point, where we could admire this expansive view from an even better angle.

From here there is a pleasant road to Clifton. Clifton is called a village but it is a village, we might say, of palaces. It lies scattered, partly in the valley, partly on the sunny slope of a hill. The fine large houses stand, now in a crescent, that design

13 St Vincent's Rock, Bristol

so much favoured in England, now in long rows or terraces, sometimes alone, sometimes forming broad streets or squares. It all displays a marvellous variety midst the gardens, the fields and the steep, wild cliffs.

Some of these buildings are lived in throughout the year, A great number of them, however, are for the use of those who come annually in the hope of finding new health in the come annually in the hope of finding new health in the lukewarm spring which rises not far from Clifton. Alas, their hope is often in vain, for this spring is used as the last resort of those suffering from that greatest of ills to threaten our short life: consumption.

Nowhere more common than in England, this disease nearly always finds its victims among the youngest and most lovable, giving them an extraordinary beauty and radiance as it destroys them. It is like the rose which, attacked by a worm, blooms the sooner and the more beautiful. There is no more heart-rending a sight than to see these young ethereal beings, breathless, already seeming half in another world, walking with difficulty across the green Elysian grass, and no more heart-rending an experience than to visit the nearby cemetery the resting place of those who have gone before, where one can read on a long, sad, uninterrupted line of tombstones their ages recorded as between twenty and twenty-five years.

HOTWELLS

A very steep road leads down the hill to Hotwells where a spring rises and where there are also many fine houses for the visitors to the spa. Close to the River Avon, it gushes forcefully from one of the rocks which rise majestically on either side. A fine building has been erected over the spring. On entering, there is a hall which serves for the visitors, who are taking the waters, to engage in conversation. Behind this is the pump-room where a pretty girl performs the duties of Hebe, pouring the lukewarm water which sparkles like champagne and is not unpleasant to the taste. When first drawn it looks a little muddy and whitish, but as it cools it becomes quite clear.

A mass of pretty trifles, rare shells, stones and minerals from the neighbouring hills, are on sale here, among them the famous Bristol stones which are found in the clefts and crevices of the cliffs on both sides of the Avon and which are very similar in brilliance and hardness to real diamonds.

The view from the pump-room windows is limited and stark. The dark red marble mass of St Vincent's rises majestically to the sky, while beyond it the Avon roars through its narrow bed of rocks and on its other side are rocky heights, terrifying and wild. It seems as if the dark river had succeeded in cleaving the rock or that it had been shattered by an earthquake to enable the waters to rush on their way. The eye can follow the river through the walls of rock for about a mile and a half, and beyond there is a glimpse of the blue hills of Wales.

Behind the pump-room a fine tree-planted terrace by the banks of the river serves as a promenade. A thousand ships come and go on the Avon and there can hardly be another spa which can boast of a similar sight. In cold or wet weather visitors stroll under a colonnade, built in the shape of a crescent and bordered by elegant shops on one side.

As far as the buildings are concerned, Hotwells appears to be a continuation of Clifton. Here, as there, they stand singly or together in fine rows with the advantage of views towards sea and river, hill and dale, for nature has provided abundantly here. There are also other enjoyments: in two handsome buildings, designed for receiving society, *déjeuners dansants* are held by subscription on Mondays and Thursdays. There is also a ball regularly on Tuesdays and on other days assemblies and promenades fill the leisure hours.

As in other larger spas, in Hotwells too, a Master of Ceremonies presides. His rules are displayed on the walls of the halls and are carefully observed. With regard to dress, they are a little less strict than in Bath though in all other matters of etiquette, particularly concerning rank, they are the same. The general arrangements in Hotwells are similar to those in Bath, except in a few minor details, and we therefore refer the kind reader to the next section.

Apart from the entertainments common to all spas, which

14   *Approach to Hotwell House, Hotwells*

are provided by the regular promenades, assemblies, balls, lending libraries and so on, the visitor to Bristol is fortunate in having the extra pleasure of being able to wander in the lovely surrounding countryside. Apart from King's Weston, there are many places within easy reach which are well worth a visit. Alas, we suffered the fate of those who did not have enough time to see everything. Anyone able to stay here for some weeks can enjoy a great variety of excursions, not least sailing on the gleaming river, when the blue cliffs echo to the music which accompanies the boats.

BATH

The distance from Bristol to Bath is only 14 miles, and we drove along an excellent road, through countryside which seemed a garden of ever-changing delight. While the season was admirably suited to the enjoyment of these pleasures, it was not however the best for learning about the style of life which sets this town apart from most others. On a previous occasion we had chanced to be here in winter and perhaps our impressions on our first visit and on this, our second stay, may, if put together, succeed in giving our readers a fuller picture of this remarkable place. But first of all, a few observations on life in the English spa in general seem to us indispensable for an understanding of the whole.

Everywhere in England etiquette is the order of the day. The British in this respect are like women and their stays. When they have been used to wearing them since infancy, they feel so uncomfortable if the accustomed restraint ceases, that they do not know how to live without it. This restraint is an integral part of their domestic life and enters into the most sacred ties between husband and wife, parents and children. How therefore could they dispense with it when at a spa, where the British, quite against their nature, must live among strangers. The fact that one lives among strangers, that life moves to a different rhythm and a somewhat changed routine, that in itself makes the atmosphere of the spa stand apart from their normal daily existence. In order, therefore, that nobody should deviate from the accepted standards and so offend company new to him, through sheer awkwardness or ignorance, each spa has its Master of Ceremonies. This gentleman (in Bath in fact there are two) sees to everything, playing, as it were the host, receiving everybody on arrival with courtesy. At balls and on other occasions he insists on the strict observance of the rules governing the whole society, concerning the hours given up to leisure, dress, rank and a thousand other incidentals. Such rules are posted in the Assembly and ball rooms so that the Master of Ceremonies can immediately refer to them. Men and women fond of dancing, should they not have been clever enough to make their own arrangements, consult him, and he will find them partners for the entire evening. He will endeavour to remove the cause of a disagreement and settle any that may have arisen. He watches untiringly over conduct and propriety.

We were intrigued to find still on the Assembly rooms walls the 'Rules fixed with General Agreement in 1742' when Richard 'Beau' Nash was the Master of Ceremonies in Bath. We think the reader may well find them both interesting and edifying.

1 That one formal visit on arrival and departure is all that might be expected of a lady of standing, or else it might be thought that she were bold.
2 On days when balls are arranged, the ladies should fix a definite hour for the servants to collect them, thus saving themselves and others inconvenience.
3 Gentlemen show their good manners to the ladies by never appearing in their company in the morning, wearing a dressing-gown and nightcap.
4 No one should be offended if someone attends card parties or breakfasts outside their own circle.
5 Gentlemen may give their tickets to a ball only to respectable ladies, unless they do not know any.
6 Gentlemen show bad manners if they push themselves in front of ladies. This is the behaviour of those who respect nobody but themselves.
7 No gentleman or lady should take it amiss if others pass

before them, unless they be persons who are not permitted to attend the dance at all.

8 Old ladies and children must suffer being seated in the second row at balls, for their time has either passed or not yet arrived.

9 Young ladies should, in their comportment, always remember that many eyes are turned upon them (unless they be coquettes).

10 Anyone who is found to spread lies and wicked gossip, is considered to be their inventor.

11 People who repeat such lies are shunned by all society, except that of others like them.

At the time of our visits, stringent rules were still in force. These were most specific even on minor points of etiquette, for example: for informal dances each ticket allowed entry for one person only; balls commenced at seven o'clock and ended on the stroke of eleven, even if that moment occurred in the middle of a dance; young ladies and gentlemen might, during the school holidays, gain admission, if introduced by a member of society; between the minuets and the English dances, there was an interval so that ladies who had precedence could take up their places, for any lady getting up only after a dance had begun, lost her precedence and must stand at the end of the line. In addition, ladies who wished to dance the minuet, must wear lappets and were requested to arrange the rest of their dress accordingly, as far as fashion permitted, while gentlemen were required to appear in full dress, it being stressed that they were not admitted in boots or half boots. Only subscribers had access to the Assembly Halls and attention was drawn to the fact that at the upper end, the first three rows were reserved for the wives of Peers of the Realm of Great Britain and Ireland, and ladies equal in rank.

The Master of Ceremonies was required to ensure that the owners of the halls pledged themselves to arrange twenty *Bals Parés* (formal balls) and thirty Fancy Balls (informal). However, these gentlemen were not required to give an account of their takings. The orchestra had to consist of twelve instruments, a harp, a flageolet and a tambourine included.

A notice pointed out that with the ever-increasing size of Bath, it was impossible for the Master of Ceremonies to learn of the arrival of every visitor immediately. He therefore hoped that these visitors would have the forbearance to excuse him if – much against his will – he was unable to call. He thereby officially asked that everybody on arrival put down his name and address in the book provided for the purpose in the pump-room. As it was of extreme importance to bar all improper company from the halls, he equally asked all visiting ladies and gentlemen to give him the opportunity of meeting them as early as possible, so that he could ensure that they received the respect and attention which he would always take great pains to extend.

All this shows that being a Master of Ceremonies is not an easy task. Those best suited to such posts are men who have lost themselves in their fortune and the great whirlpool of the world and now find themselves on their own, having saved from the general shipwreck only their strong courage, worldly wisdom, a good figure and a few acquaintances of rank. They will obtain the post upon the death or voluntary resignation of a predecessor and by the majority vote of the visitors present in the spa. They lead a very fatiguing life and their only rewards are general esteem, the revenue of a few balls arranged for their benefit each season, and a handsome present from the visitors. That they have free entry everywhere goes without saying. Their office is marked by a gold medal which they wear around the neck or as a buttonhole.

The English Master of Ceremonies bears a slight resemblance to the doctors in some of the German spas, where, during the promenade or at public eating places they flutter around both the healthy and the sick, setting everything in order, knowing everything, being everywhere and nowhere at the same time. The spa doctor, as such, does not exist at the English spas. One adheres to the prescriptions of one's own doctor, brought from home. Only in exceptional cases does one consult a local doctor or one from the neighbourhood. Public gambling is not known here and so one has not – as in Germany – to endure from early morning the unpleasant sight of these robbery-bent hyenas scavenging for their ill-gotten gains.

On arrival at the spa, as soon as one has settled comfortably, which is quickly and easily done in England, one immediately sends cards to the visitors one knows or whose acquaintance one would like to make, after which there is nothing left to do but to take out a subscription to everything and so have entry everywhere. First of all there are the Assembly rooms, then the balls taking place on certain days and the concerts which are given regularly in the larger resorts. Above all there are the lending libraries, generally found in fair numbers, which are the ultimate consolation, the last refuge of those who can find no other way to deal with that arch-enemy, time.

Once one has taken the waters early, usually during the promenade in one of the pump-rooms, has taken one's bath, breakfasted *en famille* (public breakfasts are rare), what is one to do with the long morning until one dresses for the second time before the midday meal? One cannot always ride, drive or walk; the few visits and a look at the milliners' shops are quickly done. What bliss then to take refuge in those lending libraries. There one always meets company, exchanges a few politenesses with acquaintances, staring at strangers who stare back at one. And then there are the many novels, newspapers, journals and pamphlets, most elegantly presented, which can be browsed through or taken home. And that is not all. Apart from these spiritual treasures, one also finds in these premises other more worldly ones. There are collections of all those many trifles, made of precious metals and stones which seem indispensable to the world of fashion, also all manner of articles needed for writing or drawing, from a simple sheet of paper to the most luxurious writing case or portfolio. These things are always there to be looked at or bought, and occasionally something delightful is put into a lottery, providing yet another reason for visiting these establishments.

Eating at midday is a little earlier than in London because entertainments at night begin as early as seven o'clock. Each family keeps house for itself or has meals brought in. Single men join together at the inn. Now and again one comes across a house where all the lodgers contract also for board, and so eat together. But only a few adopt this habit, as it is not considered fashionable or what the British call 'stylish'. The English do

15   *Taking the baths, Bath*

not like eating in public and it is only in the smaller spas, where the company is restricted in numbers, money and entertainment and one has to stick together more, that one encounters visitors eating in that manner. Ladies are especially reluctant to do so.

In the bigger spas one dresses for the third time after lunch. As a rule, every night of the week is devoted to a different recreation. Dinners are not customary and everybody goes to bed about midnight with the exception, perhaps, of some privileged late revellers.

Life in the English spa is much more regulated than in Germany. One knows to the last detail how every day is to be spent and there is no aimless drifting about here and there as in Pyrmont or Karlsbad. Only Sunday is a dreadful day. Playing cards, dancing and music are all forbidden, all the shops and the lending libraries are closed and there is no comfort save the evening promenade to the saloon for a cup of tea. The company lacks variety. Foreigners, those strange people from other nations who provide such a great interest in our spas, are completely lacking. With a few exceptions one sees only the natives, for even the Scots and the Irish are considered strangers.

Somehow, in England, everything in life has to go against the ordinary course of nature. Summer is turned into winter and winter into summer. Evening is made into midday and night into day. To complete these changes in time, it has pleased the powers that be to change the Season in Bath to the winter. From November to May the place swarms with visitors who rotate in a circle of endless jollifications to the point of becoming dizzy. In summer Bath is empty and it is only the very sick and infirm who drag themselves to the healing springs, quietly, sadly and alone. They can be seen on the terraces and promenades on crutches and in wheelchairs, seeking the life-giving rays of the sun. In winter there is life and pleasure while during the summer the old and lonely die sadly away.

While many are drawn to Bath by the pleasures it promises, and a few by a touch of gout, the greatest part of the visitors in the winter suffer from a special kind of sickness. Anyone who has lived somewhat too extravagantly in the world, and too merrily, and now seeks to restore his shattered finances, and others who despite their restricted means do not wish to forego entirely the pleasures of the fashionable world, can take refuge here where they will find them, if perhaps on a slightly reduced scale compared to London, but infinitely less expensive. Certainly here, too, life is very dear but still a lot less so than in London, if one wishes to live in style in that giant city. The mere fact that the hilly position of Bath makes horses and carriages superfluous means a significant saving. After a few winters in the spa one has usually regained financial stability and can once more venture out on life on a larger scale.

As society here consists mainly of members of the leisured and elegant world, the tone is as refined and aristocratically artificial as possible. There is no lack of fortune hunters but their appearances contribute to the general gaiety. Fathers and guardians of wealthy heiresses, who take their charges here in order to prepare them for their appearance on a greater stage, must certainly take great care. Many a journey to the ingenious blacksmith in Gretna Green has been planned or even initiated in Bath.

The town lies in a smiling valley, surrounded on all sides by hills of considerable height which open out only to allow passage to the beautiful river. Slowly and majestically it winds its way through valley and town, navigable up to Bristol, 14 miles away, thus enhancing the beauty of the region and providing considerable advantages through easy communication with that large port. The view of the town is wonderful and unique. When the valley had grown too narrow for it, the town extended itself onto the nearby heights where the palaces rose higher upon palaces, competing one with another in the elegance of contemporary architecture. In strange contrast with these light and lofty creations, there is, down in the valley by the shores of the Avon, the old cathedral of which King Osric is said to have laid the foundation stone as early as 676. It stands there in ancient majesty, with its centuries-old Gothic towers rising effortlessly towards the blue sky, while around it the colourful new world straddles the hills giving itself airs of superiority.

All the houses are built of beautiful hewn stone, quarried in plenty in the neighbourhood. Everything looks new, as if it had been finished only yesterday. There are squares, rows of single houses, and crescents consisting of several uninterrupted houses under one roof, uniformly decorated, giving the impression of a single splendid building. Many seem to have been placed, often at a considerable height, wherever the whim of the builder chose to put them.

The whole is not at all of regular design, yet it is incredibly attractive to look at. The large square, called Queen's Square, is particularly beautiful, with its splendid if slightly over-ornamented houses from whose windows one enjoys a superb view. In the centre of the square, surrounded by iron railings, there is a pretty garden for the use of the inhabitants of nearby houses. It is a pity it is disfigured by a small obelisk.

From Queen's Square one moves up fairly steeply by way of Gay Street to the large circular Royal Circus. The houses around it are decorated or spoilt by columns of all kinds – Doric, Ionic, Corinthian. Behind it and a good deal higher is Royal Crescent which consists of thirty very beautiful houses, having the appearance of a single one. They form a semi-crescent, built in a most noble style, with one row of Ionic columns. In front of them a carpet of green lawn runs right down to the banks of the Avon. A similar row of houses, Marlborough Buildings, stands nearby. The highest inhabited place in Bath is Lansdown Crescent, a beautiful row of houses situated, so to speak, on the crown of this town, at a dizzy height.

To name all or even more similar places and streets would be boring, and perhaps what we have said is enough to give the reader an idea of what distinguishes this town so much from all others. It is true that its very hilly position provides much inconvenience, but the splendid paving, the great cleanliness of the streets and, at night, the fine lighting combine to ease greatly these discomforts, while the police guard everything in an exemplary fashion which adds to the security and peace of mind of the visitors.

Driving in Bath can scarcely be considered. Several of the finest streets, Bond Street for example, are completely paved with hewn stone and not at all suitable for carriages. There is

16 Lansdown Crescent, Bath

no possibility at all of getting to the Assembly rooms or the two promenades, North and South Parade, by carriage. However, one need not have fear of too great exertion as sedan chairs are readily available everywhere: they appear at the slightest wave of the hand and transport their burden at a jog-trot to the highest summit. They are – like the London cabs – under the strict supervision of the police, are all numbered, and they keep their charges at a moderate level which they are not allowed to exceed.

The whole town is one enormous *hôtel garni*. All the most beautiful buildings are let as a whole or in part to visitors. The fixed price for a furnished room during the season is half a guinea per week; a servant's room costs half of that. It is disagreeable that one always has to take a whole suite of rooms, sometimes seven or eight of them, and has to pay for all this when one scarcely needs half. However there are houses which also provide food for their guests and there the people are more obliging and will let single rooms, although to be sure one's demands for elegance will have to be reduced in such establishments. Anything else one needs, apart from lodgings, can also be rented: furniture of all kinds, beds, china, kitchen equipment, domestic utensils, silver, engravings and paintings, glasses, chandeliers, tables and bed linen, all one requires, splendid or prettily simple. In the space of two hours, a large house can be equipped with all that is necessary and much that is superfluous. Enticing advertisements are posted everywhere, indicating, according to the London custom, that all that luxury and love of comfort can invent is on display behind the glass windows of beautiful shops, either for sale or to rent.

The water is very hot. Once drawn it has to stand for three hours before one dares get into it. Although it is also drunk, it is used even more for bathing. There are three hot springs. As is the custom of Karlsbad, one progresses gradually with drinking, from the weakest spring to the strongest. On this point the doctors advise the greatest care. The water is clear, with a not disagreeable taste, and is used mainly in the treatment of nervous diseases, paralysis and gout. The waters are taken in the morning between six and ten o'clock and then again a few glasses towards midday. Usually one drinks by the spring in the pump-room.

In the first half of the last century it was the disgusting habit in Bath to bathe in large common establishments without distinction as to sex. The ladies decorated their heads, which were above water, in the most modern and becoming fashion. Spectators stood on the gallery surrounding the bath and made conversation with those bathing below to while away the time. Four of these large establishments still exist, but only the lower classes make use of them in the way described. The first of these, called the King's Bath, lies close to the great pump-room; it is surrounded by a row of Doric columns and is 65 feet long and 40 feet wide, with the water at 103 degrees Fahrenheit hot. Next to this is the Queen's Bath, only 25 feet square and a little less hot. Cross Bath has been given its name after a cross which stood here at one time. It has its own small pump-room. One usually begins to drink from this spring as it is the weakest. The Hot Bath has a temperature of 117 degrees. Private baths, steam baths and similar facilities are to be found in the same building but this spring, being the strongest, is seldom drunk from and its pump-room is oppressive and gloomy.

The earliest discovery of the hot springs at Bath is lost in darkest antiquity. The ancient Britons knew them and built a town here which they called *Caer yn ennaint twymyn*, the town of the hot baths. Later the Romans gave it several names: *Thermae sudatae*, *Aquae calidae*, while the Anglo-Saxons called it *Acemannus Ceaster*, the town of the infirm. In summer it still might be called that; but if one of the old gentlemen who gave it that name were suddenly to return from Eternity to one of its ballrooms in winter, he would certainly give it a prettier name.

Bath abounds in stories and legends of miraculous cures, mostly ancient, but some from more modern times. The local inhabitants delight in regaling the visitor with them and insist on their veracity, despite the tendency to dismiss them by the doctors. Queen Elizabeth visited the town, but its present beauty and orderliness is due to Richard Nash, who prepared the plans for laying out the parks and the buildings.

SALISBURY PLAIN AND STONEHENGE

Setting out for Stonehenge, our journey once again brought us to stately mansions: this time Longleat, the seat of the Marquis of Bath; Stourhead, the home of a wealthy London Banker, Sir Richard Hoare; and finally Wilton House, belonging to the Earl of Pembroke. Stourhead has a number of most interesting portraits by Angelica Kaufmann. Although it was Sunday we were permitted to see Wilton House but a little further on, at Fonthill, Mr Beckford did not allow visitors on the Sabbath.

On leaving these beautiful houses set in luxuriant grounds, we found ourselves travelling across a vast plain. Sparse heather grew miserably here and there but nowhere was there anything to arrest the eye for a moment. The Lüneburger Heide seemed paradise compared to this.

We were in fact travelling across the notorious Salisbury Plain, a huge cemetery, studded with the graves of heroes long since gone, whose names have been lost in the course of time. Like waves, now barely visible, these rounded mounds rose just a little above the level of the grey sombre plain. Only occasionally did one make out the traces of a trench which had surrounded them at one time. The blue sky formed a silent arch above them, while no bird sang in this wilderness for there was no bush on which it could perch.

We travelled quickly, hardly noticing that we were doing so as there was nothing particularly to mark on the way; the spot we came to, seemingly the one we had just left. Then suddenly, on the horizon, we noticed something rising like the figures of ghosts, grey and shapeless. As we drew nearer and nearer it seemed to stand like a magic circle. We were still not quite sure what we saw until our carriage came to a halt and we were standing in front of Stonehenge, the oldest pre-historic monument in England, perhaps in the whole of Europe.

Enormous, gigantic stones, obviously erected by human hand, rise on a small hillock. Like high columns they stand in a large temple-like circle, two and two close to each other, joined by a similar stone forming a cross-beam or cornice which rests on their points. Some of the columns and beams have fallen,

17 *Stonehenge*

yet the complete round of the circle is clearly visible. The fallen
stones show how they were fastened as every column has at its
top a point or knob hewn out. It is all very rough and of huge
proportions. The cross-stones show two round holes at each
end into which the knobs fit exactly. This is obviously how the
primitive skill of the workers of those days made and joined
them so that they were stable enough to endure for thousands
of years. The columns also show signs of a chisel having been
used. They are four-cornered, without any form of decoration,
roughly hewn, of uneven height and girth but all of astonishing
size and weight.

They were there, as they are now, thousands of years ago
and all trace of their early purpose and origin has disappeared.
At the present time this amazing construction is thought to be
the remains of an ancient Druid temple. Here, they worshipped
fire and benevolence of the sun. While digging under the
stones, traces of burnt sacrifices were found, and who knows
but that men may have bled to death here under the sacrificial
knife of their·misguided brothers.

In the centre of this large circle the remains of a smaller one,
of less high stones, were discovered. A few of them still stand
and in their midst is a large flat stone, possibly the altar,
indicating, perhaps, that this particular part was the inner
sanctum, entered only by the priests. Unfortunately, this altar
has been broken into three by a huge cross-beam from the
outer circle falling on it. Alongside, away from the circle, lies
another enormous stone, similar to the altar one. Some thirty
steps away from the perimeter circle stand a few more columns,
each some thirty steps from the other. Perhaps they formed an
even larger circle, a kind of outer hall to the sacred shrine. It is
certain that the gigantic construction, at which we marvel, is
only a small remnant of what existed when it was complete.

How these enormous masses of rock were brought here and
what superhuman strength erected them, it is impossible to
imagine. It is equally impossible to know how they came to be
destroyed. Were they perhaps toppled by an earthquake when
the earth opened her womb and took them back to whence
they had come, those very stones which had once helped
complete the circle? It does not seem likely that they could have

been taken away for some other use for mighty strength would have been required to transport them.

What makes it all the more marvellous is the fact that the stones are of a kind of granite not found in an area of more than 30 miles around. How was it possible to bring them through dense woods, across bogs and marshes, over hill and dale? Truly, as one looks at them, one is much tempted to have faith in the old belief that Stonehenge is the work of an earlier race of giants, aided by powerful spirits. The impression made by the whole is impossible to describe. We were seized by a quiet shudder as we stood in this desolate wilderness, looking at something whose creator we found it hard to imagine for it seemed something from another world. We had time to muse at length on the impression it had made on us as we continued on our way across this great monotonous plain until, in the late evening, we reached the old town of Winchester. From Winchester onwards we encountered very bad roads. In order to make our various expeditions, we were forced to leave the main road and now we had to try to find it again by a maze of almost impassable side-roads. We often left the carriage and walked up the steep hills, as it rattled wearily onwards, and had a small reward for our pains in fine open views.

At long last we reached the little town of Chichester. We found the whole place in a state of happy uproar as if there were to be horse races. All the windows were occupied by women and girls, dressed in their best, the streets were full of people and there was an air of expectation on all the faces. The regiment of the then Prince of Wales, which is garrisoned here, was parading in full dress, marching in two lines opposite the inn. There, nobody had any time for us, and the landlord and his wife were running about, knocking their heads together. It could be no small thing that would cause such a commotion. And indeed, no, for it was Mrs Fitzherbert, the friend of the Prince, who was expected in Chichester on her way to Brighton. Two hours later she arrived, had the horses changed without even leaving the carriage or looking around, and then bowled off again. The great event was over, the soldiers disbanded, everything gradually calmed down and we too continued on our way to Arundel.

Here the Duke of Norfolk has an old castle. It had just been enlarged by the addition of a new main building and a connecting wing, and as is usual when construction is going on, the place was full of noise, dust and general upheaval. The sight of the old castle would have been imposing anywhere, but here, standing in a not very large courtyard, next to new and completely modern buildings, we felt it lost a lot of its nobleness. A few ancient ivy-clad walls were evidence that Arundel Castle must have been bigger and more imposing than it is now. The remaining part of the old building, with its fine portal, stands as if slightly astonished at finding itself next to the new edifice. The one has nothing to gain from the other; by themselves in the shade of the old trees these remains of past glory would count among the finest of their kind in England, rich as it is in monuments of the past.

That day we were destined to find all the inns in a state of unrest and commotion. In the one at Arundel the soldiers we spoke of earlier were holding a banquet in the hall next to the room allotted to us. The whole building shook with merriment each time a toast was proposed. In the next room the musicians of the regiment made music loud enough to waken the dead. The waiters had their hands full of bottles and corkscrews and while corks popped, bugles and trumpets sounded, and the rattle of the kettle-drums threatened to shake the foundations of the house. Added to this were the merry shouts of the Volunteers, now in high spirits, and as we saw preparations being made for a ball, we decided it was all too much for us and we slipped away. Contrary to our custom, we travelled on as night fell. We drove close to the sea, with a mild wind rippling its surface, silvery in the light of the moon. The sparkling waves danced and whispered mysteriously as we happily reached Brighton.

BRIGHTON

Brighton, twenty years ago a small, insignificant fishing village, is stirring proof of the miracles brought about by fashion. In its transformation, the town has even lost the original cumbersome name of Brighthelmstone and is now simply known, shorter and more elegantly, as Brighton. Pretty

English ladies have a special way of letting the word roll off the tongue and many a heart beats a little faster, on hearing the sweet sound of it being uttered.

During the summer months, the town had been the favourite residence of the Prince of Wales. It is situated only 54 miles from London which, in this country, means hardly a day's journey. It was probably its proximity to the capital that made the heir to the throne choose this, up to then, totally unremarkable fishing town. He was able to come and go as he pleased without attracting undue attention.

His presence in or absence from Brighton registered the flow of visitors to the spa. When he was absent, the town was empty and desolate; only when he returned did life and pleasure reappear. Now that we have seen the town, the longing of London's young and fashionable world to be there seems hard to understand, even admitting that we are not particularly swayed by the dictates of fashion. Its position, so close to the sea, is so unattractive that even its most ardent admirers have difficulty in finding an excuse for their partiality. They praise its air as being extraordinarily healthy and point out the great age to which the natives live. It must indeed be conceded that the climate is temperate, the town being protected from the north and east winds by an amphitheatre of, alas, very bare hills. It is dry and bracing and, in the heat of summer, a sea breeze tempers the air.

The town is small. Fine houses of recent construction mingle incongruously with small older cottages, giving the place a motley and not very agreeable appearance. The walls of the cottages are of pebble-dash, small pebbles being set into mortar, with only the surrounds of the windows and doors being of wood. The stability of these walls is much to be praised, but they look poor, especially as in England it is not the custom to whitewash the outside of a house.

Rows of spacious houses for visitors, all under one continuous roof, give the impression of a grand single palace. One forms a crescent with a pleasant view towards the sea and there are several terraces, and the so-called Parade for strolling, with these handsome houses on one side and the ocean on the other. It is laid out much in the pattern of Bath, only on a smaller scale.

There are elegant little shops where London merchants sell

their prettiest and most exclusive fashions. This is not so in other British spas where everything is supplied by the local trades-men. The custom has obviously arisen here through London being so near and the public in Brighton demanding luxuries. The local people often complain and not without just reason.

Nature has not much favoured the promenades, with bare hills surrounding the town on two sides while towards the west there is just a large expanse of cornfields, the whole being bound by the sea. As this is too shallow for large ships to come close to the coast, the view is rather dull, only enlivened a little by the fishing boats.

The main promenade is the Steine, at one time a pretty meadow between the hills, but now almost hidden by new buildings, terraces, parades and the odd fisherman's cottage. The Prince's residence, the Pavilion, is also on the Steine. It is a low pretty building, not of great size, embellished by a colonnade. The Prince had tried to establish gardens but trees and shrubs do not thrive here. The interior of the Pavilion is said to be splendid but strangers are not admitted. The large pitch-black figure of a negro holding a sundial, in the centre of the courtyard, seems odd and does not augur well for the good taste of the other ornamentation.

Another building on the Steine contains the baths. There are cold ones and hot ones, steam baths and showers, in short all that has ever been invented to flush away the evils which threaten our poor life. Sea water is used in these baths. Bathing machines, which in other resorts enable one to bathe in the open sea with propriety, are not available in Brighton, perhaps because the beach is unsuitable. It is possible, however, to bathe out of doors for there are two places, completely separate, one for gentlemen, the other for ladies, set aside for the purpose. None the less bathing in the open sea means, as can easily be understood, a good deal of discomfort here and when there is a north-east wind and a heavy swell, is actually not without danger.

The Steine seems to contain practically everything that life in Brighton means. It is however most disagreeable that the fishermen manage to insinuate themselves into this glittering circle by choosing to stretch out their nets to dry, just where one wants to stroll, so spoiling the air.

The second, though less frequented, promenade is a garden. It is surrounded by shady trees which are greatly admired here as a rarity, although one would hardly notice them anywhere else. At one end there is a small hall with an orchestra where, during the season, public breakfasts with music are held once a week. In the evenings there are occasionally fireworks, and for all these, as well as for the promenade in the park, one either subscribes per month, or pays an entrance fee each time. The same applies to the baths, to balls and other entertainments, exactly as in Bath. A specially prepared pitch for the game of cricket is generally used only by the Prince and his friends, on which occasions there is no lack of spectators.

The Assembly rooms are in two taverns or inns, The Castle Tavern and The Old Ship Tavern. In the first, one may play cards and there is a coffee-house with a billiard-table and that sort of thing. The second is similar but has the advantage of accommodation for visitors although we thought the reception inferior to what we had met elsewhere in England. The rooms of both places consist, as do those in Bath, of a dance hall and several adjoining rooms for playing cards, taking tea and making conversation. All are prettily decorated and usefully furnished.

After leaving Brighton we stayed for two days in the little town of Reigate, situated halfway to London. We had sent someone ahead to prepare our quarters and were glad, after our long wanderings, to halt for a little and take breath before once again entering the busy whirl of life in the great city. However, there was little chance of rest and quiet in this small place: stage coaches, carriages and every kind of public conveyance rolled past our lodgings all the time. It was as if all womankind had decided to emigrate from London, for it was they who formed the greater part of the traffic. The country coaches were filled to capacity, inside and out, with women and girls. Stately ladies in elegant carriages could scarcely raise their noses above mountains of dress boxes full of elegant attire destined for their future triumphs. People pushed and hurried as though there was not a moment to be lost: surely nobody ever made the pilgrimage to Loreto more eagerly, than did those crowds on their way to Brighton.

4 LONDON

We continued our journey to London and arrived there safely. We now felt a little more at home, for the expedition we had just undertaken had allowed us only very brief stops on the way. But it is difficult to feel entirely at home in this enormous city, even though within our accustomed four walls we were, we suppose, as much at home as anywhere else. The moment one sets foot into the street, however, one finds oneself in a strange world, even, we imagine, if one had spent a lifetime here. The restless hustle and bustle of a million people, concentrated in a comparatively small area, results in everybody rushing about, mercilessly pushing and jostling everybody else. After we had allowed ourselves to be absorbed in this whirl for a little, however, we began to understand to some extent what it was all about and to notice many quite small but interesting details in the endless rush.

From whatever direction one approaches this city, one always imagines oneself to be in the centre of it before one has even passed its boundaries. None of Europe's large cities, not Vienna, not Berlin nor even Paris announces itself so impressively from a distance. There are rows upon rows of houses, separated by scarcely noticeable open spaces into hamlets, small towns and villages. All seem to merge into a whole, thereby enlarging the city so that it extends over a wide area 1½ German miles long. Fine broad highways lead to it from all directions. These are well-lit by lamps, even in the towns and villages several hours away from London. The constant traffic of carriages and horsemen tells the stranger, from afar, that he is approaching the abode of nearly a million people.

It was from Shooter's Hill, 26 miles away, that we had previously seen the great capital for the first time, stretching along the Royal Thames. Now here again was the wonderful dome of St Paul's, rising aloft into the air, and beyond it the fine Gothic twin towers of Westminster Abbey, all surrounded by the spires of well over a hundred more churches. It was a good clear day but unfortunately the smoke rising from the many chimneys meant that we saw everything through a haze.

We bowled along quickly on the splendid road and like all strangers we believed ourselves to be at the end of the journey long before we had reached it. Then at last we saw the Thames in front of us and crossed the river by beautiful Blackfriars' Bridge, realizing that only now were we truly in London. Deafened by the noise all around us, we arrived at the York Hotel where we had arranged to lodge to begin with. It was situated not far from the bridge and gave us the opportunity of looking around at our leisure for a quieter place in a private house. Most strangers, who intend to stay in London for a while, do this.

A stay in a London inn is extremely expensive and the number of those where, apart from eating and drinking, one can also stay, is comparatively small. Even of these, only very few are equipped comfortably enough to make a stay of several weeks or even months desirable. This is simply due to the fact that the demand for these services seldom arises.

However without the slightest trouble one can find perfectly good lodgings, available to let immediately, complete with kitchen and cellar and all other conveniences, large or small, furnished elegantly or simply, just as one pleases. There are even available entire houses, with their own stables and any extras one may require. One has only to walk through the quarter where one wishes to stay and see notices everywhere, offering apartments to let, to the extent that the choice may truly embarrass the stranger.

The owners of these rooms are middle-class people: respectable shopkeepers or tradesmen and widows of small means. They are all eager, in the most obliging way possible, to supply the stranger with every comfort. Usually a housekeeper or the lady of the house herself will look after the cleaning of the rooms and will also cook, so that one is made to feel really at home, at one's own hearthside, between one's own four walls.

To describe London, its size, splendour and individuality, is an enterprise to which we hardly feel equal. Besides, with so many excellent people having done just that before us, it would appear unnecessary. We prefer rather to present to the reader only what we saw and took note of during our stay, adding a few small details to the large canvas which others have already painted. London is remarkable enough for one to find interest in so many small things which elsewhere might pass unnoticed.

A STROLL THROUGH LONDON STREETS

There is a story of one of the Sovereigns of the many small states of the Holy Roman Empire, who, entering London late at night, believed that the city was illuminated in his honour. Had he arrived during the day by way of one of the crowded streets of the City, perhaps Ludgate Hill or the Strand, he could just as easily have believed that the population was indulging in a dangerous riot.

Nobody who has not seen it with his own eyes can have the slightest idea of the eternal passage of vehicles of all kinds in the middle of the road, and of the surge of the pedestrians on the slightly raised pavements on both sides of it. Neither the Leipzig Easter Fair, nor Vienna, nor even Paris can serve as comparisons. All the same, nowhere is it easier to walk on foot than in London, as soon as one has grown used to the way of the locals. This is a great advantage to strangers, especially to ladies, who wish to see and take note of everything. If, as in some large cities, one is always tied to one's carriage, not able to walk even a few steps, one gets to know barely half of the place. On the fine natural stone of London's pavements one gets about remarkably well, even when the weather is not altogether favourable. In the main streets the pavements are wide enough to allow six, eight or even more people to walk abreast comfortably. In the narrow crooked lanes of the actual City it is certainly not quite so easy, as the footpaths there have to be less wide. Visitors, however, do not often venture into this quarter, which resembles more than anything an anthill and where business is the main concern and fashion and luxury really have no place.

The splendid shops and the exhibitions of every description are mostly to be found on those broad streets which somehow hold the balance between the hard-working City and that more elegant part of London which is given over to the pleasures of life. The custom of the English, when they meet people, always to give way to those on their right, greatly eases walking about and does away with much pushing and jostling. Ladies, and all those held in special respect, are always permitted to walk along the house side of the pavements, irrespective of whether this is on the right or the left. To begin with, a strange lady finds it odd when he who guides her through London, lets go of her arm the moment they have crossed the street, and passes behind her to change sides. Quite soon, however, one becomes convinced of the usefulness of this national courtesy. In the middle of the road, where hundreds of vehicles pass in all directions, order is certainly not kept as easily as on the footpaths. Broad as the main streets generally are, there is often a congestion of a variety of vehicles and horses lasting several minutes. The confusion of it all, provided one is able to contemplate it from the safety of a window, proves a very interesting sight.

Eleven hundred cabs are available all day long, in ranks specially allotted to them, yet it is often impossible to find one just when it is needed. Perhaps the Italians do not fear the rain as much as do the Londoners, for to the latter getting wet is a horrible idea, so that only a few drops have to fall from the sky for everyone who does not carry an umbrella to take refuge in a cab. Within seconds all the carriages have disappeared and one realizes that the number of eleven hundred is far from enough.

On the whole the cabs look well and in Germany they might even pass as carriages of the gentry. Only the straw with which their floor is covered makes them unpleasant. The horses are in incredibly good condition, considering they walk on paving stones every day for more than twelve hours. In fact they are as well cared for as is possible, for as soon as there is a quiet moment, the driver ties a long narrow bag around their necks, full of oats, from which they contentedly eat their fill. The police keep a strict eye on the cabbies; they are all numbered and woe betide anyone who goes beyond the official low cheap fares or offends against the rules in any other way. At such times, every passing Englishman becomes judge, for he is aware of what is going on and insists on the rules being applied explicitly. No matter the hour of night, one is quite safe in entrusting oneself to a cab, even though one may be alone or carrying money or jewels, provided someone in the house one is leaving takes the number of the cab in such a way as the driver notices.

Much has been written about the splendour of the shops and the larger stores, perhaps even to excess. All the same, it is true that nothing astonishes the stranger more than the richness and elegance of them. The brilliant displays of precious silverware, the beautiful draperies of muslin and other materials which the merchants show to the public behind large plate-glass windows, the fairy-tale glitter of the crystal shops, all this bewitches the visitor.

Objects of much less value too are displayed pleasingly to the eye. The candle-makers, for example, know how to show off their wares prettily. The apothecaries, here called chemists, decorate their windows with large glass vases, filled with brilliantly coloured spirit or water and place between them bunches of artificial flowers. At night, when the lamps burn behind these coloured glasses, each shop gleams like Aladdin's cave.

There is nothing more attractive than to visit one of the many large fruit stores, where the produce of all seasons and all parts of the world is beautifully displayed, from the royal pineapple to the modest Siberian apple, all in pretty little baskets, decorated with flowers and orange leaves. The cake shops, where it is the fashion to call in the morning and for breakfast eat several small cakes hot from the oven, also present their wares in a most pleasant manner. Everything the baker and the pastrycook have invented is to be found there, arranged enticingly on tables covered with snow-white linen cloths. Everywhere there are flowers, jellies, ices, liqueurs and

18 *Ackerman's Repository of Arts*

dragées of all shapes and colours in fine crystal jars. Then again we were much attracted by the engravers' shops where every day there were new objects for sale, sometimes genuine works of art but more often satirical portraits of the famous and occasionally also engravings of animals. The windows of these shops are always surrounded by a crowd of inquisitive people and we have to admit that it is almost impossible to pass by without one's curiosity delaying one for a moment. Booksellers, too, provide something new each day, whether books just off the press, beautiful bibliophile editions of older writers or precious engravings which one is allowed to inspect without hindrance. The so-called stationers, who deal in the multitude of things required for writing or drawing, show a thousand new articles daily, often almost unknown to us Germans, such as cardboard work and ornaments, gilt objects and such like. Then there are shops that sell nothing but cases, from the giant folder through the briefcase to the very small dainty nécessaire; shops where the most beautiful articles in steel blind the eyes in the rays of the sun; and the miniature painters who present their very fine work, usually good likenesses of well-known people, actors and public speakers, no doubt in the hope that this will engender in the passer-by the desire to see his own dear self so portrayed.

To see the many signs, emblazoned on houses in beautifully-drawn golden lettering, that alone is entertaining. How many needs are catered for, of which the frugal German is scarcely aware. One is specially struck by the fact that the Royal Family employs so many shopkeepers and tradesmen. But then every one of them from whom, by the merest chance, something has been purchased for a member of Royalty at some time, every shoemaker or tailor whose good fortune it has been to sew a stitch for a prince, has the right to boast of the fact on his shop sign, thus stretching a moment's favour into an eternal blessing. As a result the name of someone dealing in all kinds of 'remedies' appears in large letters on his house by the sea, together with the splendid legend: 'Bug-destroyer to Her Majesty the Queen'. Surely such a title has so far never been carried in any court list.

It is a wonderful relief when one leaves the rush of the City

[140]

19 Messrs Harding, Howell & Co, Draper

and gets to another part of London where everything reflects the quiet and comfortable enjoyment of life. Here there is no vulgar fighting for gain, no bustle of the crowds of workers. Everyone has plenty of time and their thoughts seem to dwell on how to spend it most agreeably.

The stores and the shops offer only what the most refined taste for luxury demands and although the goods are much more expensive than in the City, they are more beautiful, more fashionable, more elegant. For example, the shoemaker in the City sells his wares in his shop, nicely presented, and in a cleanly furnished adjoining room will take his customer's measurements, if asked to do so. In Bond Street, however, one is taken into a boudoir, elegantly equipped with a divan, fine lamps and silk curtains. The 'artist' here would not dream of touching a foot unless it had just stepped from an elegant carriage. The result is that each 'piece of art' costs two guineas. Such is the way of the world.

There can be nothing more beautiful in this part of London than the large squares. They do not, it is true, surround palaces for there are few here anyway, but there are large handsome houses, all solidly splendid. Additional amenities are the pretty shrubberies in the centre of each square, to which the residents of the surrounding houses may obtain a key by paying a guinea.

Here splendid carriages roll by, attended by blackamoors in coloured liveries and elegantly dressed men and women enliven the pavements, while there is no rush or noise. The stranger, however, who is intent on getting to know the English, is soon enough happy to leave these fashionable quarters where, after all, everything is much the same as anywhere else in the beau monde, and to return once more to see a new kind of life, not seen elsewhere, in the real City of London.

BEGGARS

One seldom encounters genuine beggars in London's streets. However, the poor know well how to kindle the fire of charity in a variety of ways. Thus on one occasion we encountered two sailors, one having only one leg, the other one arm, supporting each other as they staggered through the streets. To a wild lamenting tune they sang loudly a ballad, telling the story of their misfortune. Full of pity, John Bull listened and rewarded them with a few pence.

At crossroads where one has to step off the pavement to get to the other side of the street, there are always men sweeping the footpath and keeping it clean only to find it seconds later in a state of disorder again through the vehicles rolling by. Modestly they ask from time to time whether you might have a few coppers to spare, something one would have given gladly, even without being asked. In less frequented places, especially in the quieter part of the City, one often comes across men drawing large beautiful letters in chalk on the pavements. The letters may form names, sentences or texts from the Bible. The passer-by stops, admires the artist's work and, without being asked, will reward him with a small gift. It seems incomprehensible to us that people who do such fine lettering, could have sunk into such extreme poverty. On the Continent each one of these beggars would have made a good living as a teacher of script or a calligrapher, for it is difficult to imagine anything more perfect of its kind than the work they are doing.

One particularly remarkable character was a woman whom we met every day in one of the City's busiest streets. She was reputed to be a sister of the famous actress, Mrs Siddons, and it was said that a series of tragedies, some self-inflicted, some accidental, had caused her to sink this low. She certainly bore an unmistakable likeness to the actress and had the same tall noble figure and distinguished expression, though she was somewhat older, pale, her features hardened by her long run of misfortune. Nobody blames Mrs Siddons for being hard-hearted towards her unhappy sister, and those who believed the relationship to be true always added that this lady refused any help from that quarter, preferring to live on the charity of strangers. We often saw this curious apparition. She always wore a black silk hat, which left her face and features clearly visible, a green woollen dress, a large snow-white apron and a kerchief, also white. As she walked along, silently and with a proud air, supported on her two crutches, the crowd made way

for her, showing a kind of respect for her great misfortune. She
never asked for anything, did not beg, but the public seemed to
feel obliged, even driven, to give her something and gifts were
showered upon her. It was as if they wished to thank her for
accepting their gifts, and she, with the gracious manners of a
queen, received their offerings as her due, and then moved on
like some apparition.

LONDON DWELLINGS

Architecturally, private houses in London are not very
remarkable. As a house-owner enjoys great privileges here,
everybody strives to have his own, resulting in a city of, on the
whole, very many small houses. Anyone who does not own a
house still wants to live on his own, which narrows down the
available space considerably.

In Paris one might say that four different towns float one
above the other; in London everyone lays claim to his own
little patch of God's earth. Thus only visitors, people living
alone and those with very limited means inhabit apartments,
which, given the smallness of the houses in which they are
situated, offer very little comfort. A suite of several rooms is
unthinkable in ordinary middle-class homes; in fact, one rarely
finds two connecting rooms even in the houses of wealthy
merchants. Each storey of a house generally has only two
rooms, one towards the street and the other overlooking a
small courtyard at the back. Everywhere the stairs are narrow
and the rooms few and small. The kitchen and servants'
quarters are situated in the basement. All the doors are
remarkably high and narrow, the main doors of the house as
well as those leading into the rooms. Indeed in the larger
buildings the main doors often look just like slits in the wall
and folding doors are hardly ever found. The windows, too,
are narrow, with a wide space between them in which mirrors
are hung. These small homes gain their attraction from such
things as the fine carpets which, even in the houses of well-to-
do tradesmen, cover the floors of the rooms, the stairs and the
hallways right from the very front door, and from the furniture
of fine mahogany with its dull but graceful sheen. Everything

is clean, fresh-looking and comfortably elegant.

An important feature of the rooms is the fireplace. This is often decorated with marble or metal of some kind and the mantlepiece is generally adorned with beautiful vases from the Wedgwood factory and crystal candelabra. The cradle in which the fire burns, the fire-irons, in fact anything made of metal, are all gleaming and brightly polished. Engravings decorate the walls and at the windows are fine curtains: one can say in truth that nothing is more comfortable than an English living-room.

The bedroom can hardly ever accommodate more than one bed for all English beds are very large, so much so that three people could easily find room in one. It is the general custom not to sleep alone, so that sisters and girlfriends share a bed without any ado, and when the husband is from home nearly every woman takes one of her children into her bed or, at a pinch, even the maidservant. Englishwomen are afraid of being in a room alone at night as from infancy they are not accustomed to it. Feather quilts are quite unknown though one does find feather mattresses which have lately been increasing in popularity. The ordinary mattress, however, remains more common. Only the very poor have beds without curtains or rooms without carpets.

EVERYDAY LIFE

The largest and most industrious section of London's population, the tradesmen and shopkeepers (both count as one here) lead a dreary life on the whole. Heavy taxes, the rising cost of everyday necessities, much aggravated by the desire for a certain luxury in dress and the like, force these people to live very frugally, in fact in a state that in other countries would be considered near poverty.

Banished for all eternity to the shop and the darkish back room next to it, they forego almost any pleasure. The theatres are too far away and mostly too expensive; the wife of even a well-to-do shopkeeper goes there perhaps only twice in a year.

They hardly ever escape to the country and several of them assured us that in ten years they had seen no trees other than those in St James's Park. During the week they can rarely leave the shop from nine o'clock in the morning until midnight. Very often the shop is the wife's responsibility while her husband sits in the back-room, mentioned before, looking after the accounts. It is true that all the shops are closed on Sundays, but so are the theatres, and as all employees assert their right to go out on that day, it is the lady of the house who stays at home.

The wealthier merchant scarcely leads a more diverting life. He is far behind the heads of the rich merchant houses of Hamburg and Leipzig in his participation in social and public enjoyments. To some degree this may be due to the custom of the country, for the womenfolk prefer the seclusion of their own homes and are not much used to a social life and to moving in high circles, preferring not to disturb the calm but rigid conformity of their domestic life. The men, on the other hand, like to look for their pleasures outside and seek these in the coffee-houses and the taverns.

The families of these merchants live the better part of the year, sometimes the whole of it, in the country, in pretty houses of varying size, which they call cottages, though they surely deserve a grander name. Here the women and children enjoy the fresh air, keep up good neighbourly relations while leading a life of decorum, albeit somewhat boring. The head of the family spends the day in his London office, and in the evening travels back to his loved-ones in an hour or two on excellent roads, either on horseback or by carriage.

There is really nothing to say about the everyday life of the great and noble: in no country do they truly reflect the nation but rather resemble each other everywhere, in Russia as in France, in England as in Germany. Besides, so much has already been written about the luxury of their lives, which take no note of summer from winter nor day from night, that further comment is unnecessary. So we shall maintain silence and only mention it when we find, in passing, something worthy of note. In our travels we have always sought to get to know the customs of the real people of the country being visited, and for this one has to look neither too high nor too low, for it is nowadays preserved only in the middle classes.

20   *Messrs Pellatt & Green, Glass and Crystal*

A DAY IN THE CITY OF LONDON

He who goes to bed late, rises late, so runs the maxim, and it follows that the golden morning sun has fewer worshippers in London than anywhere, although here, on the whole, gold is held in high respect. Day does not begin until nine or ten o'clock. Suitably dressed, the whole family then gathers in the breakfast-room, the gentlemen wearing boots and frock-coats, the ladies dressed in indescribably charming snow-white garments, fastened right up to the neck, with graceful little caps. The negligé is the glory of the English women: it combines great elegance with the utmost simplicity, whereas their dresses tend often to be unnatural and over-elaborate.

There is nothing more inviting in the world than an English family breakfast, and the hour spent at it is considered the most agreeable of the day, often pleasurably extended. The quiet flame of the fire in its polished cradle burns brightly even, if the weather should be damp, in summer. The elegant tea-service is attractively set out on a table covered in snow-white linen and next to it is fresh unsalted butter, cooled in water, the whitest bread in the world, rusks, hard-boiled eggs and perhaps, after the Scottish fashion, honey and orange marmalade. Hot rolls, a kind of buttered warm roll, and toast, slices of bread toasted slowly over the fire and then spread with butter, these must never be missing. They are placed on a special silver dish close to the fire where the kettle sings away merrily as it boils.

With all this, breakfast would not be complete without the latest newspapers which have an important part to play. In praise of Londoners, it must be said that they have completely banned that regular feature of the German breakfast-table, the tobacco pipe. This dirty pleasure is left to the lower classes and only a retired old sailor or a hardly civilized country squire would enjoy it quietly within his own four walls.

The lady of the house makes the tea and without any doubt she does so not only with much more formality than we do, but also better. The cups are carefully warmed with hot water, the tea is measured out and the hot water poured on it in accordance with a strict routine. Then, to seek praise for all this trouble, everyone is asked in turn whether the tea is to their liking. Everything is done slowly and with the quiet dignity the English give to all their meals for they do not like to let anything spoil the enjoyment of the moment.

At breakfast the newspapers prove the only exception to this rule and both ladies and gentlemen soon get caught up in them eagerly. These newspapers do not only supply political news but also the latest events in the theatre, family affairs and above all local gossip, cheerful and sad, edifying and scandalous, true, half-true or completely invented. Everything is read and everything discussed so that conversation does not suddenly come to a halt as otherwise it so often does.

After breakfast the men turn to business and go to their offices or wherever their profession may take them. As far as is possible, all work is completed in the morning which, in spite of the late start, is long enough as no one has dinner before five or six o'clock. After the meal, unless fate is unkind and makes more work necessary, everyone likes to relax.

Again, it is after breakfast that many men visit their habitual coffee-house, where a great deal of business is transacted. Local letters and messages await them there, while it is also the place for meetings with friends, to talk over important matters and make appointments. The hostess of the coffee-house, on her high seat near the entrance, will take all messages and pass on the information promptly, accurately memorized, to her clients, all of whom she knows personally for they seldom fail to appear every day at the same hour. This habit of being available each day at a definite place is extremely valuable in this enormous city. Many unnecessary errands and much time, otherwise lost, are saved in this manner. It also contributes to domestic peace, for next to the impeccable cleanliness of his dress, nothing is nearer to the Englishman's heart than that of his home, its stairs and its carpets, so the fact that so many matters which might create disorder or at least unrest in the home, are dealt with away from it, is of the utmost help.

The ladies too now set to their business. They reach for their morning hats, as every time of day has its special dress and it would be noticed if a lady, even in a carriage, were to be seen during the hours of morning without a hat. Although she were wrapped in seven veils, everyone would stare at her as something from another world. Moreover should she venture even a few steps in the street, hatless, she would be completely lost for the rabble would follow her as mercilessly as if she had committed the most shocking indiscretion.

So, well-armed in large hats and with kerchiefs and shawls we now take the air, for fashion dictates that, even during the warmest hours of the day, one must wrap up most carefully. As our circle of close acquaintances is small, we do not have too many visits to make, and these are mainly, as in all big cities, to a few homes in the neighbourhood. Paying calls in London is usually simply a question of leaving one's card but we do, however, have one indispensable visit to make, to a woman in childbed. In England, as elsewhere, this is essential, though here such calls are acceptable somewhat later than is our custom.

We find the lady in a splendid room and an even more splendid large bed. Pillows and bedcovers are embroidered with fine needlework, edged with lace, while the hangings of white French muslin, pleated into pretty folds and lined with green silk, float down from the canopy, allowing one to see the bedposts of mahogany and even more precious woods. The lady's bedgown is adorned with flounces of the most expensive lace, the fineness and exquisiteness of everything proclaiming great wealth. The main topic of conversation is dictated by the new arrival's wardrobe which is displayed on a side-table. He himself is not visible, being in the nursery with his wet-nurse, for breast-feeding among mothers of the upper classes is not as common in England as it is in Germany.

There are some excellent shops in London which sell nothing but things for children, at very high prices too. All the goods from these shops are displayed in extravagant heaps in the lying-in room. Nothing is forgotten, not even a large pin-cushion in which the pins of all sizes are arranged in artistic patterns, looking like fine, rich, silver embroidery. These things will probably be rarely, if ever, used for by their nature they are too dainty and fragile for anything but display.

Having at long last finished looking and admiring, we set off shopping. This means going into at least twenty shops, having

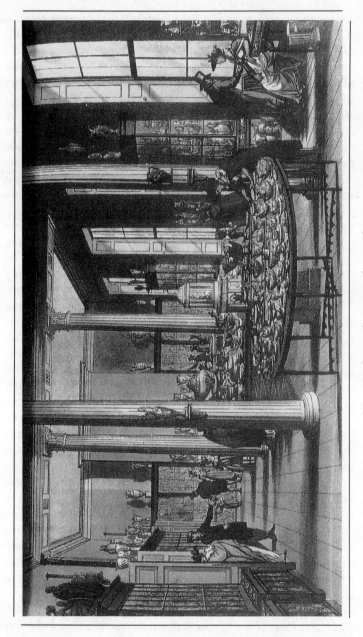

21   *Wedgwood & Byerley, China*

a thousand things shown to us which we do not wish to buy, in fact turning the whole shop upside down and, in the end, perhaps leaving without purchasing anything. It is impossible to admire sufficiently the patience of the shopkeepers, who endure this nonsense without ever dreaming of showing annoyance. Very grand ladies go shopping in a carriage and, without leaving it, have half the shop brought out to them, to the great discomfort of the shopkeeper and the passers-by on the pavement. The story goes that a group of sailors whose path was obstructed by just such a coach, standing with its door open, strolled through the whole performance without any ado, each wishing a courteous 'good morning' to the lady inside.

The great variety of exhibitions of works of art, as well as natural curiosities, offers agreeable and relaxing breaks when at last we have tired of keeping the shopkeepers in a state of perpetual motion. The promenade in St James's Park equally provides a diversion but, charming as it is, it is less often frequented. There is, however, never a lack of people strolling about there but only on rare occasions does one find it as populated as, for example, the terraces of the Tuileries are on any day. There are far fewer idle men in London than in Paris and English women do not go out as much as the ladies of Paris and, if they do, they prefer a shopping party to all other promenades.

The cake shops, about which we have spoken earlier, open right onto the street, as in fact do other shops, and so it is quite respectable for ladies to visit them alone. The only exception is the establishment of Mr Birch, near the Stock Exchange; there one may not be seen without a male escort. The smallish breakfast-room is at the back of the house, at the end of a long corridor. Even if the sun should be shining brightly outside, no daylight penetrates the interior of the place, which is lit by wax candles. The rooms are furnished in a decent fashion, though not in any way specially distinguished. Here one always finds parties of ladies and gentlemen, supping their turtle soup in silence and eating a couple of small hot pies. Nothing else is available but the pies are said to be the best in the world and, most certainly, nothing can surpass the turtle soup. Nowhere else do they know how to prepare it so excellently, at least so the Londoners say. What we admired much more than the soup, however, was the composure with which the ladies and gentlemen enjoyed the mixture, spiced as it was the Cayenne pepper and Madeira, which burn both the tongue and the palate. The former owner of the place, a Mr Horton, amassed a fortune of over a hundred thousand pounds in a relatively short time, simply from the sale of these little pies and turtle soup and his present successor, a Mr Birch, seems well on the way to following his example. Nevertheless, the prices are very modest and, like everywhere else, they are strictly fixed. The amount everybody consumes is very small, but the number of consumers is enormous which accounts for the large profits.

Towards five o'clock, the time has come to think of returning home to the obligatory changing of dress before dinner. Today we have been asked out to dine but even if we were to spend the evening *en famille* at home, it would be unseemly and quite unheard of, provided one was in good health, to remain in one's morning dress. Even the men take off the suit they have worn to the Stock Exchange, appearing in more elegant attire.

Dressed in our best and feeling somewhat restricted thereby, we drive to dinner at half-past six. Londoners are not particularly hospitable for they dread the way in which prices have risen and even more the etiquette, so much a part of all social gatherings here, which places such a heavy burden on the lady of the house, who anyway prefers the peace of her home. Large dinners are therefore given only for special events, such as the presence of visitors whom one wishes to honour. Otherwise, the Londoner prefers to take his friend to a tavern rather than to entertain him at home. There, tête-à-tête or in a larger, but always private circle, they indulge in wine, politics and light-hearted banter. At home they would be frightened by the presence of the women who, superficially, are treated with the greatest respect but, as is the case with such people, one tends to keep out of their way.

But back to our dinner. We find the guests assembled in the drawing-room, which accommodates no more than twelve to fourteen people. After the conventional greetings, the ladies take their seats in easy-chairs on either side of the fireplace while the gentlemen warm themselves at the fire, not always in the most decorous manner. Laboriously, with a sparsity of words, the conversation flickers between life and death until at long last the welcome call to the dining-room is heard. This is situated either on the floor above or on the floor below because, as we have said earlier, the houses of even very rich people are rather less than spacious and convenient.

The table is ready set, except for glasses. Since the English now travel a lot, there are napkins at their tables, at least certainly when one has a dinner party. Some years ago they were only to be found in houses which tended to do things in the foreign manner. In those days the tablecloth hung right down to the floor, which we suppose it still does when dining *en famille*, and everyone took it on his knees upon sitting down, using it as we would a napkin. The lady of the house installs herself in a chair with arms at the upper end of the table, while her husband sits in a similar chair at the other end. The guests then take their places, according to a plan arranged by the master of the house, along either side, in ordinary chairs, as far as possible men and women alternately. The dishes for the first course are already on the table.

Nowadays English cuisine has its admirers in Germany too. We are not among them and we confess that we shuddered at the thought of bloody meat, fish prepared without any salt, vegetables underdone in water, and hares and partridges which like all other roasts are cooked without being larded and without butter, just in their own juices.

The lady of the house now serves the soup, rather thin and lavishly seasoned with cayenne pepper, after she has first asked each guest by name whether he wishes to have any. There is an endless series of questions and answers between host and guests at the English table which proves a great embarrassment to the stranger who, even if he has a fairly good knowledge of the English language, finds it impossible to know all the technical expressions. Every time a dish is served he is asked to say whether he wishes a lot or a little, with sauce or without, which part of the poultry or fish, whether he likes it well or underdone, this last question being particularly disconcerting to the visitor. These questions resound from all parts of the table at once, for a few friends of the house usually help the hosts in serving. After the soup, all dishes are served at the same time, not one after the other as in Germany. These consist generally of a large sea fish, a salmon, cod, turbot or the like, which, had it been salted in the cooking, would be excellent, but as it is prepared here, is almost inedible. There are also puddings, vegetables, tarts and all kinds of meat and poultry, again cooked without salt, butter or any other form of seasoning. steamed, grilled, roasted or just plainly cooked in their own juices. Pepper, however, is generously used and, should a thin dry butter dough be laid over a dish, it is then graced with the name of a pie.

The half-raw vegetables must look very green and fresh and only at table does everyone put as much melted butter on his portion as he wishes. Potatoes are an essential part of any meal and they are excellent, steamed simply. Puddings of all kinds would also be very good, were they not often too rich, consisting almost entirely of beef marrow and such things. Tarts, the triumph of the English kitchen, consists of semi-ripe fruit, cooked in water and covered with a dry dough. The pickles which accompany the roast are really a wide variety of vegetables, sweet-corn, unripe walnuts, small onions and such, preserved in a richly-spiced strong vinegar, and they are also excellent. With these products and with soy and other piquant sauces which are made and sold in London in bulk, there is a big trade all over the world. These sauces, the mustard, oil and vinegar, all in a fine cruet-stand, are ready for the use of the guests and there is a salt cellar for every two people.

The salad is prepared by the lady of the house with great formality. The lettuce, a very tender juicy variety whose leaves are small and elongated, is cut into very small pieces. We have never encountered this kind outside England, just as our cabbage lettuce is not known there. Untiringly all these dishes are offered to the guests, who are expected dutifully to praise everything, protesting that never in their lives have they tasted veal or mutton of such excellent quality and so beautifully prepared.

The ceremony of drinking at table is even more tiresome,

especially for ladies from abroad to whom it often gives real trouble. There they sit, deafened and frightened by all the strange goings-on, when suddenly the master of the house stands up, raises his voice and asks a lady, and out of courtesy it is always the stranger first, for permission to drink a glass of wine with her and at the same time would she prefer a white wine from Lisbon or red Port. French wines and those from the Rhine are only served with the dessert. Embarrassed, she makes her choice and then in a loud voice, the servant is asked to bring two glasses suitable for the wine chosen. Bowing to each other gracefully, the two leading characters say, in chorus, 'Sir, your good health! Madam, your good health!' They then empty their glasses and hand them back to the servant. A little later a different voice offers the same invitation and the ceremony is repeated over and over again until every gentleman has made the round with every lady and every lady with every gentleman at least once. It is not an easy feat for those unused to strong wine. One must not refuse as that would give offence: at the same time one must, by an inclination of one's head, indicate a wish for the good health of all those at the table, and, even more important, watch vigilantly to see if anyone among the guests should pay one this compliment. It would be the height of ill-manners for a lady to drink without being requested to do so. She must wait, however thirsty she may be, but fortunately the request seldom fails to come quickly. The gentlemen must invite a seconder for every glass, while a third is free to join in, having first asked leave in a seemly fashion.

It can be seen that in this way one is kept fully occupied, replying to the questions about eating and drinking, the many toasts to people's healths and keeping a watchful eye for the proposal of one's own, with the result that interesting table-talk has little chance of developing. It is, in fact, considered unseemly for anyone to try to start a conversation and if he did, the master of the house would immediately interrupt him, saying: 'Sir, you will lose your dinner. We shall discuss such matters afterwards.' The ladies, anyway, from sheer modesty, speak as little as possible, and strangers cannot be too careful in avoiding the desire to carry on too lively an exchange, for it

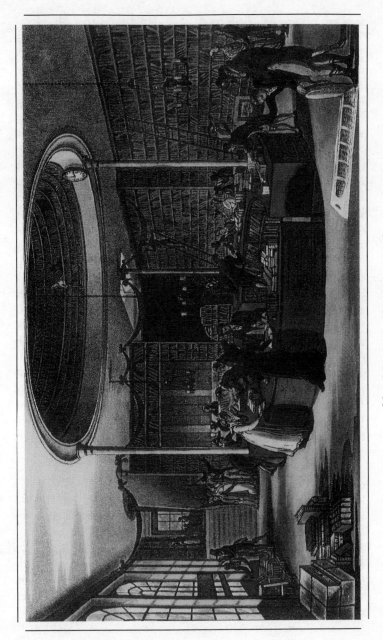

22　*Messrs Lackington, Books*

does not take much here to be considered monstrous bold.

Having got the first difficult act of eating over, the table is cleared, the crumbs carefully brushed from the tablecloth to make way for the cheeses of various kinds, along with butter, radishes and another salad, this time eaten without any dressing other than salt. This entr'acte is short and immediately followed by another. Every guest now has a small, finely-cut crystal bowl filled with water set in front of him, together with a small napkin. This is for rinsing the mouth and washing the hands, acts performed just as if one was alone in one's own house. To see the whole assembly engaged in this exercise, reminded us of a circle of tritons, as they can be seen sitting on fountains, spouting water. In fact the ladies show a certain grace in taking off their rings before dipping the tips of their fingers; the men deal with things a little more boldly.

After this cleansing ceremony the whole scene changes. The tablecloth and everything on it disappear and the beautiful, highly polished table of mahogany shines in front of us. Bottles and glasses are now placed in front of the master of the house, fruit is brought in and every guest receives a setting for dessert, a glass and a small red-checked or red cloth folded in four. This one must not unfold as it is used only for placing under the glass. The fruit is now handed round and as with all the preceding dishes, is offered by the host with the usual questions. On the whole it is bad, sour and half-ripe. Hazelnuts, which are the Englishman's favourite nut and which he cracks year after year, are never missing but sweet confections and bonbons are not much in evidence.

Thereafter the bottles begin to play the leading role; everyone pours as much as he wants for himself, a little or a lot, according to taste, and then passes them on to his neighbour. The only condition is that the glass must never be left empty and must be drained with each toast. Allowance is made for the ladies, however, should they only wish to sip a little. The host now proposes several toasts; he drinks to the health of his friends who then return the compliment to him and the lady of the house; the Royal Family is never forgotten on such occasions. Several of the guests express 'sentiments', that is to say, short phrases or maxims such as: 'Merit is to

win a heart and keep it.' They often refer to the ladies and are
repeated in a loud voice while drinking. All one can hear now
are the toasts, encouragements to have another drink, and
reminders to keep the bottles circulating but fortunately, soon
after due honour has been given to the King, the lady of the
house rises from her chair and, with a little bow, gives the
signal to the other ladies to rise and trip along modestly behind
her and out of the door. Even when a husband and wife eat
alone, tête-à-tête, Madam leaves her husband alone with his
bottle after the meal. Whether then also he proposes toasts, we
cannot really tell.

With the ladies out of the way, the men begin to feel more at
their ease. All restraint is now shed, for they are alone by
themselves, with the pleasure of wine, politics and many a
risqué joke, which with difficulty they restrained themselves
from telling in our presence. Their boisterous talk and laughter
let the whole house know that they are very well at ease. But
we, the poor ladies, what becomes of us? There we sit round
the fireplace again, staring at each other and stifling a yawn.
Not even coffee is served to cheer us up a little. To do
needlework in company is considered shocking and it does not
take us long to inspect each other's dresses, so we sit there in a
most disconsolate humour, feeling altogether bored with life.
How we should love to fall asleep but that too would not be
seemly. At last a wretched hour has crept by. We have talked
about the weather and the theatre, although this is not such a
common topic here as in other countries, as one attends less
frequently. The stranger has been asked ten times how she likes
London and ten times she has dutifully replied: 'exceedingly
well'. Finally, at long last, the lady of the house decides to end
our misery and asks the gentlemen to come in for tea.

It is said that a quick or a slow response to this invitation is a
clear indication as to who rules the house, the husband or the
wife. Yet even if they linger a little, the gentlemen will
eventually arrive, perhaps a little high in spirits and a little
talkative, though may it be said in their honour, we have never
seen anybody drunk on these occasions.

The hostess now makes the tea with much ceremony. The
inevitable questions are once again asked; how does one take

one's tea, whether sweet, whether with a lot or a little milk. In some houses it is served by a servant, but this is the exception to the rule as most English ladies are loth to have their place at the tea-table taken from them, a place they greatly cherish. As well as tea, a very poor, thin coffee is offered.

The conversation is now a little more animated although only rarely does a cheerful, pleasant dialogue develop, for the gentlemen have already said all they want to say in the company of the bottle and the ladies are tired and do not talk much anyway. After tea one drives home as it is too late for the theatre, although one might stay for a game of cards, if invited.

Whist is the only game usually found in society. Here the counting is different from ours and one can only lose at the most seven points in a rubber, of which three are always played, no more, no less. The playing-cards are large and clumsy and very expensive, making them one of the few manufactured articles where the English rank below other nations. It is not customary to use money at the card-table and one does not tip the servants. It is well known that the English are very good at Whist, their national game, playing seriously and in silence, but what is not generally known is that it is not the players who fix the stakes but the master of the house who decides for what his guests will play. One must submit to this rule without question if one does not wish to give offence. Some hosts, for sheer ostentation, insist on very high stakes, others more sensibly do exactly the opposite. It is therefore advisable for the visitor to make inquiries about the custom of the house before taking part in a game, as otherwise he may find himself unpleasantly embarrassed.

After the game one sits down to a cold evening meal of oysters, lobsters, tarts and the like. This is quickly dealt with and, happy to have survived the day's pleasures, one drives home late, well after midnight, through streets still swarming with people. All the shops are open and lit up and, anyhow, the street lamps are always burning until the sun begins to shine.

There is another kind of social gathering which the upper rank of the middle classes, about whom we are talking here, has copied from the more exalted circles of the country's great families. These gatherings are called routs and are the equivalent of our assemblies in Germany. In England one always associates the word assembly with a gathering in a public place, arranged by subscription. The lady of the house plays host at these routs and sends out invitations to them. A few days prior to the event, friends are sent tickets, usually about three times as many as the rooms will accommodate comfortably. Clearly, for such a party one needs a larger home than the ordinary, one that contains at least a few connecting rooms.

At ten o'clock, often much later, people start to assemble, squeezing through to greet the hostess, who has usually taken up a position not far from the entrance door. They take a seat at one of the many card-tables which, placed closely together, fill the whole room. Tea and refreshments are handed round as long as the servants can make their way through the multitude. Only when at last it has become so crowded that no one can any longer breathe, when the general noise is so great that nobody can understand a word anyone is saying, when there is a lack of chairs and anyway no space to put them down, has the pleasure reached its peak.

Eventually at two or three o'clock in the morning the fabric of the gathering begins to disintegrate, but slowly, just as it built up. One drives home, having had what is considered to have been a delicious evening in the grand style. Then the lady of the house, her senses surely numbed by the noise, utterly worn out after having been eternally on her feet and by all the greetings she has had to extend, can at last retire to her room, proud, none the less, in the knowledge that she has achieved the greatest glory of her social life.

SUNDAY

For the working classes on the Continent, Sunday is a wonderful day. Even old men begin to look forward to it on Saturday night, rejoicing at the thought that, after six hard working days, they will have their families around them in a happy mood, in clean and festive dress. Children begin counting the days until Sunday as early as the previous

Monday, knowing that there will be no school and that they will be free to enjoy themselves and play to their heart's content. For older boys and girls there is the blissful prospect of music and dancing under the lime trees or at the inn.

It is true that for members of the beau monde in the towns, any day may be Sunday if they so choose, but for all sections of society, the Lord's Day is not merely a day of rest, but also of joy and social pleasures and, above all, for family reunions. There are few who do not look forward to it with happy anticipation. They may even go to the theatre, after spending their evenings during the week working.

Things are entirely different in London, where music and dancing are strictly forbidden, the theatre must not even be thought of and all shops and exhibitions are closed. The fanatical pedantry with which the sanctity of the Sabbath is guarded here, surpasses even that of the Jews who prohibit only work, not play. A few of the noblest families of the realm were recently admonished in the churches as Sabbath-breakers and grave sinners, and abused in the newspapers. Their only crime was to have enjoyed a concert on Sunday in the privacy of their homes. It also happened on occasion that guests at a party on a Saturday night, stayed until after midnight, dancing and playing cards and were thus accused of desecrating the Lord's Day even before it had begun.

'Is it really true that people play cards on a Sunday in Germany?' a lady asked us. 'No day better than a Sunday, when one has nothing to do anyway,' was our reply. 'Good Lord,' sighed a second lady, continuing as if to reprimand us: 'One cannot blame them for they do not know any better.' And with that she cast a pitying look at us poor heathens. 'But they would not play for money?' a third one asked. 'Certainly for money – sometimes a lot of money.' The company recoiled, shuddering at the very thought. 'God bless us,' said the fourth lady, 'only once did I play cards on a Sunday – and then not for money – and to this day, I cannot forgive myself.' Two minutes earlier, the four ladies had sighed bitterly about the Sunday, a day which did not allow them to play even a rubber. Out in the country, they suffered the most terrible boredom, while the gentlemen consoled themselves with the bottle.

A true Englishman divides his Sunday between public worship, domestic devotions and the bottle. His wife passes the time remaining after her prayers, with some good friend, discussing the characters of every dear neighbour, who has to be judged by her very strict standards. Gossip, without question, is permitted on a Sunday. Children, alas, fare very badly, as special schools have been set up for them on Sunday evenings. They are marched there in a procession, after having already had to recite the rather senseless and dull liturgy of the Church of England twice at church and once at home.

But the visitor from abroad is worse off by far, for he is totally unacquainted with their code. He may chance to open the piano when immediately the landlady will come into the room and with a curtsey, remind him that this is the Lord's Day. He may look at a book, when a visitor will call and notice that it is some worldly matter, upon which he delivers a well-meant admonition. By now a lady, being somewhat irritated, may sit down by the window, and without giving it a thought, pick up some knitting. Lo and behold, in no time a crowd will gather in front of the house and with much noisy scolding, cause the landlady to appear again and this time express herself somewhat less politely than before. And should she then so occupy herself away from the window, the servants, upon entering the room, would show their justified horror, in their faces, at least, if not in words. Indeed, should you even want to play a game of Whist with a compatriot in your room, your own servant has the right to denounce you at the nearest Justice of the Peace and you will not escape punishment.

So what should you do with a day which occurs fifty-two times a year? You may undertake short journeys, season and weather permitting, ignoring the fact that the road tolls are doubled on the Sabbath. No, in winter and in bad weather, the only thing is patience: nothing else will do.

5 PUBLIC ENTERTAINMENTS IN LONDON

THE THEATRE

The different nations of Europe may be recognized not only by language; they are different in the way they walk, in the tone of their voices and in their gestures. Each of them has diverse characteristics, difficult to define, but none the less evident and unmistakable.

The Fine Arts, too, are greatly influenced by these natural or acquired differences. No Dutchman paints like an Italian and no Frenchman like either; they must all be true to their own national backgrounds. The forms, the movement, sky, the light which we have been accustomed to from infancy, stamp us indelibly with distinguishing features. We can only reproduce what we carry deep in our own selves and the distinction between different schools of painters lies more in the sky under which these schools develop than in the masters who are believed to be their founders.

The art of the theatre shows these national differences even more clearly and, were it possible to watch a play without hearing so much as a word, the experienced observer would still be able to tell at once whether he was watching an English, French or German performance. All three may be excellent in their own way, yet each may disappoint the stranger. For he, not sufficiently acquainted with the individuality of nations, will judge things according to the standards he has brought with him. Only gradually will he discover that what at first struck him as disagreeable, unnatural, even exaggerated, is actually sincere, true and admirable.

If one considers a theatrical performance as a perfect,

rounded whole, we Germans are not superior to other nations, although we have many excellent actors. The Weimar Court Theatre, favoured by the chance combination of many rare and extraordinary circumstances, was perhaps the only one in Germany where now and again one could watch presentations of masterpieces of the most excellent writers, which by creating a complete whole, achieved almost perfection.

That the German actor has to be everything to everybody is a disaster; through it he is prevented from developing the special talent most suited to his personality. In Paris and London this is different. Every actor devotes himself to those parts best suited to his own individual identity. Age is considered much less important there than with us. More fair-minded than we are, people understand how much is required of the artist if he is to reach a high degree of perfection in any of the arts. No perfect artist is ever born. Years of application and study are required in the training of a great talent and often youth has gone, before this talent reaches its full potential. This is recognized in France and England where people prefer to be deceived by make-up, dress and lighting, rather than forgo the greatest enjoyment art can provide, simply because the actor is some years too old.

The best German actor is he who is most moderate in gesture in timbre of voice, rhetoric and posture, for moderation and seriousness are in the nature of the German. To our neighbours we seem cold for the very reason that we consider them over exuberant. A Westphalian peasant might in the same way fear that his counterpart from Provence or Gascony was about to strike him dead when all he is doing is bidding him 'Good Morning' in the manner of his own country.

If one considers a perfectly constructed piece of art to be a whole, abiding by strictly laid-down rules, French tragedy must surely rank above all others. Time and place are rigorously adhered to, while each word and each line find critical judges in the stalls who make no allowance for the slightest offence against these established rules. Laws concerning what is right or wrong, unknown to any other nation, tie the playwright and actor alike. Both have to observe these strictly defined boundaries. The work of art, so meticulously created, dazzles, astonishes and demands admiration but does not engage our sympathy. A chill, which we hesitate to call boredom, overwhelms us. The poses struck by the most famous actors, beautiful and artistic as they may be, somehow always remind us of those conventional figures found in French paintings, and of which even the greatest masters have not been able to free themselves completely. The spirit of tragedy is not what one would expect to be the spirit of a nation which habitually looks on the bright side and accepts whatsoever fate might hold in store. The language itself, with its lack of modulation, runs contrary and is unsuited to reciting. Everything seems artificial, like listening to a carefully trained singer to whom nature has denied a really musical voice. Where the French excel is undoubtedly in high comedy. There one finds the esprit, life, wit, humour and that exquisite conversational tone which in everyday life distinguishes the French from any other nation.

English theatre is at the other end of the scale. There are no rules to limit the writer or the actor. Unrestrained, both allow their genius to take over. Everything is at the writer's disposal: verse and prose, a constant change of scene, an extension of time into eternity together with every possible theme. All the same, the lack of good new tragedies exposes the difficulty of making successful use of these unlimited possibilities. Only Shakespeare's gigantic talent was able to use them fully, and he still stands alone, with the public revering him as their only true poet and flocking tirelessly to his masterpieces.

English comedy provides a faithful, if sometimes exaggerated picture of domestic and social life, stressing the drawbacks, the virtues and comic situations, encountered in the different strata of society. The peculiarities of different parts of the country, especially those of the Scots and the Irish and their dialects, heighten this comic aspect and are presented with great accuracy.

Comedies of character, of which the French have produced masterpieces, where everything hinges on one single role, worked out in minute detail, are unknown to the English. Instead all plays abound in figures which to us appear to be caricatures, although they do not seem so to this singular nation. Nevertheless, if these strong features were to be softened and moderated a little, the prototypes might well be met everywhere in social life.

This is especially true of the better-drawn of these caricatures, which we in Germany might also find entertaining. We have in fact more in common in the things that amuse us than is generally believed.

Even though strict rules apply in England as to propriety in mixed circles of men and women, the public is quite indulgent where the theatre is concerned. Women who in social life are shocked at the slightest word offending their delicacy of feeling, watch quite happily scenes from which any French woman would angrily turn away, which indeed the whole Paris public would counter with strong indignation.

The English tragic actor plays his role more naturally than his French counterpart and with more bravura than the German. He imitates nature too faithfully and often goes beyond the bounds of propriety. Wild expressions of pain, loud cries of physical suffering, convulsions of madness, the agonies of the dying: the public is spared nothing and certainly considers that what it is seeing, is the highest form of art. With hair standing on end, the English public applauds most heartily when everybody shudders with terror.

The size of the theatres forces the actors to speak every line over-loudly, as the sailor seated in the most distant corner expects to hear and understand everything for the sixpence he has paid, just as well as the grandest lady in the first box. Clarity of speech is therefore the first thing which the English public demands from the actor. He must articulate every word and every syllable with the greatest care, and in doing this, mediocre actors often achieve a most disagreeable, even ridiculous, effect. Only the best of them know how to deal with the problem and even then with great effort.

Better actors, too, tend to emphasize certain set speeches, extolling patriotism and liberty, which, they know in advance, the public will applaud every time. They address passages to the public, taking no account of their fellow actors at all, only re-entering the actions of the play when the speech is ended. At certain times the actor even recites his part, pausing sufficiently between each phrase, so that there is time for applause. After that he falls silent again, making the whole appear to be melodrama in which the public wholeheartedly played its part.

Reciting in English anyway has a singing kind of sound without much modulation, a kind of pathos which, to the stranger, appears affected. It is difficult to describe, but the attentive observer will also notice it in everyday life in any highly emotional conversation. It is a rhythm peculiar to the English language: every language has its own.

In comic plays, particularly in farce, the English perhaps surpass all other nations. It is the well-known innate seriousness of this nation which makes its rare moments of gaiety all the more delightful. Jokes are not always of the subtlest order, indeed they are often a little coarse and clumsy but they do make the public laugh. Some actors, Munden, for example, only need to appear and the house is shaken to its foundations by the most noisy merriment. This is to say a lot for a nation which considers laughter in general unseemly and permits the educated a smile only. Here art allows nature to win the day and the rules of restraint are forgotten.

Operas are seldom heard, an English recitative being unthinkable, while the Englishman considers the change from the spoken word to song unnatural. On the whole the people do not care much for music, although sometimes short operas are performed as an epilogue. There is no lack of good male and female singers who can render such works agreeably enough to the English ear.

THE ENGLISH PUBLIC AT THE THEATRE

This subject deserves a section of its own, for the attitude of the English public at the theatre is surely unique in the world. The despotic rule it has over what happens on the stage is quite unknown elsewhere in Europe. Not even in France, where the audience is far from forbearing, far less in Germany, would such behaviour be found. Often, we must confess, when we paused to consider what the German public suffers through the indulgence they show to their favourites, we longed for these performers to spend a few months on the English stage, so that they might appreciate how well off they were at home.

Nevertheless, taken as a whole, the ways of these islanders cannot be justified at all. Every word spoken too inaudibly, every line or gesture ill-made, every hesitation are mercilessly censured. Only an actor making his debut is shown much forbearance and encouraged in every way. This explains, of course, why we never saw a London actor who had not learnt his part properly. The prompt box, which usually kills so much illusion, is banned completely from the stage. Instead, hidden from the audience, there is a prompter in each of the wings of the stage, who diligently follows the text and is ready to assist the actor, should, just for once, his memory fail him.

As elsewhere, it is the public at the very top of the house that has the loudest voice. Every little song, every aria which pleases this lofty crowd, has to be repeated two or three times. And there is much that pleases them. Even the renowned Mrs Billington had, in our presence, to deign to sing a bravura aria and a duet twice over. Should there be unrest or some dispute in the pit or the gallery, should someone fall ill and have to be taken away, there is at once a demand to the actors from above to stop the performance until order has been restored or the people causing the disturbance have been thrown out. Sometimes the noise grows so loud that the actors have to leave the stage. When they return, they are received with applause, and continue exactly where they left off.

How, with all these interruptions, the illusion can be sustained, is not considered of importance. The main thing is that for his money everyone should see and hear all that there is to see and hear. At times the spectators become the actors themselves. Once, when we were at the theatre, a sailor decided to sing a little ditty during the interval. Immediate silence was demanded from aloft and the audience obeyed. The sailor, for what he was, sang well enough in a quite tolerable voice, without stagefright even though among the listeners were some of the most distinguished people in the realm. He received much applause and was asked to sing again. This time he tried to be too ambitious, exceeded his ability and had to give up in the middle of a roulade, now to be greeted with general laughter.

ARRANGEMENTS FOR THE SPECTATORS AT THE TWO GREAT LONDON THEATRES

All performances begin at half-past six, and even this hour is on the early side for a public which generally only dines at about six o'clock, and often much later. The performances last so long that anyone lacking the English patience must surely tire, for only seldom does one get home before midnight. Short and sweet, somehow, is not a characteristic of the English: they like long sittings everywhere, in parliament, at table and in the theatre also.

Every night two pieces must be played, one in five acts, and an epilogue which often consists of two or three acts. This is usually a farce, occasionally a short opera and often some nonsense adapted from recent English novels and so, full of gruesome, dark horror. Whether the second play matches the first or whether it is in sharp contrast to it does not seem to trouble the audience: it is enough that the spectator should have full value for his money.

Both the large theatres, Drury Lane and Covent Garden, are open from the end of September until the end of June. Then they close and the smaller theatre at the Haymarket opens for the summer. During May and June it is the custom to put on benefit performances for the senior and better-known actors: these form a part of their salary and often last until after one o'clock. In order to give the public its fill, all kinds of small extras are inserted into the entr'actes, sometimes a little song, sometimes a dance. These usually so please the spectators that they have to be repeated two or three times with the result that the performance goes on and on.

The boxes are very roomy and contain several rows of seats, set one above the other, and placed in such a way that one can see well from all of them. The same can be said for the pit which, without stalls or *parterre noble*, stretches from the orchestra right to the back of the house. In all rows of the boxes, seats cost six shillings, while the pit costs a little more than half of that. There are two galleries above the boxes where seats are one or two shillings per person, and then, high above in the last gallery, completely in the background and almost invisible, are enthroned those worthy people of whom we talked before and who usually set the fashion. Low divisions separate each box from its neighbour. Brightly lit, like daylight, and filled with spectators, they make an enchanting sight. Etiquette dictates that all ladies attend the theatre in full dress if they wish to sit in the front rows of the boxes, especially in the first and second tier. No lady is admitted with a large hat though a small dress one, ornamented with feathers or flowers is allowed. In the pit, however, they can appear in ordinary clothes with large hats which they must remove without objection, if asked to do so. Women of the middle class and gentlemen of any rank frequent the pit. It is quite a respectable place but one has to arrive early, often before the house has opened, in order to secure a good place, as it is not possible to reserve seats there.

No lady is admitted to the front two rows of the boxes, without, in the first place, having inscribed her name in a book provided for the purpose and so reserved her seat. This is in order to keep the public nymphs of the town from occupying these seats which are intended for the more respectable families of the realm. These other ladies are allotted special seats at the back of the theatre.

By inscribing one's name, one has the right to reserve several seats in whichever row one desires, until the end of the first act. One may send one's servant or, what is more common, pay a shilling to the box attendant who, for this sum, will seat somebody in them. These seats are therefore considered reserved until the end of the first act, but after that anybody has the right to take them. Nobody is permitted to pay for more seats than he requires, and even if he did, or even say took a whole box, it would serve no purpose. The Englishman maintains that nobody by paying money should be allowed to deprive somebody else, who also pays, from enjoying a public spectacle, as long as space merits. For this reason there is no system of subscriptions in English theatres. Even the Royal Family have to make an advance reservation of their box, which, by the way, has little to distinguish it from any other, as it is, without discrimination, taken up like all the others, should no one from the Royal House be attending the performance.

After the third act anyone is admitted at half price, a custom which is most unpleasant for the more elegant section of society. Making much noise, these night birds, the very people it is desirable to keep out, swarm in and only the strictest precautions prevent them from occupying the first row of the boxes. They are the worst members of society though they are certainly dressed in accordance with the rules, and they spread themselves over the whole house, which is why no lady would ever go to the theatre without a male escort. A gentleman would never offer his seat to an unknown lady sitting behind him for fear of placing his neighbours next to an unsuitable person. This is an example of where a foreigner, being unaware of the custom, could seem, by trying to be courteous, to be exactly the opposite.

DRURY LANE

The auditorium of this theatre is one of the biggest and finest in the world. While we did not see the exterior in its finished state, it seems to be somewhat clumsy in style, a common fault in so many of London's public buildings, and, in spite of its great size, to be dwarfed by an unusually high roof. However, it should be noted that this roof is of great benefit and importance, as it houses not only the mechanism for lifts and other machines, but also the safety curtain which, in the event of fire during a performance, can be lowered at once and so protect that part of the theatre which holds the audience.

Within the theatres there are four rows of boxes, not counting the galleries, all painted in light colours and decorated with good taste. At least fifty crystal chandeliers and many more mirrored wall-brackets are arranged elegantly for the illumination of the whole, yet, despite the several hundred candles burning in them, their brilliance seems to vanish the moment the curtain rises and the stage lighting floods the area like the brightest sunshine.

The stage sets prove worthy of the whole. The backdrop is not a true curtain for it does not roll up but instead divides into

23   Interior of Drury Lane

several parts, depending on what is required by the production. These parts can again be divided into smaller ones which slot into each other and can, if necesary, be raised. In the same way, when they are lowered, they fit together as if by magic, so that not the slightest gap is seen between them. This arrangement has a great advantage in that the scenery is not damaged or creased by being rolled or folded and never shows those rippling movements our curtains do, making the spectator think of an earthquake, even in the most peaceful scenes.

The most brilliant stars in the theatrical firmament happened to be at Covent Garden during our stay in London. Nevertheless, Drury Lane remained rich enough, especially in the comic domain, to give us the pleasure of most excellent performances. Above all Mrs Jordan was brilliant, she being the mistress or, as some say, the secretly wedded wife of the Duke of Clarence. He did her every honour in the eyes of the world, always having her driven to the theatre in his carriage with his own livery. The sight of this exceedingly charming woman on the stage, made one forget completely that she was long past her first youth and had become a little too plump for the younger parts. The cheerful roguish expression of her pretty face, her agreeable, sonorous voice, the naïve grace and naturalness of her movements proved so irresistable that one could ask for nothing more.

We must recall here one special performance at Drury Lane which pleased us above all others: *Much Ado about Nothing.* In Germany we sometimes see a shortened version of this play under the title, *Die Quälgeister.* Even then it succeeds in entertaining, in spite of the author's endeavours to debase it by putting the Shakespearean characters into awkward, tight uniforms of the military. What a delight it is then to see this play in its original brilliance, with only a few cuts to comply with the code of morality. Mrs Jordan as Beatrice and Mr Bannister as Benedict were truly in their element. The scenes of badinage between them, where one jest swiftly follows another, one must see, as played by them, to believe that lines learnt by heart can be rendered so convincingly. The slow and somewhat laboured speaking of dialogue which we have mentioned before, had here, as with all good English comic actors, completely disappeared. Everything went quickly, yet in this large house, no one in the audience lost so much as a syllable. To be sure, when the language reverts to verse and seriousness returns, so does the solemn preaching tone. Constable Dogberry and his companions were extraordinarily amusing with their broad peasant dialect, causing the whole house to shake with uninterrupted laughter, so that when the actors appeared on the stage they often had to pause, in order to be heard eventually.

Mrs Bland, a short plump, rather elderly favourite of the public, was said to be an excellent singer because she made a great noise, yet at the same time pronounced the words very clearly. In the entr'acte she sang a popular English romance,

'Poor crazy Jane', the simple lament of a girl, jilted by her lover
and so driven mad. The music was nothing special but the song
had to be repeated twice to loud applause. In this country the
text counts for more than the music and it so happens that such
descriptions of human misery give the greatest pleasure to the
English. Their feelings are rather like their taste for cayenne
pepper: only something very strong stimulates the heart and
the stomach.

The final item of the evening, or what one could more
suitably call here the night, was a grand pantomime, performed
mainly by Italians, a spectacle we had never seen given so
perfectly anywhere before. A magician sat on his throne,
surrounded by his attendants. In the background, behind iron
railings, were old Pantaloon, Harlequin, Columbine and the
faithful servant, Pierrot, all slumbering in coffins, apparently in
the deep sleep of death. The magician has to make a journey
and it is necessary for someone to sit on his throne in the
meantime and be capable of holding up his sceptre without
falling asleep. A small roguish goblin, played incomparably
well by a Signor Grimaldi, is selected to perform this
honourable task and shows himself not a little proud of the
fact. The magician warns him most earnestly not on any
account to fall asleep, and then departs in his dragon coach. All
goes well for a while. The foolish goblin is out of his mind
with joy at sitting on such a magnificent throne. Then sleep
begins to creep over him and, though he tries steadfastly to
stay awake, it is in vain. He even tries to take a strong pinch of
snuff from a large box, which makes him sneeze three times
and upon each sneeze, he shoots at least three feet high into the
air, turning several somersaults before landing back in his seat.
However, sleep triumphs and as he loses consciousness, the
sceptre slips from his hand. The magic spell is broken and a
scene of great confusion follows. Harlequin and his friends are
now in constant flight, having risen from their coffins in great
delight. They rush about in every direction, performing a
thousand different escapades, all the time pursued by the
goblin. There is a continual change of scene, each more splendid
than before and the transformations, which followed in quick
succession and variety, are truly magical. The eye has hardly

time to take it all in. The mimics, just like the scenery, were all excellent and one comic turn followed another so rapidly that the house resounded with non-stop laughter. Everybody laughed, everybody was happy, but surely nobody, when he reached home, would be able to recount what he had actually seen. The show ended at about one o'clock.

COVENT GARDEN

While this theatre is not as large as Drury Lane, it is equally elegantly decorated and somehow appears even more splendid and magnificent. The judicious placing of different-sized mirrors around the theatre magnifies the brightness of the masses of candles. On this stage it was often possible to see the most famous actors together in one performance. First and foremost there was Mrs Siddons who, since we saw her last, has left the theatre. She was a tall, regal figure. It seemed as if Melpomene, as depicted by the ancient masters, had left her pedestal to walk among mortals, so stately and beautiful was she, everything in true proportion. Her whole being seemed so suited for tragedy that it was almost impossible to think of her as cheerful, let alone laughing. She had an extremely melodic voice, with an inimitable tone of sadness, soft yet penetrating at the same time. She was well past her first youth but time had marred her beauty only a little and nobody missed the youthful charm in these noble features. She was fairly plump, but this too was no impairment because of her height. She would in fact have been perfect had she not, at times, given in to the temptation, in order to please her public, of misusing her great talent by over-acting in a rather terrible way. For instance, as Isabella, in *The Fair Penitent*, when in the fifth act she plunged the dagger into her bosom, she died with loud, convulsive, heart-rending laughter which went on for quite some time, making the audience's hair stand on end. Of course the English like that sort of thing, even if some of the ladies suffered convulsions and faintings. Her real triumph was, I think, the role of Lady Macbeth, which provided ample opportunity for her talent. The very sight of her in the sleepwalking scene made one's blood congeal.

24 *Interior of Covent Garden*

Her brother was Kemble, who rightly deserved that honour. Although he, too, was now past his prime, his figure was still noble and handsome, and if, at times, he seemed a little monotonous, his acting was always well thought out and credible, making one recognize who had been his mentor. Young Siddons, the spit of his mother, and his wife who combines youth and beauty with a talent for gentle, suffering and loving parts, also distinguished themselves. They are respected partly for what they have already achieved through their training, and partly for the hopes they hold out for the future. It is hard to imagine the part of Juliet being played more gracefully than by the young Mrs Siddons.

Cooke was a master of a different kind. Nature had denied him a good figure, but rewarded him instead with a most expressive face, especially for the parts he chose for himself: tyrants, villains, cold, daring, haughty characters which he played exceedingly well. His greatest triumph was as Richard III. Never before was that part played as he played it, nor will it ever be again. He made the part his own, so much so that his enemies even maintained that he played this character in his other parts, in all of which one could see Richard. His figure, his tone of voice, the way he walked, everything was absolutely true in his playing. When he appeared unashamedly wicked, one shuddered before his grim resolve; when he showed pretence, he deceived the spectators; when he, with cold disdain, mocked those around him, even his own ugliness; when in wild despair he shouted, 'A horse, a horse, my kingdom for a horse!'; when with false meekness he conquered Lady Anne's heart at her husband's coffin – in all these situations he was the same, a great and true actor.

When one remembers the splendid scenery which is quite common here, it seems sad that, because their integral worth always guarantees a full house, Shakespeare's masterpieces are often neglected in this respect. The glamorous sets tend to be lavished on modern plays which have little else to recommend them. One has, however, to see Shakespeare's work especially in this theatre for this is where one can find the great actors who excel in the main parts. The supporting roles are often played unsatisfactorily and the slow speechifying, in a somewhat barking fashion, of the mediocre actors at first seems ridiculous and later becomes unbearable. All the same, it must be difficult to speak loudly and still retain the right modulation.

It is a pity that all those plays of Shakespeare still in the repertoire, are performed in Garrick's version. Like so many of his kind, he deluded himself into thinking that a great actor is a greater writer and therefore took unwarranted liberties with the master. In *Romeo and Juliet*, for example, Juliet awakes while Romeo is dying, thus creating an impossible scene, and the Nurse is left out of the play completely. *Hamlet* is performed pretty close to the original, except that Fortinbras does not appear at the end. Hamlet is Kemble's favourite part, which he plays in the minutest detail as if he had just finished reading *Wilhelm Meister*.

What Cooke and Kemble were to tragedy, Munden, Fawcett and Lewis were to comedy, especially Munden. Stupid servants, silly boys, eccentric old men, these were his speciality, with Polonius in *Hamlet* his triumph. We have never encountered anyone who excelled him in pulling faces and adopting foolish postures. Things can be just as tumultuous at Covent Garden as they are at Drury Lane. Once, during a benefit performance of Kotzebue's *Menschenhass und Reue*, adapted by Sheridan as *The Stranger*, a production particularly well done in the comic parts, a young man appeared in the entr'acte and performed a hornpipe. Quite undeservedly, for he danced very badly, he seemed to take the fancy of the distinguished audience. A repeat was demanded but the young gentleman would not oblige by appearing a second time. Then the noise began and it seemed that the whole house was falling in, like the walls of Jericho when the trumpets blew. The uproar was beyond belief and, witnessing such a scene for the first time, one could not but be afraid. One of the actors came on the stage and stood waiting for the shouting of the crowd to abate for a while. When at last that moment arrived, he stepped forward and with a deep bow asked the audience's permission to sing a song, assuring them that immediately afterwards the other gentleman would dance again. He was simply resting for a little. The applause was now as loud as the rebuke had been before and so he sang a silly song, of endless verses,

[179]

about a Yorkshireman. This had to be repeated twice, though naturally the singer did not need to be asked to do so. The moment the song ended, the dancer reappeared, was allowed to dance calmly and, that over, was hissed and sent on his way.

During the next interval, an actor imitated the best known members of the two theatre companies, doing so to perfection. This is something which would hardly be tolerated in other countries. The manner of walking, of speech and delivery, everything was absolutely right, and with loud applause the audience shouted out the names of the actors being imitated. It was very interesting to hear the same part of a tragedy several times, presented in quite different ways. Of course this entire performance was followed by an Epilogue, for without that the audience would surely not have gone home quietly even though the new day had almost dawned.

The greatest uproar we experienced in the theatre was at a performance of *Pizarro*, Sheridan's version of Kotzebue's *Die Spanier in Peru*. Up to now the play had been performed only (though many times) at Drury Lane for, as is well known, Sheridan was a co-director there. Now it was announced for Covent Garden with Mrs Siddons as Cora, Kemble as Rolla and Cooke as Pizarro. All the boxes for that day had been reserved long in advance and in the theatre there was a great air of expectation.

The management of Drury Lane, however, could hardly be expected to watch such a triumph take place at Covent Garden with indifference and so took extraordinary steps to prevent it. To begin with they announced that they would present the same play that night, something unheard of, as in the history of the London theatre never had both houses presented the same play on the same night. Then, the day before the performance, the management hosted a splendid dinner in Mr Cooke's honour. It goes without saying that, in the true English manner, a great deal was drunk upon that occasion and the hero of the day was taken home in a pretty inebriated condition. The next night the audience at Covent Garden was the most brilliant gathering to be seen there for a long time. To begin with all went extremely well, until Cooke came on as Pizarro. Despite all his exertion, he was unable to utter one audible word, trying in vain several times and in the end being reduced to silence. The actors at Drury Lane knew only too well the weakness of their former associate and had counted on it. They knew that every day after having been the worse for drink, Cooke was completely hoarse and quite unable to act. His complaint only lasted a day which is why they fêted him the night before. The anger of the public knew no bounds and the rage of the sea, tossed by the wildest gale, hardly gives an idea of the incredible roar that came from the pit and the galleries. In the boxes people were reasonably quiet; the ladies trembled and grew pale as corpses, a few even fainting and having to be carried out. The actors were forced to remain on the stage and Mrs Siddons and Kemble, looking very hand-some in Spanish dress, had to face the terrible uproar, looking anxious and embarrassed, for as soon as they seemed to be about to leave the scene, the audience threatened to storm it. Cooke stood in the background, looking quite shattered, while the noise continued for a full hour, making us wonder how the people's lungs withstood it all. Eventually Kemble tried to apologize for Cooke's indisposition and to propose another play for the evening. He could, however, hardly make himself heard against shouts of 'Pizarro! Pizarro!' from a thousand throats. Others shouted 'Cooke is drunk', paying scant attention to Kemble trying to assure them most humbly of the contrary. As the roar increased from minute to minute, the actors seemed to take counsel together, after which Kemble stepped forward and asked the public if they would allow young Siddons to play Pizarro, book in hand. This request was greeted with loud applause, the storm abated, Cooke sneaked off the stage and the play continued from exactly where it had been broken off.

We found it hard to understand the composure with which the company, especially Mrs Siddons and Kemble, carried on playing after such an upheaval. They truly surpassed them-selves. The scenery was magnificent and young Siddons, in spite of reading his lines, much better than one might have expected. Everything was forgiven and forgotten; only when Kemble announced that the play would be given on the next day, were there shouts from all sides: 'Tell Cooke not to get drunk again.'

OTHER LONDON THEATRES

Of the summer theatres, which are really meant for the Nobodies who are doomed to spend the summer in London and which only open when Drury Lane and Covent Garden close, the Haymarket is the most notable. It is not particularly large but beautifully decorated inside in white and gold, and the lighting is excellent. This theatre concentrates mainly on comedy, farces and short operas. However, we happened to see Mr Elliston in the episode of Gardenio and Lucinda from *Don Quixote*, a performance which left the audience in tears. Elliston is an actor who might well have become a rival to Cooke and Kemble but he was not allowed to get ahead and has, in fact, spent the last couple of years in New York where he enchants everybody and melts hearts like wax. The performance ended with a short comic opera which made up for the terrors of the first piece, drying the tears of the second gallery and the general wailing and chattering of teeth, and sent everyone away laughing.

Among the others are Astley's Amphitheatre, the Royal Circus and Sadler's Wells. They also provide entertainment for the Nobodies during the unfashionable season. All have light fare, such as pantomime and ballet. Astley's Amphitheatre was a family company and, during our stay in London, Mr Astley suffered the misfortune of seeing his theatre burn down for a second time, destroying his own house next door, where his poor mother died in the blaze. The Royal Circus offered more or less the same kind of entertainment but boasted an excellent tightrope-walker. Sadler's Wells we decided not to visit. It is situated some way off and as we were given to understand that beer and alcohol contributed somewhat to the success of the performance, this made us a little apprehensive.

There is also, in the village of Chelsea, the beautiful Rotunda at Ranelagh where, from February until the end of May, concerts are held. They are frequented by the beau-monde, rather different from those at Vauxhall and rather more boring. The audience is impressive, but does not seem to be enjoying itself.

25 *Theatre Royal, Covent Garden*

THE ITALIAN GRAND OPERA

From Covent Garden, the pride of the nation, we now turn to the Italian Opera. Although the most distinguished people in the realm are its patrons, this kind of theatre is hated by the man in the street as it seems to go in every way against the national temperament. John Bull visits it but once and pokes fun at it for the rest of his life. The foreign language, the strange behaviour and, above all, the French dancers appear to him to be sacrilegious on his own dear soil. The whole thing would have collapsed long ago were it not for its patrons' great vanity, their love of display and a preference for things foreign. It is quite clear that opera cannot thrive here and that, in spite of the vast sums spent on it, it vegetates miserably.

The theatre, even larger than Drury Lane, has five rows of boxes, apart from the pit and three galleries. In spite of the brilliant lighting, it is over-decorated with paintings which makes it seem darker than other theatres. The decoration was in rather poor taste with hosts of little cupids swarming everywhere amidst thousands of scrolls and garlands. The whole effect was colourful, but not bright. It is the brilliant meeting place of the nobility, to whom it mainly owes its support. In addition, anyone laying claim to being fashionable, well-educated and having style, at least pretends he frequents the place regularly and that he is enchanted each time, even though, keeping his mouth carefully closed, he has had to suppress many a yawn during the performance. The boxes, upper and lower, are all let at prices which, in many a small town on the Continent, would pay for the lease of a whole house or even buy it.

Twice a week, on Tuesdays and Saturdays, from December to June, one sees in the boxes the most beautiful, famous, rich and distinguished ladies in the kingdom, all dressed in their grandest finery. Glittering with diamonds they sit in long rows and provide a sight which surpasses the actual spectacle on the stage. Those who do not have a subscription are seated in the pit, which is considered to be on the level of the boxes, and where one must also appear in full dress. The tickets cost half a guinea and the ladies appear beautifully adorned, while the gentlemen have on their dancing pumps and their cocked hats under their arms. If people do not observe the rules of dress, they are placed in the first gallery which costs half as much as the pit, though whether from there, on the sixth floor, one can see or hear very much, we beg leave to doubt.

Fate intended us to see *Calypso*, a work by Winter. We had no choice, as it is the custom for several weeks running, to perform the same opera and the same ballet until the singers and dancers are tired. It would appear that the public in the boxes does not tire of seeing the same thing over and over again, and pronouncing it excellent each time. The famous Madame Billington sang the part of Calypso, which was little to her advantage. One might overlook the fact that she is well over forty, were she not so impossibly fat, more so than anyone we have ever seen on the stage, and if only she had tried to make up for her lack of youth and a good figure, by her acting and her expression. Unfortunately, she thought it beneath her dignity to be an actress and instead simply stood motionless and sang, believing that in so doing she was giving enough. The English considered her to be the finest singer in the world and, indeed, her voice was excellently trained, pure, full and particularly in the high notes possessed of great volume. Yet expression and manner of delivery were lacking completely and she sang everything exactly as prescribed, one thing after another like clockwork, adding now and again little cadences and trills to astonish the listeners. Thus she believed she had attained the highest reaches of her art, for no singing in the world means more to an Englishman than holding a trill for a quarter of an hour.

Most of the other singers, male and female, were Italians and most were less than mediocre. The worst was the second lady singer whom, we were told, the management had engaged only because the costumes of her predecessors fitted her to perfection. The orchestra was praiseworthy and the sets pretty, although they hardly compared with those of other London theatres. The establishment seemed to be run in a parsimonious fashion, unworthy of the large sums spent on it and the quality of the audience who attended.

At long last we were delighted when Signor Telemaco, with a jump into the air, changed the mood of the music, as we were much looking forward to the Ballet. Alas, this too was in three acts and never seemed to come to an end. It was a moral, sentimental affair. Mademoiselle Parisot, L'Arboire and his wife were excellent, as were others whose names escape me, but then the leading dancers always are, for every year first-class artistes from Paris are engaged for the season at extremely large salaries. The others, and especially the walk-on parts, however, showed up badly against them, both in their art and in the costumes they wore. Nowhere is there a trace of that magic with which the Paris Ballet transports us into another world. We reached home after one o'clock, as tired as if we ourselves had taken part in the dancing. We had left the house at seven o'clock that night.

VAUXHALL

It is difficult to imagine anything more charming and brilliant than this fairy-tale garden, situated a short distance from London on the banks of the river Thames. This is particularly true on Gala nights, as they are called on the occasion of a Royal birthday, when there is extra and even more resplendent lighting. One can find a happy throng of perhaps fifteen thousand well-dressed men and women strolling between the beautiful shrubs and trees in the glimmer of the many sparkling lights. Music fills the mild summer night and there is an atmosphere of relaxed pleasure. One might have entered the paradise of the Mohammedans.

Merely to enter this magic spot dazzles and surprises. In the centre of a large square, surrounded by fine trees, there is a raised orchestra platform, lit by a multitude of coloured lights, glittering against the dark night sky like a fairy palace built of precious stones. The fantastic construction seems to float in the air, yet is solid enough to carry safely about a hundred players. Behind the trees, festooned with lights, are roofed arcades with little arched alcoves at the side. There too lamp after lamp is hung, in fact there seem to be lights everywhere, sparkling in splendid glowing colours. Leading from the square are a

26 *The Chinese Pavilion, Vauxhall Gardens*

[187]

number of well-lit walks, and indeed some dark ones as well, but these would never be used by fashionable society. At each end of the lighted walks are little halls, decorated with statues, transparencies, flowers and garlands of crystal, offering shelter from the cold, wind or a sudden shower. In some of these, far from the orchestra, small ensembles of musicians play. Well-dressed attendants stand round the square, ready at all times to bring to the tables any food or drinks which might be required.

The orchestra is composed mainly of wind instruments. We heard a concerto for trumpet played here superbly well, the musician being in the service of the Prince of Wales. The most popular English singers, except perhaps the most distinguished, also perform here, singing arias, folk-songs and part-songs. Music generally sounds well in the open air, but the effect of these mighty sounds, coming from the sparkling fairy-temple into the silent night, is something difficult to describe. Yet in spite of the large throng, there is no great noise from people, as they generally walk in silence or just whisper and listen to the music until a bell calls them to a distant part of the garden. Here one is confronted by an extraordinary automaton, a moving clockwork picture representing a waterfall. The waters roar and turn to spray. Below is a bridge over which pass vehicles, animals, people on foot and on horseback, everything seeming completely life-like.

From here, one strolls back to the orchestra who generally play some grand aria or special piece, and then on along the brightly-lit walks to visit the various halls. Time flies so quickly and when another bell rings, one suddenly realizes it is midnight, and one is being called to a different part of the garden to witness a fireworks display. This is pretty, although not to be compared with the dazzling splendour of Vienna's Prater. After this the crowd disperses, each little circle of friends repairing to one of the boxes where they can dine and watch the beau monde go by.

Later, dancing takes place on the green lawns. The ladies to be seen dancing may well not be of the highest virtue, for in London a young girl of good repute would hardly expose herself so publicly. Besides, we noticed that nearly all the time it was the same ladies who danced and so presumed that the management had engaged them to be present. Nevertheless they danced happily and decorously and, as all were young, pretty and well dressed, the illusion was complete and no one asked who, in truth, they were. Usually day dawns over these pleasures, but fashionable society tends to leave before two o'clock. Only then do things deteriorate somewhat, becoming a little too wild and bacchanalian for one to wish to be present.

CONCERTS

Famous virtuosi, who in a few years amassed a fortune in London which they could not have done in a lifetime at home, know very well how much the English love music. They are not really a musical nation, for they are lacking in talent as well as an ear and a sense of taste. As we have already remarked, the words mean more than the tune and clear enunciation more than the singer's art.

This is certainly true of the man in the street and the middle class. Society, however, those people who have had the opportunity to travel and to gather a wider knowledge of things, enjoy acting as patrons to foreign talent and reward it in a princely manner. On special days, many of these people hold musical assemblies in their houses, attended by well-known foreign musicians. Lucky is the performer who arrives in London with even one acquaintance or address, for it may well be the making of his reputation.

A number of grand subscription concerts is given during the winter in London, for which many notable foreign and native virtuosi are engaged. They are fairly expensive and are mainly patronised by the fashionable society. The most brilliant of these take place during the last two, so-called, winter months, once a week in a fine high-vaulted hall in Hanover Square. Adjoining the hall are two splendid rooms for conversation. The concerts are mainly devoted to vocal music and we never took greater pleasure from a concert than we did from one of these. The brilliant audience was quiet and attentive while London's best singers vied with one another. Madame Billington, whom we liked much better at the concert than previously at the opera, Madame Storace, Madame Dussek, wife of the famous pianist, sang most agreeably, the latter also playing the harp in a masterly fashion. We were specially delighted with the tenor Braham who at that time had perhaps the finest voice in existence. He is actually an Israelite, called Abraham. There were arias, duets, music for four voices and quite a number had to be repeated, for as we have noted before, the Englishman, high or low, likes to get his money's worth and demands it, without ado or respect for person. The artist has to obey, even if it is hard for him and in the end it is considered an honour to be 'encored' as they call it here.

At the end of the concert, a boy of seven, the son of the manager, sang a little Italian song. He was quite good for his age, and his appearance showed the kindheartedness of the English who always like to encourage budding talent. The boy too was asked for an encore, even though it did require a certain amount of patience to listen to the child's small voice just once, immediately after Braham's beautiful, manly singing.

ST JAMES'S PALACE, THE PARKS, AND KENSINGTON GARDENS

There can be no prince, not even the ruler of the smallest state scarcely visible on the map, who has a less impressive residence than the King of England. Looking at that ancient, crooked and dilapidated building, which boasts the fine name of St James's Palace, one can hardly believe one's eyes. For much of the time King George III does not live in the place and the large bed with its red velvet curtains in the levee room is merely there display. All the same, according to time-honoured tradition, court festivities are held in this regal rat-hole. However, the royal personages only arrive there just before these begin, perhaps incognito, preferring to live in the Queen's palace, Buckingham House. This is a slightly more modern building, simply constructed of bricks, and far from being splendid, is neither very large nor beautiful. It is situated in St James's Park, a favourite promenade for Londoners, and is adjacent to the Palace.

This park is simply a very large fine meadow, crossed by footpaths, with a canal flowing through it and groups of stately old trees scattered here and there. It is all quite artless, yet extremely pleasant, and the pastoral peace which meets one immediately on entering contrasts strikingly with the noise of the great city one leaves behind. At the western end of it is Buckingham House and its gardens, with Green Park stretching alongside it. This too is a charming meadow, laid out as a promenade with a few trees. Hyde Park, which borders both, is much larger and stretches out towards Kensington Gardens. Through this a clear, silvery stream winds, and the cows and horses grazing on the banks add to the tranquil charm. Everything is fresh and green so that the city might be a hundred miles away.

Entering Kensington Gardens from Hyde Park, one could well believe that one had wandered into some ancient heathen grove where the magnificent trees rise in sylvan glory to ornament the scene. The gardens belong to the King and during the season they are open, to a properly dressed public, from eight o'clock in the morning until eight at night, proving a popular place for a walk in the air. They are not laid out in the latest fashion, but in an older style, with broad avenues in a straight line, and a certain symmetry of which landscape gardening does not now approve. This makes them well suited for strolling in a large city, and the sight of the promenaders taking the air under the splendid trees leaves a charming and lasting impression. Kensington Palace, situated in these gardens, deserves this name merely because of its owner. The Royal Family never go there, the residents being private people allowed to live in it by the King.

Each Sunday afternoon in fine weather, St James's Park swarms with well-dressed walkers, who are certainly Nobodies but look as fine as if they were Somebodies. All who have laboured throughout the week in the shops and offices of the City and who do not have, for some reason, to stay at home, hurry into the open to get some fresh air, see the green trees, or even, perhaps, just to display their Sunday finery.

While the sight of this crowd is most enjoyable, even more interesting is Hyde Park in the spring. On a fine Sunday, between two and five o'clock, the fashionable world drives, rides on horseback or simply walks there. The most beautiful carriages and the finest horses pass through Hyde Park's main artery towards Kensington at this time. No hackney coach or public conveyance dares show itself to remind us that there are people in this world who are neither rich nor distinguished. But it is a fine sight to see so many grand coaches and fine horses, the beautiful women and the heads of the charming children looking out of the carriage windows. This is the most obvious proof of the wealth of London's population. The paths, too, are crowded with people on foot who have descended from their grand carriages to walk and to greet their friends. It has been estimated that on such days there could be up to a hundred thousand people enjoying the beauty and the blue skies of the parks and Kensington Gardens, making a brilliant spectacle.

In winter too, thousands of people will gather there, especially when, during the severe cold, the canal through Hyde Park is frozen over. It is then that the skaters come out to show their skill and everybody rushes to admire them. Pavilions are specially built to provide refreshment and warmth and, most important, help in case of accidents for which, in fact, an establishment has been specifically provided on the bank.

THE KING'S BIRTHDAY

This day is the most important of the year for London society. It is celebrated on the 4th June, which is the actual birthday of King George III. It comes at the divide between winter and summer and sets the tone for the twelve months to come, in fashion, in carriages – everything, in fact, is ruled by this great day. Certainly this was the case while the old King was able to appear in public, but his later ill health is bound to have created many changes in the customary ceremony of the day. However, the main events have undoubtedly stayed the same and will do so as long as there are kings of England.

For months before the big event, all the saddlers, coachmakers, jewellers and fashion designers are thrown into a frenzy of activity; new garments and finery must be created, jewels remounted, splendid carriages and liveries acquired. It is essential to shine brilliantly on this day, just for one hour, for the whole ceremony does not really last much longer. The newspapers do their best to perpetuate the display and for many days afterwards their pages are filled with long columns of descriptions of absolutely everything, down to the little details of the tassels on a lady's dress or the stitching on a gentleman's gala wig, and of course the carriages and the liveries. But to what end, for perpetuity on paper is nowadays of short duration.

At one o'clock in St James's Park we noticed many people around a small back door of the palace, where they waited to see the King alight on his arrival from Buckingham House. As a thunder of cannon announced the impending festivities, we were struck by the expression of joy, love and expectation on the faces of the people, for they cling with great affection to good old George, during whose long reign most of them were born. Anxious to avoid being jostled by the large crowd, we decided not to wait for his arrival and walked up St James's Street, a fine broad thoroughfare leading to the main entrance of the Palace. Here, from the balcony of a private house, we were able to watch the stream of wellwishers comfortably.

It was a colourful and cheering sight. All the balconies were filled with happy faces, packed close together and even the roofs swarmed with spectators. On the street below, a great throng of well-dressed people overflowed from the footpath so that there was scarcely room for the carriages to pass. Many had ground to a halt and from them pretty women and children looked with curiosity at the colourful crowd. The Horse Guards paraded in front of the Palace, and at the gates stood richly-clad court servants together with the King's hundred Yeomen, a kind of Swiss Guard. Their dress has remained unchanged since the fifteenth century and is strange to behold. The people call them 'the King's Beefeaters' and their well-nourished figures seem to deserve the title. Their ancient English uniforms – scarlet, trimmed all over with gold, a shining silver escutcheon on front and back, with a flat cap decorated with coloured bows – all this, while appearing strange, contributed to the dignity of the occasion, taking us back down the centuries. This impression was enhanced when a group of people emerged from the Palace – apparently the Royal Fire Brigade, in a strange scarlet uniform – where they had delivered their congratulations, and made their way in procession to a nearby tavern, there ceremoniously to drink the King's health. Before them, trumpeters blew the popular 'God save the King'.

Through all this throng, an endless stream of carriages moved slowly, taking wellwishers to court. They supplied the richest and most varied sight, for nowhere else can one see more splendid vehicles of the latest designs or more handsome and proud horses. Livery servants walked slowly in step by the carriages and the coachmen, enthroned on their high-fringed boxes, controlled the impatient, snorting horses. Each wore a big round wig which would seem to be the mark of the coachman here, as are moustaches in other countries, and it is a case of the nobler the gentleman, the larger the wig. The grandly dressed personages who sat in the carriages seemed to be a little bored with their slow cavalcade. Looking down on the scene from above, the ladies seem very graceful in their over-elaborate finery and sat there stiffly with an anxious air. They looked rather like the contents of a box from a fashion shop which had been spilled out into a formless mountain of gauze, flowers, feathers and a thousand other pretty things.

The Lord Mayor and the Sheriffs of the City, in the formal black dress of their office, wearing thick gold chains, drove in heavily gilded state coaches, of old-fashioned design, though in fact these were of recent manufacture. To most of the coaches clung the equally gilded servants in their fine livery and large feathered head-dresses. Some rather rusty-looking Court coaches (reminding us of those in which we used to drive to Pillnitz from Dresden) took advantage from time to time to make use of their privilege by leaving the line and passing to the front. The Dukes of York and Gloucester, as well as other members of the Royal Family, sat in glass-coaches so that they could be seen clearly from all sides. Among all this splendour, one noticed quite ordinary hackney carriages, carrying mainly officers and members of the clergy; indeed a wag next to us insisted he recognized three bishops in one of them and so, he commented, they each drove to court for a sixpence. Alongside these conveyances, the bearers of the sedan chairs trotted slowly along. They were brilliantly dressed and the door of each chair was emblazoned with the coronet of an earl or a duke, indicating the high rank of the lady seated within. All were accompanied by liveried servants.

This procession continued uninterrupted from one to six o'clock. The moment they arrived at the Palace, the ladies and gentlemen alighted, dropped a curtsey and a bow to the King and Queen and, perhaps hardly being noticed in the throng, moved on to make way for new arrivals. This was the sum of the pleasure, which it had taken so much in money, time and preparation to attain.

After the official ceremony, the Queen gave a family dinner, the only one in the whole year. This was followed by a concert for which the court poet, known as the Poet Laureate, has to compose a special ode each time. Only a very few of the noblest in the land are chosen to be invited. At one time this concert was followed by a ball which lasted for two hours at the most, and at which the strict rules of rank and etiquette prevailed, but for some years now the other pleasures of the day have had to suffice. In the evening a number of public buildings, the theatres and the houses of shopkeepers and tradesmen who are by royal appointment, were attractively illuminated, bringing the important day to a suitable end.

BOARDING SCHOOL FOR GIRLS

During our little Sunday excursions around London, we would often meet a crocodile of thirty or forty young girls on the footpath by the main road. Dressed in snowy white, with pretty straw hats, they provided a charming sight as they walked piously to church. They walked in pairs, one behind the other, some in the first flush of maidenhood, others still fresh as rosy children. They were accompanied by several mistresses whose duty it was to supervise strictly the propriety of their promenade, carefully watching at every step their expression and any excessive sign of emotion such as a tiny skip for joy or a little cry of delight. Sometimes a similar crocodile of boys approached from the opposite side, making for the same destination, accompanied by their teachers. Each greeted the other in a friendly fashion but the pupils only dared give sidelong glances and carried on walking in obligatory seriousness. They were all pupils of one of the many boarding schools, being shepherded ceremoniously to church twice every Sunday. County towns and villages swarm with these institutions, all of them flourishing, as in England practically nobody has his children educated at home, where they would create too much disorder and unrest. As soon as the boys and girls leave the nursery, they are sent off to boarding school and only return when their education is completed and they are almost grown up.

Girls in these institutions learn a little of everything and nothing very thoroughly. They are taught history and geography yet an Englishwoman hardly ever knows what things are like outside her own country, much less what has happened in times past. They are also given lessons in French and Italian but this is of little use to the foreigner who does not speak English, for he will be hard put to find a lady in society who can converse with him in a foreign language. Music and drawing are treated very superficially and usually forgotten as soon as possible. The girls learn to embroider, make paper flowers, little boxes out of gilt paper and all manner of things from cardboard, not to mention vases from eggshells and a thousand other trifles. However, the knowledge of what is required to run a household is generally a mystery to them. The main purpose of the headmistresses in these establishments is to see that their pupils shine brilliantly once a year when the parents and relations gather at the end-of-term celebrations. Several months before this, all serious teaching stops and everything is concentrated on preparing the children for the important day. They are taught monotonously and mechanically the pieces of music with which they will delight the audience, while drawings are made with the assistance of the teachers. Most important of all is to train them for the ball which will take place in the evening and to this end the dancing-master hardly ever leaves the place for weeks on end.

A lady of our acquaintance whose daughters were at a

boarding school in the little town of Southwark, near London, took us to such an event. The headmistress of this very large school received us with great courtesy and took us into a hall, at one end of which sat the highly delighted mothers and other relations. The pupils themselves were on display at the other end of the room, seated on several rows of benches, one above the other, arranged like an amphitheatre. It really was a charming sight. Imagine fifty young girls from eight to sixteen years old, in perfect health, simply but well dressed in their school uniform of snow-white short dresses and blue shoes, their only adornment a silver net over their hair and a silver sash. There they sat, glowing with youthful expectation and happiness.

Under the guidance of the dancing-master, the ball at long last began. The girls had to dance with each other, all quite modest dances, no waltz, no shawl-dance, no extravagant movements, rather a kind of minuet for six or eight couples which the master had composed specially for them, and which is possibly danced nowhere in the world but in establishments such as this one. The more skilful dancers each had a little solo to show off how well she could perform and at the end she was praised and embraced by her loving family. Only two poor little Dutch girls stood sadly and alone in a corner. Nobody seemed to bother about these young foreigners who had been sent over from their own country to be educated here. As fellow strangers we felt sorry for them and called them over, telling them that not long ago we had arrived from their country. We soon had the pleasure of seeing their eyes light up with joy too. After the display dances, which proved a little long and boring, a few English and Scottish country dances followed. Now happily free from constraint, the children jumped around in a lively fashion and a few young cousins and brothers were even allowed a turn on the floor with them.

With silent emotion we watched their carefree joy. These lovely, dancing creatures were preparing for life, which at this moment when we are writing, has long since embraced them with all its many consequences. Their bright eyes were full of expectation for the future, confident that it, too, was to be a dance of joy. It may well be that now those same eyes are filled with tears of longing as they remember the carefree days, irretrievably lost. We thought of their future with foreboding and took our leave of them in the midst of their happiness, with silent prayers for their well-being.

BOARDING SCHOOL FOR BOYS

Boarding schools for boys are generally run by members of the country clergy, who take a lease of or buy some large, fine building, not far from the church where they preach, and combining the business of education with their actual profession, these reverend gentlemen are able to enjoy a life of relative ease. We had the opportunity of getting to know well the establishment of Mr Lancaster in Wimbledon, 8 miles from London. It is considered to be among the best, and Lord Nelson had two of his nephews educated there. Essentially, they are all very much alike and differ only in the number of pupils and the grander or more limited scope of their arrangements.

The very reverend gentleman in Wimbledon did not concern himself at all with the teaching. He remained invisible to his pupils, spending the whole day in his study where he taught English to a number of youths from abroad who lived in his house as boarders. Only when school was finished at midday, did he appear at his high desk in the schoolroom to receive the teachers' reports. Four teachers lived in the house. The teaching all took place in the same room, with each master having a small high desk and the pupils, in platoons, changing from one to another on a different schedule each week. This continued without interruption for four hours, from eight to twelve. The day opened and closed with a prayer, according to the service of the Church of England, when, in a Christian manner, the boys remembered the King, the Royal Family, pregnant and nursing mothers, and so on. They were taught the Classical languages, geography, history, writing, arithmetic and French. Those who wished to learn fencing, music, dancing and drawing had to pay extra and, for these subjects, teachers came down several times a week from London. Other subjects worth knowing, such as we teach our children in Germany, were completely ignored.

The pupils ate together, pretty poorly, under the supervision of the teacher on duty that week. At certain times he drove them to the village common where they played under his guidance, at other times they played in a large courtyard. Every day they bathed in a large outdoor bath, even in winter when the ice had first to be broken. The whole routine, the teaching, the punishments, the way the children were treated, was carried out according to laid-down rules, without any regard to age, character or ability. It would have been difficult for it to be otherwise, with sixty of them between the ages of six and sixteen. The supervising teacher changed every week and no doubt then thanked God to be rid of the burden, and able to relax a little at the well-provided table of the reverend gentleman, and recover from his exertions, with the boarders and the rest of the household. No teacher got to know his pupils very closely as the children were only under his care for about twelve weeks in the year and that at different intervals.

The special boarders had a wonderful life, however, for they provided Mr Lancaster with three times as many guineas as the other pupils. Of course they took part in the lessons but they ate well at his excellent table and took their recreation in the pleasure garden and the orchard as they pleased, while the others had to stay in the dreary courtyard and were beaten pitilessly should they ever sneak into those forbidden regions. They were in fact the children of the rich, and thus at an early age it was impressed on the pupils that much was conceded to the rich and money should be the goal towards which to strive.

If a boy committed a misdemeanour, failed to learn his lesson or caused a disorder at play, the teacher would, as a punishment, make him learn by heart a page of Latin or Greek. Should he not, within a certain time, have achieved this, his name was written on a piece of paper which was laid on Mr Lancaster's desk. In the evening Mr Lancaster called all the offenders to his study, however many there were, all together, and calling them 'Sir' or 'Gentleman' asked, without any further investigation of their crime, whether they could perform the task set for them. Of course, they answered 'No', and without further ado were asked what they deserved. The reply was 'to be beaten', whereupon the reverend gentleman promptly carried out the sentence with his own hand, often to seven or eight, one after another, with no regard as to whether the boy was six or sixteen, and in a most disgraceful manner.

If two boys had had a quarrel or fought each other, and one accused the other, even were his complaint clearly justifiable, his claim was not acknowledged as long as the accused denied the deed. The plaintiff had to call witnesses and even if he and they were obviously lying, the accused would be punished unless he in turn could call other witnesses to prove his innocence. It was all coldly formal, as in the English court. No thought was given to getting to know the character of the child, his sense of appreciation of right and wrong, or to encouraging a love of true justice.

We refrain from making any comments on such a system of education. Everyone may draw his own conclusions as to what can be expected to be the eventual outcome of such treatment at an early age, and reflect on the advantages we have over these proud islanders.

Every Sunday morning the pupils gathered in the schoolroom. Mr Lancaster was not the parson in Wimbledon but in Merton, a village half-an-hour away. He was in the habit of trying out his Sunday sermon on the boys, early in the morning, before preaching it at midday in his parish church. He combined it with the Church of England service with the result that the whole took a full hour. At eleven o'clock, dressed in their Sunday best, the boys were then arranged in pairs in the yard, and, in the company of four teachers, marched to the church in Wimbledon where with a sermon, hymns and the litany, they had to remain a further two hours. In the afternoon they were herded to church again in the same manner and at eight o'clock at night there was another long service in the schoolroom where, yet again, the King and the Royal Family were remembered. Between all these services of worship they had to read the Bible and were permitted to take a little walk in the company of one of the teachers. All games or amusing diversions were frowned upon and sternly punished.

THE BRITISH MUSEUM

This rich collection, housed in a fine building, is worthy of the great nation whose name it bears. The untiring collector, Sir Hans Sloane, laid its foundation in the middle of the last century by handing over his own very remarkable museum. Later, several other large collections came together in a similar fashion, the whole combining to produce the present degree of perfection.

Perhaps its greatest glory is Sir William Hamilton's vases. We lingered some time to admire the beautiful shapes which have been so skilfully conceived by the English manufacturers and which have been instrumental, throughout Europe, in banishing those ugly, misshapen forms, so fashionable for so long. Our domestic utensils have in this way gradually attained the agreeable shapes they now have.

We found together here the things which reminded us of the golden age of the Romans and the Greeks – jewellery, signet rings, lamps, masses of small articles from the tombs of Pompeii and Herculaneum, the Penates of the Ancients, brought to light once more. It all conjured up a vivid picture of how civilized their everyday life was and in those rooms we felt we lived with them.

We passed quickly through the halls containing the National History collections, stuffed animals, minerals and a considerable collection of coins. When one has limited time, as we had, one has to be selective and this may mean sacrificing much that is interesting. It is, however, better to look at a few things leisurely and well and to take away with one a clear and deep impression, than to spend just a few moments taking in everything, which anyway is tiring and confusing and of very little lasting benefit. Thus we only glanced in passing at the curios brought back by Captain Cook from the fifth continent, which fill an entire room.

Several rooms contain bookcases, housing the well-stocked library behind metal grilles. Apart from a great number of old books, many very rare, this library contains nearly everything published in England up to the present, for a copy of all books,

[201]

printed under licence, must be submitted here. In the room where the manuscripts are kept, we spent only a short time. It contains writings in all forms: on palm leaves, hieroglyphs of the Egyptians, and convoluted illuminated texts of the mediaeval monks, alongside letters and manuscripts of famous people of latter days. It is in fact a paradise for the discerning historian who has the time to browse, and what interesting information is to be found by the lover of anecdotes and scraps of news about the illustrious! A rummage through a desk or a portfolio would result in many volumes of letters which might be of interest and indeed benefit to our age. Also stored away here, in many large cupboards, are the letters of English kings and queens, and many men who influenced their times.

The curators were very kind and helpful in showing items of special interest, such as a whole volume of letters from Queen Elizabeth to her favourite, the Earl of Essex, somewhat ambiguous in their sentiments. Her handwriting is strange. It is obvious that the very large lettering, not beautiful but full of flourishes, was formed slowly and carefully, but in spite of the very flattering words she wrote so precisely to her lover, one might quote, in a slightly different sense, the words Schiller put into Mary Stuart's mouth: 'No heart speaks from these strokes.' There are letters, too, mainly in French, from this unfortunate rival of Elizabeth. We were particularly moved by one, loving and trusting in tone, which she wrote as she reached the English border, showing no forboding of the sad fate which lay ahead of her as she stepped into that foreign land.

A long letter from Cromwell to his dear wife in Edinburgh was full of pious sentiments and counsel to maintain her Christian humility. It was written during the legal struggles against the ill-fated king and we found it most edifying. We were also shown a rough draft of a long speech which, it appears, William the Conqueror intended to make to the English people on his arrival from France. Written in his own hand, it is badly spelt and full of corrections and deletions, and states that he had only crossed from France, due to his love for the English and his desire to make them happy.

Among the more recent manuscripts, we noticed Pope's

original draft of the *Essay on Man*, again full of corrections and alterations. Not without reason does one of his contemporaries refer to him as 'paper-sparing Pope'. The entire poem is written very badly and is practically unreadable, on various scraps of paper, envelopes, visiting cards, invitations, even in the margins of old newspapers. The whole has been cobbled together, as well as was possible, with pins and silk threads. There is also a short manuscript in Rousseau's own hand, which we would have loved to read, but although we were told that it had been published, we were never able to find a copy.

In the centre of this room, framed under glass on a desk, lies enthroned the most sacred document of the English, the Magna Charta. For a long time it was lost and the rumour is that it was discovered only in the nick of time. It had fallen into the hands of a tailor who was about to take his scissors and cut it into little strips of paper for making measurements. Even though now a little faded and ravaged by time, it is kept safely here for posterity and looked at reverently by every true Briton.

We should have liked to return to the museum another day but the rules made this difficult. As so many strangers wish to visit it, one is allowed to go there only once. Just a few people are admitted at the same time, and permission has to be obtained a long time in advance. The general public is allowed in on a Thursday morning, but there is neither pleasure nor profit in being herded through the rooms by poorly-informed attendants in the company of a lot of other people. Anyone wishing to use the museum for the purpose of research, however, can under certain conditions obtain a permit from the authorities. A quiet room, well supplied with all that is necessary in the way of writing materials, is set aside every day for this purpose.

OTHER LONDON MUSEUMS

London offers a great variety of interesting exhibitions and museums, such as Somerset House which, with its magnificent staircase, is in itself one of the finest buildings in the city. Part of it houses the Royal Academy of Painting. Then there is Merlin's Museum, mainly devoted to mechanical exhibits, and Week's, also with mechanical inventions, but here concentrating on things of more interest to the world of elegance, automata of great ingenuity: a silver swan, a black spider, little goldfish playing in a bowl, so many mechanical playthings, not to mention flowers made of jewels and bunches of grapes of rubies – in fact a veritable fairyland from the thousand and one nights.

Sir Ashton Levers, on the other hand, who spent his lifetime making his collection, shows the mineral products of Mother Earth, shells from the depths of the oceans, beetles, butterflies, worms and a marvellous variety of stuffed animals. One can also see the collection of things which Captain Cook brought back from his travels, something we knew about from books and engravings, and a wonderful display of artefacts made by savages. Here one could spend a year and still not have seen everything.

MR WHITBREAD'S BREWERY

What preparations to make a jar of porter! What commotion, what cranking and rattling of machinery! Beer barrels larger than a house in the Highlands! Cooling vats as wide as an ocean! Mr Whitbread's brewery would seem worthy to brew the invigorating infusion for Odin's heroes in Valhalla.

But to be serious, this brewery really is one of London's most important sights. The old King once visited it and took breakfast in the brew-house, an occasion which cost the owner some fifteen hundred pounds. The English satirist, Peter Pindar, endeavoured, in his 'Instructions to a Celebrated Laureate', to persuade the official poet to record this famous event in verse. Among other things the King asked Mr Whitbread how many barrels he owned, to which that gentleman replied: 'Laid closely together lengthwise, they might well stretch from London to Windsor.' Windsor lies 22 miles from London but, in view of the size of this huge establishment, Mr Whitbread's assertion does not seem all that impossible.

A steam-engine, situated in the basement, is the mainspring of this whole immense enterprise, and is the cleanest, simplest and least noisy we have ever seen. It has been calculated that it does the work of seventy horses, working day and night. Initially it supplies the necessary water, and carries the ready beer through subterranean channels across the road, into another building, where it is put into barrels. It brings these barrels, ready for loading, from the cellar. It grinds the malt, stirs it in the 20-feet deep vats and then transports it, with the help of a screw-like contrivance, up to the very top of the building. There, are found the very large but shallow tanks, only a few inches deep, which are used for cooling the beer. We were assured they would cover five English acres. The porter only needs to stand in them for six hours to be completely cold.

While everything in this vast establishment gives the impression of extreme cleanliness and order, working with apparent ease, every day something new has to be invented to improve what already seems to be perfect. Great stress is placed on the saving of fuel required by the three large vats, each containing five hundred barrels. The brewery employs two hundred workmen and eighty extraordinarily large horses. These are perhaps the biggest animals of their kind in existence and the shoes of one, which had to be put down because of illness, weighed 24 pounds. They are surely the giants of their breed.

In a building, higher and bigger than a church, stand forty-nine large barrels in which the beer is stored until it is decanted into smaller ones for distribution. Through remaining in the larger containers for a while, the quality is said to improve greatly. If Diogenes had had the good fortune to live in a barrel of such size, the philosopher could easily have entertained twelve people at a round table and still had room for a pretty little boudoir for himself. The largest of these barrels has a kind of gallery at the top with a stair leading up to it. It is 27 feet high and has a diameter of 22 feet. It is hooped from top to bottom with iron bands at intervals of 6 inches. Towards the bottom the bands are very close to one another. All the barrels are made of strong oak and several contain 3,500 ordinary barrels. The famous barrel at Heidelberg would lose its place of honour in this company.

When we finally left the brewery, we felt somewhat intoxicated from the smell of the beer, in fact the atmosphere made one feel that one might be able to live on air. The men employed there, however, did not look at all as if they were willing to experiment in that way.

GREENWICH

At London Bridge, in the midst of the noise of the ever-busy City, we took one of the boats that play on the Thames for the public's convenience, exactly like hackney cabs. Like them, they are numbered and under police supervision. This bridge, the oldest of the three which span the river in London, had for some time been marked for demolition, to make way for an iron one, resting on a single arch. In its present form, the arches were far too narrow for the mighty river it spans. The wild and turbulent Thames rushes beneath it and every year takes its toll of those foolhardy enough to try to navigate here in spite of the obvious dangers.

As far as the eye could see, a forest of masts stretched away from us as we passed downstream. The river is as busy as a well-frequented main road, with launches and small vessels of all kinds constantly passing to and fro, while large ships, arriving at or leaving the port, sail majestically among them. From all sides one hears the merry cries of the crews; the shouts of welcome and farewell resound in the air. The large number of workmen, busily unloading and loading the boats, the wharfs along the shore, all this demonstrates that London is one of the great trading centres of the world.

From the moment we left London, the banks of the river offered us varied and charming views. At last, 5 miles down river from the City, the Greenwich Royal Naval Hospital came in sight, standing large and splendid in its pretty surroundings, with a fine terrace onto the river. This Hospice, which the nation maintains for those of its heroes who are weary from fighting the wild elements, is something it is justifiably proud of, for the world offers little to compare with

27 *View of Greenwich*

it. It consists of four separate buildings, which, seen from the water however, give the impression of one single palace, embellished with columns, balustrades and all the splendour of recent architecture. A large terrace, with a delightful view towards London, runs right along the front to the river to which one can descend on broad stone steps. It was here that George I set foot in the country he was to rule, and the beauty of Greenwich must have filled him with high expectations for the future, as he drove towards St James's.

The buildings are constructed in fine stone and one has specially to admire the chapel, decorated with extravagant splendour, where marble columns support a finely painted ceiling. There are halls where the veterans can stroll in inclement weather, the largest being all of 106 feet long, with a cupola and another fine ceiling. On a hill, at the other side of an agreeable park, is an observatory.

It was a commendable and humane idea to build this refuge on the banks of the Thames, with its view of the ships coming and going. The veteran heroes from the sea still have this recollection of their world in front of them, while the young sailors setting off into the unknown can draw comfort and courage from the sight of this eventual haven. There are close to three thousand men here, housed in princely fashion, well fed and looked after. Every two years they get new, decent and comfortable clothing, while every week they receive a not insignificant sum in pocket money for their small needs and pleasures. In the case of illness, they are carefully nursed, and here, unlike the practice followed in so many other institutions, they are not separated from those things that have been important in their lives. They can constantly relive events of the past with their old comrades and cheerfully fight again all the battles won, before the paintings on the walls of their dining- and living-quarters depicting these very scenes.

We found the dormitories particularly well furnished. In long airy halls, which in winter are heated from several large fireplaces, a row of cubicles, similar to the berths of ships, is installed on the side facing the windows. Each has a small window on either side of the door opening onto the hall and is large enough to take an English-size wide bed, a table, a chair and a chest. Everything in these rooms is neat and tidy. There is a carpet, clean curtains on the windows and bed, the walls are decorated with engravings and on shelves are arranged their pretty tobacco boxes, tea caddies, glasses and cups. Each man is free to hang what he wishes on the wall, be it a picture of the King or the Queen, a famous hero of the sea, a battle, a view of a port or even an amusing caricature.

One-hundred-and-forty widows of courageous seamen also live in the place, where they carry out all the work usually performed by women, including the nursing of the sick. In all ways they are as well cared for as the men. The orphans of seamen are also looked after, and several hundred boys are trained in a separate part of the building to follow in their fathers' footsteps. Another three thousand veterans, for whom there is no room in the Hospice, are accommodated in boarding-houses.

ST PAUL'S CATHEDRAL

The external appearance of St Paul's Cathedral is well known from engravings and, sadly, one can gain a better impression of the building as a whole from these than one can in reality. In the vicinity there is no point from which one can view it advantageously for, although after St Peter's in Rome it is the largest church in Europe, it stands too closely surrounded by a graveyard, houses and many narrow streets. In the interior also, there is no spot from which to see the whole, for here the architecture seems to get in the way, making a clear view impossible.

Despite all these faults, this magnificent building still makes a profound impression. Apart from the area in the transept of the cruciform church, furnished for services, and the occasional statue, the building seems quite empty. An awe-inspiring silence and feeling of loneliness seems to hang over everything and there is nothing of the clutter of paltry furnishings that men seem to need to help them make their approach to God. It is a temple in the finest sense of that word. As we stood in the centre of the church, looking up where the dome extends well nigh into eternity, 'a second heaven into heaven', a solemn

28 Interior of St Paul's Cathedral

shiver overcame us: it was not a sensation of uplift but rather one of fear. The few people around us seemed to disappear from view and their very insignificance emphasized the overwhelming proportions of this mass of stone.

It became difficult to alter that first impression until we remembered that it was these puny men who, by their concerted efforts, had built this astonishing edifice and that one single man from among them had conceived the design in his mind long before it reached up towards the sky. He had, in fact, even thought of it originally in much grander form than it stands today, and he alone directed the strength of the hundreds who had worked there and were unable to understand clearly what they were achieving. Now the master and his labourers are at rest but what they accomplished will stand, defying the march of time, even as the glorious ruins of Palmyra and Persepolis, when the populous city has long since become a desert.

Having regained our self-confidence, we now walked around, our every step resounding in this vast cavern, and when someone shut a door at the foot of the steps to the gallery of the dome, it seemed to us like a clap of thunder. We climbed up to this gallery from where we had a wonderful view aloft and below. Above, one has the impression of a second church rising, as the vault of the dome is so immensely high, even from here. Below, the floor is made up of large black and white marble squares, looking like a fine mosaic from this great height. This is known as the Whispering Gallery because, if one puts one's ear to a certain part of the wall, one can hear quite clearly someone whispering at the other side.

Climbing on a little further, we emerged into the open air, onto a little gallery round the lantern of the dome. We had hoped from this highest point to have a fine view of the city and its surroundings. It was a clear day but unfortunately the coal smoke from the many chimneys hid the view below us while that slight haze, peculiar to the English sky, obscured the distance. The boisterous noise of a group of sailors, whom we heard ascending, made us hurry to descend.

As we wended our way home down Ludgate Hill, a very crowded street next to the cemetery, we noticed all the pedestrians standing still, gazing anxiously at the cross on the top of St Paul's. This is fastened above the globe of the dome's lantern and from below looks very small. With the help of binoculars, we were able to discern one of the sailors whom we had encountered in the church. He had contrived to get himself onto the cross and at that horrible height was delighting in taking up breath-taking positions, waving his cap, standing on one leg, driving the spectators into a state of terrified admiration. Of course a man like him, accustomed to standing high on the rocking mast of his ship, in the midst of the wild ocean, had long since lost any feeling of dizziness and probably found this firm, motionless spot quite safe in spite of the great height, whereas all of us below remained frozen with terror at the mere sight.

THE TOWER

'We are going to see the lions.' So say the families of the gentry and the yeoman farmers when they are about to make the pilgrimage to London to see the capital's sights. These lions, part of the Royal menagerie kept at the Tower, serve collectively to describe the things to be seen in the city. Alas, these noble animals and their residence have, through their popularity, acquired a certain notoriety and a foreigner of good breeding would hardly be expected to visit the Tower at all. Nevertheless we decided to go there, fully aware of the dangers involved in doing something so unfashionable and out of keeping with the precepts of good society.

We found the Tower and its lions at the farthest end of the City, close to the banks of the Thames. This old fortress, with its watergate to the river, lies gloomy and sullen, the scene of countless horrors, its grey towers looming over the surrounding moat. Here is the Traitor's Gate, through which many unhappy creatures were brought by barge down the Thames and the doors of which often closed behind them for ever. As we entered through the main gate, which has just room enough for a carriage to pass, our attention was drawn to the small barred windows above it. They are those of the room in which the terrible Richard III had his brother's two young sons suffocated as they slept, innocently unaware of the fate in store for them. We felt no desire to enter this murder chamber.

An old legend says that Julius Caesar was the founder of this fortress. History, however, tells us that it was William the Conqueror who laid the foundations in the middle of the eleventh century, as part of his plan to hold his much-loved Londoners in awe. It is evident from the haphazard character of

29   The Bloody Tower, the Tower of London

the whole that there had been no definite plan at its inception
and that the building had been continued in a similar manner
during the reigns of successive kings. The Tower is, in fact,
almost like a small town, containing as it does within its
precincts, several streets, a church, stores, barracks for the
garrison, houses for the officers, the arsenal, the mint, quarters

for the officiating priest and other diverse buildings. It is surrounded by a broad moat and between it and the Thames there is a terrace on which are mounted sixty cannons, fired on ceremonial occasions. As is usual with fortresses, it is closed at sunset. The Yeomen or Beefeaters who happen to be on duty act as guides to visitors. Here they are obviously in their right setting, as their dress and appearance help to transport us back to earlier dark centuries. The Mint and the buildings connected with it occupy about a third of the Tower site and are not shown to visitors. We were therefore left with the White Tower, the Crown Jewels and the lions. We began with a visit to the last.

The lions are housed here in especially strong cages, along with panthers, leopards, tigers and other inhabitants of the wilds. They are fierce, stately beasts and it is clear that they are well looked after. According to the English custom, each has, apart from its sleeping-quarters, a 'living-room' in the cage where visitors are received. All boast Christian names, those of the lionesses being particularly grand. Here one finds Miss Howe, Miss Jenny, Miss Charlotte and Miss Nanny, rather as if one was at an English assembly. Many of these animals were born and bred in the Tower and it is strange that these very ones are the wildest and most intractable.

The Crown Jewels are shown in a peculiar and somewhat apprehensive way, quite different from the liberal manner of the Green Vault in Dresden. The Beefeater who was our guide opened a small door through which we entered and, as instructed, sat in a row on a bench. The door was then locked behind us and we were blinded by the unexpected darkness. As our eyes grew accustomed to it, we found ourselves in a small, dark, stone vault, just like a prison and gradually perceived before us a strong iron grille behind which sat an old woman between two lights. This dragon-like guardian of subterranean treasures then proceeded to show us a great number of precious objects, many of them quite unique and of ancient workmanship. There were, for example, a golden eagle whose neck contained the oil for the anointing of kings and a golden spoon into which the bishop pours the oil at the coronation and many old table requisites of gold and silver. We were shown the sceptre, decorated with the fleur-de-lis, the imperial orb, many crowns and other such things, some of them still being used at coronations and on other ceremonial occasions. A pearl of inestimable value, an emerald of truly enormous size, and a very beautiful ruby decorate the crown which the King wears in Parliament. In the case of the Prince of Wales, his crown is placed in front of him in parliament as a sign that he is not yet entitled to wear it. All this splendour glitters with precious stones and, in that gloomy cell, it seemed to be a fairy treasure guarded by an evil spirit. Its value is said to be more than two million pounds sterling, and that does not include the precious stones whose value cannot be estimated.

From here we went on to the White Tower, which is neither a tower nor white, but a large square building in the centre of the fortress, old, grey and timeworn to look at. Its battlements are crowned by four lookout turrets, one of which had been made into an observatory. On the first floor we saw the trophies taken from the Spanish Armada, very old and many of them ingeniously devised instruments of death. Among them was a great number of thumbscrews which the Spaniards carried with them, so that on landing they might use them to extort information from the defeated English, possibly about hidden treasure.

In the hall there is a life-size figure of Queen Elizabeth about to mount a white palfrey. The figure wears the clothes that Her Majesty did when she addressed her people after the remarkable victory over Spain. We should, however, not advise any actress dressing to take the part of Elizabeth, to take this as a model. The good lady looks quite terrible, especially the hair, crimped into the shape of a high, broad tower and no longer looking like real hair. The dress also has an incredibly tapering waist, forced into a corset. Here, we also saw the axe which severed the head of beautiful Anne Boleyn, and many other of the sad mementoes with which the Tower teems.

Old armoury is displayed in another large hall. We would never have believed it possible for these murderous weapons to provide such a pleasing sight. Here they had been elegantly arranged in a spirit of invention and taste. The walls shine with bayonets, pistols, daggers and swords. They have been

[215]

arranged in a series of designs, forming a church window, an organ, coats of arms, stars and even snakes. The ceiling rests on pillars of muskets, festooned with pistols.

In yet another large hall, all the kings of England stand in a long stately row, mounted on horseback and in full armour, from William the Conqueror to George II. The armour, much of it very splendid, is that which the owners actually wore in their lifetime. That of George II was particularly grand, all over gilt, but our Beefeater guide assured us, rather naïvely, that he had never worn it. Old John of Gaunt, son of Edward III, must have been a man of exceptional height, for his armour is 7 feet high and his lance and sword in proportion. Henry VIII, too, must have been an imposing gentleman for the suit made for him in his eighteenth year is only slightly smaller than that of John of Gaunt.

THE PALACE OF WESTMINSTER

In these remains of an ancient palace, built by Edward the Confessor, now resides the goddess Themis. Like the kings of England themselves, she is ill-housed and both inside and outside her residence shows signs of decay. As we were curious to see the place where so many remarkable decisions had been made, that arena of the most famous orators in the world, we decided to go there one morning.

We began at Westminster Hall, lofty and vaulted, some 275 feet long by 74 feet wide. The English maintain it is the biggest of its kind in Europe, the ceiling of which is not supported by columns, a claim we would not contest, though, despite its size, we did not find it very grand. The walls are without decoration and, viewed from below, the artistically carved oak of the ceiling is not very imposing, if only because of its brown colour. It is said, however, that when examined closely this ornamentation in the Gothic taste is not without a certain merit.

In olden times, this hall was used for great feasts and for the carousing of kings. Richard II is said to have once entertained many thousands of people in it at the same time. Parliament often sat here and it was the High Court at which the king himself presided. It was here that the unfortunate Charles I was tried and convicted and, even today, it is the scene of rare legal cases involving a Peer of the Realm or someone of consequence. Generally, however, it is now used by advocates and their clients, waiting for their turn to be called to the courts. We saw many of the advocates walking up and down in their black gowns and large, powdered wigs. It was all very informal, no guards, no ushers to keep order, with everyone walking where he pleased. We, too, moved around unhindered and, stepping behind a curtain at the side of the hall, to our astonishment suddenly found ourselves in a dark, not very impressive room which reminded us of a small village church. Here, in an elevated place, sat a black-gowned gentleman with an enormous stately wig. He was speaking in a very precise and emphatic manner but because of the many people passing in and out, making as much noise as they might at home, we were unable to understand a word he was saying. True, from time to time someone cried 'Silence', but nobody seemed to take much notice and the noise continued unabated. Around a table sat thirty to forty other gentlemen on benches, also in black gowns, wearing white, somewhat smaller, wigs. They all seemed to be listening attentively to the speaker, as well as was possible under the circumstances. To our amazement, we learnt that this was the High Court of Chancery and that the gentleman on the dais was the Lord Chancellor, Lord Elton. Those surrounding him were the judges, gathered in this noisy place, to take decisions in important lawsuits. However, it is possible, it appears, to appeal against their decision to the Upper House.

Full of wonderment at the informal manner in which business of the greatest importance was dealt with here, we wandered around the old palace for a while, up and down stairs, along ancient, vaulted corridors, and found ourselves finally in the court of the King's Bench. Things here did not seem any better than in the High Court, with the same noise and disorder prevailing. On a dais presided two gentlemen in wigs, one of whom was the Chief Justice, Lord Ellenborough. Before them, behind barriers, stood a couple of poor devils, with woeful countenance, whose fate was apparently being decided. This court deals with criminal cases and some excellent jurists, such as the famous Mr Erskine, often appear for the defence or the prosecution. It is to be hoped that these eminent gentlemen are granted more attention than seems usual here. Nowhere did we ever see, what is undoubtedly the most serious business in the world, namely the decision between right and wrong, guilt and innocence, reward and punishment, life and death, dealt with in such a casual way. There was no trace to be seen of that essential seriousness which should mark the conduct of every court. It is impossible to comprehend how the judges and advocates can tolerate all this noise without losing the purport of their cases. We left hurriedly and decided not to visit two other courts, also in the Palace of Westminster, where undoubtedly things happen in the same way.

Parliament was unfortunately not sitting, but we wanted at least to see where the Upper House meets. It is a medium-sized hall whose walls are covered by faded tapestries depicting the victory over the Armada. These are said to have artistic value, but the ravages of time, duly assisted by dust and dirt, reveal little of their erstwhile glory. At the far end of the hall stands the Royal throne which, with its canopy, looks for all the world like an old-fashioned red damask four-poster, picked up in some junk shop. Next to it on the right-hand side, is an equally insignificant old armchair for the Prince of Wales, while on the left there are six chairs for the other princes. In the centre of the hall are four large square woolsacks, covered in red material, on which sit those lords who at the same time are Judges. The remaining lords take their places on a few rows of seats along both sides of the hall. The picture is completed by a large fire-place, with a wrought-iron screen in front of it – presumably to ensure that in the heat of the debate, nobody falls in. Such is the appearance of the hall where often the fate of millions is decided, in which meet the most powerful members of a nation which would dearly love to be the law-maker for the whole globe, a nation that has never adopted the laws of another country. It may be that this very unpretentiousness is the telling proof of that pride which, based on supreme self-confidence, disdains ostentation.

In the Lower House, apart from the throne and the

woolsacks not being there, the furnishings are much the same and do not seem any brighter. The walls, however, are panelled in wood and on one side there is a gallery for those who wish to attend the sittings as spectators. Women are not admitted at such times. Few of them would, we are sure, endure arriving at nine or ten o'clock in the morning and remaining there until midnight. It must be said, however, that care is taken that one should not starve for a caterer always has refreshments ready for members of the Lower House, in a coffee-room under the same roof. Strangers also are permitted to partake of refreshments from his table, but must beware, for it is customary to find, on returning to the gallery, that one's place has been taken.

The hall of the Lower House was originally a chapel, dedicated by King Stephen to his patron saint. The ambitious Edward III restored it in the first half of the fourteenth century and later Henry VI put it to its present use by dividing it and making extra corridors and rooms at the side. Unfortunately this work almost destroyed one of the finest examples of Gothic art. When, several years ago, part of the panelling was removed in order to enlarge the hall, to everyone's surprise behind it were revealed the remains of the rich decoration of the original wall, giving an idea of the splendour that had once been there. Priceless remains of the art of the period came to light, including carvings, paintings and gilding, fresh as though made only yesterday, together with distinct traces of the old high altar. The walls at the side and the ceiling were covered with fine carvings, and there were armorial paintings, life-size figures, and a superb depiction of the Adoration of the Shepherds. All these things, of priceless value to students of the history of art, had been desecrated in a barbaric manner to produce this sad, unimpressive hall, as if, in the whole of London, no other room could be found for the gentlemen of the Lower House to meet. Of all this splendour only one fine Gothic window remains intact through which the sun now shines dimly, as though he missed the former glory.

From the outside the whole building looked sad and dilapidated, as did the fine church opposite, famous Westminster Abbey. Little trouble and money are spent on the preservation of these ancient monuments, with the result that they seem to be slowly sinking into decay.

WESTMINSTER ABBEY

This resting place of the illustrious dead stands sad and dreary, itself somewhat resembling a graveyard of centuries past. It is only possible, from the outside, to guess at the old splendour of this Gothic church, built in the straightforward cruciform style, for here, as with St Paul's, there is no spot from where one can properly survey it as a whole. Two fine square towers crown the high basilica, each of them, in the Gothic style, surmounted by several smaller ones, rising gracefully into the air. A magnificent porch leads into the sanctum.

From the entrance on the west side, one can immediately realize the plan of the whole. The abbey stands before one, in lofty splendour, like a petrified forest. The high vault of the roof, seemingly created and placed there by some supernatural power, rests on slim but strong pillars, arch upon arch rising lightly and airily into the distance. Each pillar is in reality a group of five slender ones. The veiled sunlight, filtering through the high stained-glass windows, casts an awesome twilight over the ornamentation embellishing this great church. Everything that is old here, is impressive and elevates the spirit: everything new, contrasts disagreeably. Most strange is the modern altar, made of white marble in the so-called Greek manner, standing as it does in the beautiful old choir where the kings of England used to be crowned.

The many monuments, which overload the church, destroy the unity of the building. There is little sense of order for they stand about as though they had somehow been rescued from some disaster and put down anywhere as a temporary measure. Apart from that, few of them really seem to deserve a place as works of art. In these imposing surroundings many look insignificant and walls and brackets have had to be made to support them. While it is a worthy intention of the nation to honour its great men in this great Abbey next to the tombs of kings, one cannot help but wish it had been done in a more harmonious fashion. The high purpose has been obscured, as everything is arranged in a topsy-turvy way and one has to penetrate dust and cobwebs in order to look at this or that monument tucked away in a far corner, so much that is important and beautiful being hidden by the clutter of the mediocre.

There is one corner dedicated to people of literary talent. It is called, very unimaginatively, Poets' Corner, and while we found there Goldsmith, Händel, Shakespeare, Garrick, Chaucer, Butler, Thomson, Gay, Johnson, Milton, Dryden and many others, we looked in vain for Swift, Sterne and Pope. The aisle is narrow and to be among the great, many a celebrated name must be satisfied with a humble corner due to the lack of space. A medallion of Goldsmith, through talent and fate so closely related to our Hölty, is placed over the door. Händel sits writing, as if listening to the music of the spheres and ready to transcribe it all on paper. Garrick, royally attired, steps from behind a curtain, looking surprised and delighted by his new surroundings. Shakespeare leans thoughtfully against a pedestal, pointing towards a parchment with this inscription from *The Tempest*:

> The cloud-capp'd towers, the gorgeous palaces,
> The solemn temples, the great globe itself,
> Yea, all which it inherit, shall dissolve
> And, like this insubstantial pageant faded,
> Leave not a rack behind. We are such stuff
> As dreams are made on, and our little life
> Is rounded with a sleep.

Among the other monuments which are scattered around the rest of the church, that dedicated to Lord Mansfield is held in special esteem by the English. It was made by the younger Flaxman and both it and that of Lord Chatham, father of the famous William Pitt, cost six thousand pounds each. Lord Mansfield is clad in the flowing robes of an English judge, not very suitable to sculpture, and sits in a slightly inelegant position on the judge's seat, one hand resting on his knee and the other holding a rolled document. Next to him, but a little lower, stand Wisdom and Justice, while behind, Death, extinguishing the torch of life, is daringly represented by a beautiful naked female figure.

Lord Chatham stands on a high pedestal, in the stance of an orator; the virtues weep at his feet but it is not clear whether they are touched by his speech or whether he is saying such things as would make virtue cry. There is a strange memorial to the unhappy Major John André, who was hanged by the Colonists as a spy during the American War of Independence and is remembered here.

There are twelve chapels adjoining the church, where the ashes of kings and members of several noble families are interred. Although their ashes are here, no king has had a monument erected to him in the Abbey since Elizabeth's time. We enjoyed looking at these old monuments, nearly all of them large, square sarcophagi, on which the statue of the departed lies in full ceremonial dress, hands folded on breast, quietly at rest, as if sleeping. Here were none of the caricatures such as we found in *Aux petits Augustins* in Paris where, for example, François I, Marie de Medici and Charles IX are portrayed lying on their tombs in the most horrible contortions of dying, hair in wild disarray, and practically naked. We stood, deeply moved at the tomb of Mary Stuart, laid to rest not far from her deadly enemy and murderess. Time had rendered the face of her statue almost unrecognizable.

The oldest of the twelve chapels contains the tomb of Edward the Confessor which is decorated with mosaics of coloured stones, many of which, alas, have been broken or removed. Edward I also rests here and, next to him, Eleanor of Castile, his wife, that model of matrimonial love and fidelity unto death. In 1274, before he was crowned, Edward went on a Crusade to the Holy Land. Disregarding the long and dangerous journey, Eleanor accompanied him, for she preferred to bear these discomforts rather than be parted from her dearly loved husband. Fortified by her closeness and fired by her courage, he was soon victorious, causing great devastation among the Saracens. The infidels, however, took cunning revenge by sending out assassins who managed to wound the king in the arm with a deadly poisoned arrow. The murderers, it is true, perished in their turn by the swords of Edward's faithful men but the King was carried unconscious to his tent. The doctors declared that he had no hope of life unless one of his servants would suck the blood from his wound, thus sacrificing his own life to save that of his sovereign. In silence they stood around his deathbed, they who had often defied death in its most terrible shape, yet none was prepared to make this supreme sacrifice for his future King. Eleanor then threw herself on the arm of the King, none daring to hold her back, and soon, thus saved, he opened his eyes. No words can express the emotion he felt when he realized how he had been brought back to life and beheld Eleanor there, afraid to clasp him to her bosom for fear that she might poison him again. Trembling with joy, she watched him from a distance. Then it was realized that the poison had had no effect on this pure angelic creature. Why, we do not know. It is sufficient to record that Eleanor continued for many years to live at the side of her husband, soon sharing the throne and only coming to her rest some nineteen years later. This is what the legend tells us and it is far too beautiful a story to disbelieve, even though many historians make no mention of the event. On this sarcophagus also are to be seen the figures of those resting below. While, at that time, art was in its infancy, a guardian angel seems to have watched over the work so beautifully wrought by the sculptor's chisel and saved it from the ravages of time. Eleanor's radiant face, her gentleness and warmth of heart seem to have been preserved for eternity.

The tombs of Edward III and Henry III are in the same chapel. That of King Henry is in the antique fashion, decorated with porphyry, mosaic and gilding. His statue, cast in metal, stands on it. Here are also to be found the ancient chairs on which the kings sit at their coronations. Below one of them is the Stone of Destiny on which the Kings of Scotland were crowned and which, as readers will recall from earlier in these memoirs, Edward I brought to Westminster from Scone.

Immediately adjoining this is the chapel of Henry V, which because of its splendour, is one of the most remarkable. Alas, the poor King lies there without his head, and the orb and sceptre seem to have been torn from his hands. As was usual at a time when the taste was for solid grandeur, it had all been made of pure silver and, even in this sanctuary, did not escape the greed of villainous thieves.

There are nine more chapels, consecrated to various saints whose names they bear, containing many objects of great interest to the antiquarian. They provide an excellent history of the artistic taste and way of life in the Middle Ages, as for example, the wooden monument to the Saxon King, Sebert, who was the first to build a church at this place.

We found especially intriguing the tomb of an Earl of Leicester, due to its similarity to that of the famous bed of the Graf von Gleichen. Here the noble earl lies in his robes of chivalry in the centre of a very wide sarcophagus and next to him, on his right-hand side rests his first wife in graceful modesty. The wide space on his left, however, lies empty. His second wife refused, even in death, to take second place to the first and on her deathbed gave orders to prevent this happening. She was buried elsewhere, and all memory of the jealous lady would have disappeared, had her act of foolishness not ensured that she was remembered.

All these chapels are under one roof in Westminster Abbey, with only the last and most beautiful, that of Henry VII, being added later. It seemed to us, however, to be in a quite inexcusable state of neglect. The roof is very badly maintained and it would only need time to continue to take its toll for a little longer, for everything to disintegrate into a beautiful ruin, attractive elsewhere, perhaps, but hardly in a place dedicated to the memory of sacred ancestors. Outside it is decorated in a splendid Gothic manner, and is of good proportions. Its main ornament is a series of fourteen towers of pierced stonework. It is entered from the church through a massive arch of hewn stone, guarded by three gates of gilded wrought-iron. The carved work of the ceiling, the vaulted arches supported by elegant pillars, the magnificent windows, all these are once again evidence of the grandeur of Gothic architecture, which it is impossible to praise too highly. If only the chapel could find a friend and admirer, as did Cologne Cathedral in the Boiserée brothers, who would restore and preserve for time to come its now decaying glory. In the centre of the chapel stands the tomb of Henry VII himself, made of black basalt, decorated with gold bronze and surrounded by railings of the same material. Six bas-reliefs and four statues by the Florentine artist, Pietro Torregiano, embellish the work.

Alongside these remarkable and venerable works of art is to be seen an extraordinary display of wax effigies of the kings and queens in glass cases. These veritable scarecrows should have been destroyed long ago for the only interest is in the clothes they wore in life. If Queen Elizabeth, in particular, knew what a hideous picture she presents here to posterity, that vanity, which was so characteristic of her life, would not let her rest easily in her grave.

6 LONDON'S SURROUNDINGS

WINDSOR

The stately old castle of Windsor stands on a height on the south bank of the Thames, about 20 miles west of London. From there one can enjoy a wide view of the rolling countryside around, making a fine contrast with the Castle's rather stern aspect, with its ancient walls and ivy-clad towers.

It was built by William the Conqueror a short time after he had made himself master of England. Henry I enlarged it and surrounded it with a wall. Later Edward I made the Castle his favourite abode and later still Edward III was born there. The latter's affection for the place of his birth made him rebuild it to a new ambitious plan and it eventually became his summer palace. King Charles II also spent much time on embellishing Windsor and since his time it has remained a favourite residence of English kings, especially in the summertime. During the reign of George III many alterations and improvements were again made. The moat was filled in, a hill which limited the view towards the east was levelled and fortifications pulled down. Despite all this, the castle still retains its venerable and ancient look, even if some of its early imposing character has been lost.

There are two courtyards, the Upper Ward and the Lower Ward, separated by the so-called Round Tower, the home of the Commander of the garrison. On the north side of the Upper Ward are the state apartments and the audience rooms, on the east the apartments of the princes and on the southern, those of the high court officials. The Lower Ward is remarkable for St George's Chapel. The apartments are

30 Windsor Castle looking Eastward

[227]

decorated with wallpapers and paintings of various value and they all show the effect of the ravages of time. The most striking of the rooms is St George's hall, the chapter hall of the Knights of the Garter. It is 108 feet long and at the end of it stands the royal throne with the Cross of St George in a halo above it, surrounded by the garter, borne by putti, inscribed with the well-known motto: *Honi soit qui mal y pense*. The state apartments are hung with many pictures which the visitor, for lack of time, can only glance at in passing. He is told the names of such great masters as Titian, Poussin, van Dyck, Holbein, and many others, but a Holy Family by Raphael and an Adoration by Paul Veronese are pointed out as the highlights of the collection.

The most striking feature of Windsor Castle is the vast terrace, unique of its kind. It stretches along part of the north side and the entire eastern side of the castle, and is 1837 feet long and proportionately wide. With the view of the Thames, winding its way through the rich countryside, between the villages and country dwellings which enliven its banks, and the park-like woods, this is a sight beautiful beyond description.

The family of George III do not live in the Castle itself, but in a modern building which one can see across a stretch of lawn from a corner of the terrace. There is also a second building there which houses the Princesses. Quite near to Windsor, the Queen has another small house, a rather middle-class ordinary place called Frogmore with an unremarkable garden, of which she is very fond. Small picnics on her daughters' birthdays and little family *déjeuners* with a few favourites from her ladies are held there.

To get a true idea of the Royal Family's life at Windsor, one should really have seen it before the tragic illness of George III. Here they were released from the barriers of etiquette and strict seclusion which surrounded them in London, where if one was not actually being presented, it was difficult to catch more than a glimpse of them, for in their rare visits to the theatre or out driving or horse-riding they passed by too quickly for one to gain a real impression. During their stay at Windsor, however, they could be seen every Sunday morning, in their simple morning dress according to the English fashion, congregating to attend the service in St George's Chapel. When the King was well, he never missed, even on weekdays, seven o'clock devotion at the Chapel Royal in the Upper Ward of the castle to which the public was also admitted. Later in the day he could often be encountered, in a simple dark blue coat and a round brown wig, visiting the farm buildings or in the stables, for all the world looking like a prosperous tenant farmer. In his early days, rural economy was his favourite interest and he was not displeased at being known as Farmer George. On a bright summer evening the whole family would take a stroll on the terrace. The scene there was a most interesting sight. On one side was the castle with its ancient walls and battlements and towers, and on the other the view of the rich countryside, the river, field and forest in the glow of the setting sun. Nearby moved the colourful throng, composed of all ranks of society, of all ages and of many nationalities, for no stranger would lightly miss the opportunity of visiting Windsor from London on a Sunday. Among them were those from the surrounding countryside, gentry and farm labourers, mixing with the staid city dwellers, their portly spouses and dainty daughters.

Like all the others, we fled to Windsor of a Sunday and joined the motley crowd on the broad terrace which now seemed almost too narrow. At seven o'clock two military bands appeared on the ramparts, one at each side of the terrace. Both played 'God save the King' in a rousing manner, neither paying much attention to the other, which mattered little as the distance between and the great noise of the crowd meant that they hardly heard each other anyway. They loved this tune and played it, without much change, the whole evening. Soon afterwards the Royal Family appeared, a single constable with his staff walking in front to make way for them. The people crowded around on all sides. First came the King with the Queen at his side. Whenever he recognized someone, he spoke to him or gave him a friendly nod, regardless of rank or standing. Anyone new, who caught his attention, aroused a lively interest and the satirist, Peter Pindar, has recorded his habit of repeating a certain one-syllable word several times. He always addressed a few words to the astronomer, Herschel, whenever he saw him and the Queen, too, was exceedingly friendly towards her countryman. The promenade seemed to give her less pleasure than her husband, on whose arm she walked, due in part to the high-pointed heels she wore. In her grey taffeta dress, which she lifted high, and her old-fashioned little white coat, this very small lady did not look at all regal. The King was inclined to stop suddenly, or make a turn on the spur of the moment, seemingly forgetting that he was escorting her. The two eldest Princesses walked behind on the arm of a lady-in-waiting, the second, Mary, having an interesting face, and they were followed by the Princess Elizabeth and then the youngest sisters on the arm of their brother, the Duke of Cambridge. They followed the King back and forth, stopping when he stopped, moving on when he did. In the course of one and a half hours, we must have passed them at least twenty times for as soon as the King reached an empty part of the terrace, he turned and came back. These promenades gave him such pleasure that he seldom returned home before dusk. We, however, grew weary before he did, and when we left the terrace he was still moving happily around.

The little town of Windsor has not a great deal to recommend it. Stretching along the high hill on which the castle is built, the streets are steep and uncomfortable for driving or walking. The inns, too, we found disappointing, considering their proximity to the Court. The village of Eton, home of the famous college, lies on the other side of the Thames, joined to the town by a bridge. The architecture of the school buildings is not distinguished but there is a fine Gothic chapel which enhances the scene. Henry VI founded and built this college in 1440. There are sixty boarders who are educated at the King's expense and in addition sons of good families attend as paying pupils. As at Oxford and Cambridge, their education is conducted in a rather strict and monastic way, even in matters of dress. Each August the scholars are examined and a chosen number will continue their studies at Cambridge. Those twelve who most distinguish themselves in the exam, gain the right to become, after three years, Fellows of the University, an honourable and profitable status. Eton has a notable library, and the college is surrounded by well-kept gardens.

KEW GARDENS

Kew Gardens, particularly famous from a botanical point of view, are reached by a road which, starting from Hyde Park, leads past beautiful Kensington Gardens and then along a seldom broken row of villas for about 4 miles. These houses, each bordered by charming lawns and gardens, are the homes of wealthy London families. The men of the family are engaged in business in the City while their wives and families enjoy here the pure air and all the amenities of rural surroundings, far from the smoke-laden atmosphere of the town. We have already commented on the delight we found in the cleanliness, taste and opulence of these half-urban, half-rural dwellings. We find it difficult to resist eulogising again, when one recalls the feeling of domestic peace and comfortable well-being the sight of them induces, even in the passing traveller.

At Kew, it is only the gardens that are remarkable. The King's residence is small and insignificant and is only used by him and his family on their frequent morning promenades to this favourite place, or to escape from court for a little. They never live here and indeed it would in no way be worthy of such guests. While we were there, a massive building, to be a future dower house for the Queen, was under construction. We have rarely seen anything quite so awkward and clumsy as these masses of stone being used in a completely unsuitable pseudo-Gothic style.

The Royal Botanic Gardens at Kew contain a wide variety of plants from all over the world, and if they do not surpass all others in Europe, they certainly equal them. The fact that the English flag is to be found fluttering in all parts of the globe, has meant that practically everything growing on this earth has found its way to this little plot, even from the most distant shores. From the cedar of Lebanon to the modest heather, everything finds here the care, the soil and the climate it requires, so that nothing vegetates miserably but all grows luxuriantly, green and flourishing. The King was greatly interested in botany and spent much time and money on these gardens, taking pleasure in seeing them thrive. The famous amateur scientist, Sir Joseph Banks, took them under his special supervision and put his botanical knowledge, which he had gained painfully in dangerous and distant parts of the world, to work in this fertile field, until eventually something very special and perfect resulted. The climate, made milder through the current of sea air, and the naturally warm soil of England contributed to the establishment's success, for here winter never entirely deprives the fields of their green carpet and flocks find their food in the open all the year round. It was to be expected, therefore, that any plant from a mild climate would soon become naturalized. Many plants that have to be kept indoors and only exposed to the air in the summer months in Germany, even in the far south, here flourish in the open as they do in their native lands. We think of the large-leaved myrtle and the scented heliotrope among many others.

It is a great pleasure to stroll on the finely-raked gravel paths between the flower-beds of different shapes and sizes and be delighted by the ever-changing play of nature with colour and form. Then one enters the large greenhouses and in each finds a new world. In one are the rarest products of sun-scorched Africa, in another the exotic plants of South America, and then in a third, the plants from more temperate zones. Everything is here in one place, different yet somehow making up a pleasing whole.

What one might refer to as the living flowers in the air are also cared for at Kew. A large aviary has a great number of strange, brightly coloured birds flitting about happily, apparently feeling quite at home in what seems at least to be relative freedom. In an open part of the garden one sees the golden pheasant and the marvellously patterned though more common ordinary variety, while next to them strut peacocks, some of rare breeds, and other species of exotic birds. In the centre of this part of the garden is a pond with an island on which the Chinese pagoda has been built, and here the water birds in great variety swim around or walk on the shore on long spindly legs. These colourful creatures seem just as much at home as they would in their own country.

On a broad green meadow we saw another amusing and

unusual spectacle: some forty or so kangaroos hopping about in complete freedom. Nature has produced nothing more ridiculous than these strange animals. They walk upright and, with the help of their long tails, they are able to make terrific leaps into the air. Their short little forelegs are not used for walking but are held in front of their chests in a droll fashion. Standing upright, they appear to be of a man's height. Their young survey the world with curiosity from the mother's pouch in which she carries them. On occasion, should Mama take too daring a leap, one of the babies may fall out of the pouch onto the ground. Quickly it is retrieved and put back. We saw two little males get very angry with each other and, standing on one leg and their tail, they dealt severe blows with the long sharp nail on the other leg. We watched their eccentric behaviour for a little and found ourselves laughing out loud at their antics.

When we wanted to see the actual 'pleasure grounds' of Kew, our old troubles beset us again. These gardens were shown to the public only on a Sunday and we were there on a weekday. When no persuasion, no entreaty, no remonstration had any effect, we grew annoyed and vented our irritation between ourselves in German, in quite an audible manner. By great good luck we were overheard by a German gardener who was working nearby. On catching the sweet sounds of his mother tongue, his heart was moved and, settling matters with his fellows, it was agreed that he should take us round and be our guide.

The promenades were most agreeable, with many tall trees arranged in groups, these shady plantations alternating with walks among flowers and small shrubs. We found a small, beautifully planted little flower garden with a pond in which goldfish played. Unfortunately these gardens are again far too cluttered with buildings of all sorts. There are lots of temples, dedicated to Bellona, Pan, Eolus, Peace, Solitude, or whoever else. There is a temple of Confucius, a wilderness with a Moorish building, a pseudo-Chinese pagoda, a mosque, Roman ruins, in short too much to be in good taste. None of these buildings is in itself particularly attractive, yet equally one could not condemn them as being unworthy of the place.

Nevertheless one cannot but wish for much of it to be removed, for it insults the eye of anyone who has had the opportunity of admiring the lovely simplicity of English parks.

RICHMOND HILL AND HAMPTON COURT

An agreeable path leads from the gardens at Kew to those at Richmond. Here there had also once been a clutter of buildings erected by successive kings and queens, but happily these have disappeared and only one belonging to the present Queen remains, a simple and unpretentious place she visits with her family. There is an observatory, built by the King, said to be remarkable for a number of instruments made by Dr Herschel, but we did not visit it, the earth around us being too beautiful for us even to think of taking a glance at the sky.

From the stone bridge here, spanning the Thames, one has a fine view of the river and of Richmond Hill rising beyond it. It is not very high and when one has climbed to the inn built at the top, there are even more romantic views of the valley. There may be more exciting and extensive panoramas, but nothing can replace the feeling of calm and joy of living which seizes all who behold it. Everything combines harmoniously to make it unparalleled in England, or anywhere, for where else would one find such a combination of meadow, garden, field and wood? The Thames flows through it, not yet the mighty, broad river of the capital, here navigable only by small vessels, not the great ships bearing rich cargoes.

All around one can see the white gables of the farmhouses, the columned façades of the grander villas, the towers of distant castles and the spires of churches in villages and small towns. In the distance can be seen the grey towers of Windsor on their hill, and, nearer, the great palace of Hampton Court. Down below is the house of Strawberry Hill and the village of Twickenham, consisting of pretty little houses, while close to the river bank stands the villa once occupied by the distinguished poet, Pope.

From the windows of the Star and Garter Inn on Richmond Hill, an excellent and well-organized hostelry, and one of the finest in England, one can at a single glance take in the

31 Richmond Hill looking Southward

splendour of a whole scene, whose magic would be well-nigh impossible to capture by brush or pen.

Opposite is the entrance to a park, some 8 miles in circumference, and here it is nature that caters for the rambler, not art. Tame deer graze midst the splendid trees. These animals had been brought from Hampton Court, since the old King seldom went there any more. Gaps in the woodland continually open up new vistas, so that one is constantly observing things from a different point of view.

Greatly attracted by what we saw, we descended to the banks of the Thames again, to have a look at Hampton Court, the King's largest palace, but not lived in by the Royal Family. Its rooms are now given by the Crown to deserving people as a residence for their lifetime.

The palace was built by the famous Cardinal Wolsey in the time of Henry VIII and reconstructed by Christopher Wren under William III. It is imposing, more through its size than its architecture which is not of outstanding beauty. Of the several hundred rooms, we saw sixteen state apartments and, once again, a fine collection of pictures. The much praised cartoons by Raphael were, alas, no longer there and it seems they have disappeared without trace. The gardens are large and impressive, but they lack the intimacy achieved when planned and cared for constantly by the owner. The extensive greenhouses hold, among other things, the biggest vine in Europe.

STAINES, SLOUGH AND OATLANDS

We drove past Hampton Court for several miles, inland from the Thames, through the beautiful park of Claremont and the little town of Cobham until we came to Painshill. Claremont Park is not open to visitors but in any case the exterior promises nothing extraordinary, although we have heard the interior and its works of art much praised. We had visited the gardens of Painshill several years ago, on a previous visit to London, and admired its long and beautiful pathways. We therefore approached, full of the anticipation of meeting an old friend. It was, alas, a day of thwarted hopes for we were not admitted. A short time ago the property had been bought by a rich London banker who no longer allowed the public to admire this paradise for which he had paid his good guineas. We could only look sadly at the beautiful trees, longing for their shade and then turn back to the Thames and the little town of Staines. Here we were cheered by a happy and colourful crowd of race-goers who were making merry, and they soon enabled us to forget our ill-luck at Claremont and Painshill. Once again, the scene reminded us vividly of fairs in Germany which from time to time bring life and pleasure to small towns and villages.

Next to the inn at Staines, a high and daringly arched bridge spans the river. While not quite as big as that at Sunderland, it is otherwise exactly like it and it is certainly worth the journey from London to see it alone, especially if one does not have the good fortune to travel to Newcastle and Sunderland. Light and graceful, it seems to make a daring leap across the river. Even the *Pont des Arts* in Paris, despite its fine railings embellished with orange trees, cannot in any way compare with this delicate arc, apparently thrown into the air by some supernatural hands.

From Staines we took a pleasant route through fertile country along the Thames to Salthill, where an inn, set in its own grounds, offered us every comfort we desired. It is a favourite place for those making excursions from London, especially strangers who wish to enjoy at leisure the beautiful surroundings of Windsor for a few days.

Quite near Salthill, in the little village of Slough, is the house where Dr Herschel resides. It was given to him by the King, and is a large but not attractive place in which he has lived for several years. We came armed with a letter of recommendation to our famous countryman, and he and his sister, a person of similar intellect and education, received us in a friendly manner. In addition to helping her brother in his scrutiny of the sky, this lady also helps to make the doctor's terrestrial problems as agreeable as possible. Both of an age, this exceptional brother and sister enjoy a happy life in quiet rural peace. The Royal Family, under whose special patronage they live in entire devotion to their scientific work, honours them in every way, especially during the King's summer residence at

Windsor. They are much loved and respected in the neighbourhood, and whenever we mentioned their names we heard
nothing but praise.

In spite of his great age and the discomfort inseparable from
his work carried out in the damp English nights, perhaps more
unpleasant than elsewhere, Dr Herschel enjoys robust good
health. He was most engaging company, undemanding, and
captured his audience immediately. Although they had remained
German subjects and they unmistakably bore the stamp of that
nation, as a result of their long sojourn in England, they had
forgotten their native tongue to the extent that they found it
difficult to express themselves fluently in it. We were shown
his astronomical instruments most willingly. The giant telescope in his courtyard he regarded more as a rarity and nearly
always used smaller ones. He confessed that he had made all his
important discoveries using them, maintaining that it was not
the size of the lenses but diligence and accuracy in his
observations that had gained him the reputation he had.

Dr Herschel belongs to that remarkable breed of people who
enter this world in poor and miserable conditions, their parents
unable to provide them with an education worthy of their
talents, but who have the resolute will, clear sight and unfailing
courage to forge ahead through the storms of life. He was born
in Hanoverian country in 1738, son of a poor musician with a
large family, who could do no more for him than give him a
solid grounding in his own profession. The boy soon found an
opportunity to learn French, and happily his teacher was a man
of wide education who was able to kindle in the young mind of
his eager pupil an interest in logic and mathematics. During the
Seven Years War he accompanied his father with the band of a
Hanoverian regiment to England. After a while, when the
father decided to return home, the son took the chance of
remaining in England and trying his luck there. In London
however, he was lost in the crowd, unnoticed and repelled, his
star as yet unrisen, and it took all his firm determination not to
lose courage. He resolved to leave the unfriendly capital which
had rejected the unprotected, unknown stranger and to travel
north. After much wandering there, he settled in Halifax. A
position of organist had fallen vacant there and after a trial

period his application was accepted. Apart from the few hours he had to devote to his job and a few more when he gave music lessons to earn money, he spent all his time studying languages. He began with Italian, then took up Latin and finally attempted some Greek. All this he accomplished without any help. Still alone and without a teacher, he progressed to more serious subjects. He acquired a complete grasp of something very close to him, the theory of harmony, then pressed on further to mathematics and the kindred sciences. In that way he passed a number of profitable and agreeable years in Halifax. Then he was called as an organist to Bath where he found more work in his chosen profession by playing at the Assembly Rooms, at concerts and in the theatre. Yet, despite the increased work and the temptations of the brilliant life around him, he remained faithful to his studies and spent many long hours of the night pondering on these abstract matters.

He now occupied himself almost exclusively with astronomy and optics. A friend lent him a telescope and with great pleasure he observed the stars in the firmament through it, resulting in the irresistable desire to own for himself the apparatus for studying astronomy. He consulted a friend in London about the purchase of a large telescope but the price was so enormous that he did not have the means to make the purchase. Instead of being downcast, he boldly decided that he would make an instrument himself. He had only the poorest resources, but after many vain attempts, he at last succeeded in 1774, in observing the sky through a 5-feet long Newton reflector, made by himself. He now aimed higher, and still clinging to his job as his livelihood, made a series of instruments bigger than any seen before. Often he would rush from the theatre or the concert hall during the intervals, to look at the stars, always succeeding in returning to his music desk in good time.

His astronomical discoveries, which became known all over the world, date from this period. He became famous and news of his reputation reached the King. In 1782 he was taken under Royal protection and thus freed from his fatiguing professional duties. The King granted him a pension for life and provided him with the house in Slough where we had our happy encounter with this remarkable man and where, until his death a few years ago, he listened to the secrets of the spheres.

On our way back to London, we travelled by way of Oatlands, the lonely rural home of the late Princess Friederike of Prussia, consort of the Duke of York. It lies a short distance from the Thames at the farthest end of the valley we had seen from Richmond Hill. This Princess, daughter of King Frederick William II, lived here almost all the year in monastic solitude. The Duke came only seldom to Oatlands, and then with a few friends who made little change to her solitary life. Her main occupation was making beautiful embroideries, which she worked at with her ladies well into the night, going to bed when morning dawned and rising when the sun began to set.

The ill-fortune which had accompanied us on this journey and had frustrated us so often still seemed to hang over us. Here, once again, we had arrived on a day when visitors were not admitted. The stout, irritable lady, who was the wife of the caretaker, assured us that we should have come on a Sunday and an equally stout and cross Berlin pug dog, standing next to her, growling and showing its teeth, seemed to confirm this assertion. In spite of these inauspicious omens, we decided to use our powers of persuasion and fortunately had some success. We told her we had come specially from Germany across the sea, hoping to be able on our return to tell our countrymen what our Princess's house was like, and how she fared. This seemed to touch the heart of the old lady, who became noticeably more friendly. Putting the pug on his cushion, she wrote a little note to Madame Silvester, a German favourite of the Duchess, and eventually emerged, specially dressed to accompany us personally to the Castle. Now wagging his tail, the snarling pug waddled along quite sociably beside us. We proceeded through a fine large park, then entered a flower garden full of beautiful and rare plants. A crowd of large and small monkeys sported around in it, some long-tailed and some short. The Duchess loved them and indeed all animals that could be trained to domesticity, so that there were birds, parrots and dogs in great numbers in and around the house.

The house is neither big nor splendid, but simple and

furnished in almost a middle-class style. In fact, its greatest ornament is the fine artistic embroidery, worked by the Duchess and her ladies. We found the walks in the grounds most pleasant, although here again there was nothing remarkable apart from a grotto, somewhat fantastically decorated with fossils from Derbyshire and containing a large marble basin. Around it lie the graves of all the Duchess's favourite dogs and monkeys, each with its own stone and inscription. It reminded us vividly of the cemetery which Frederick the Great had had constructed at Sans Souci for his four-legged friends, among whom, in a moment of gloom, he had once had his own tomb prepared.

Wanstead House in Middlesex is not very large, and has little to distinguish it, except that the Prince de Condé found refuge there. His wife declared it to be inferior to the kennels of her father's house at Chantilly, now destroyed, and indeed she may have been right, for those magnificent buildings opposite the palace, with their finely decorated façade, were more like a royal residence. The elderly Prince held his small court here, where they kept to the old ways, observing the manners and dress of the time when they lived under Louis XVI.

CHELSEA, HAMPSTEAD AND HIGHGATE

London abounds in charming outlying villages where in beer-gardens and tea and coffee-houses one can spend the day pleasantly in the open, as the Viennese do when they go to the Prater. There is, however, one problem in London. If only the Londoner could take time to relax from his daily routine, his essential round of work which leaves him never a moment free (since everything is so expensive in this country where even the air one breathes does not seem to escape taxation), he would be able to escape more often to these charming places. But despite all this, once or twice a year everybody tries to visit these retreats, which we have only time to mention in passing. Chelsea is really quite near, yet it appears to be completely in the country. Here one finds the Royal Military Hospital, smaller than its Naval counterpart at Greenwich, but run on the same lines and worthy of mention for its superb architecture by Sir Christopher Wren. Hampstead is situated about 4 miles outside the city and is one of the pleasantest excursions one could make. There are many in London who have, in fact, never got beyond Hampstead and think it to be the end of the world. There are magnificent views over London and the countryside, even if these do not quite rival Richmond Hill. Apart from Lord Mansfield's Kenwood House, there are few grand dwellings, as it is not far enough into the countryside for the aristocracy. Highgate, at a similar distance, is not so beautiful and is less frequented for pleasure, as it is traversed by a busy main road.

We also journeyed out to Roehampton, by way of Chiswick, and visited many houses of the great aristocracy, such as Sion House, and of the wealthy men of the City, bankers and merchants, all set in incomparable verdant surroundings.

THE WEST INDIA DOCKS

On the northern banks of the Thames, close to London, are to be found the warehouses and the wharves which form an indispensable part of any nation's maritime trade. It is an area of restless activity, of constant noise and of the hubbub of the people working there. On this highway to the markets of the world, the nearby rural pleasures seem to be very far away. Close to the city lies a giant man-made construction, the docks built to serve the West Indian trade. They were built not so long ago by a consortium of London merchants at a cost of 600,000 pounds. The cost is being recovered for the syndicate by means of a levy on goods discharged there, and as it is the law that all ships to and from the West Indies must use this artificial harbour, they will be well compensated. The docks consist of two basins, the smaller of which is used for loading, and the larger, which can accommodate many vessels, for unloading.

The whole makes a very imposing sight: broad quays, large splendid warehouses, like palaces, the bustle of the men at work on the ships, all this impresses the visitor who is also surprised to see the space completely occupied with goods so that it almost seems too small for its purpose. These docks are an invaluable advantage to trade as vessels carrying goods of great worth can be separated from the ordinary cargoes and lie here safely guarded from possible theft. Formerly there was much confusion, for the ships from the West Indies arrived usually in convoys and a scrimmage would take place for the privilege of landing goods first. Now all is arranged in a quiet and orderly manner and there is little damage or loss.

Opposite these splendid docks lies Greenwich, a refuge of peace and quietness easily reached by a regular ferry-boat. Then it is only a few steps to the beautiful park, where in the silence one can forget the rowdiness of the money-grabbing world of commerce which lies not so far away. Beyond the park is Blackheath, ill-famed as the haunt of the English highwayman. Its reputation is worse than it deserves, for, on the whole, the number of these fiends seems to have diminished in recent years and the reports of robberies and murders in the newspapers are often invented to fill some empty space or add a little spice to their rather dull contents.

KNOLE, COUNTRY RESIDENCE OF THE DUKE OF DORSET

From Blackheath we made a short excursion into Kent, to an area different from the one which we had seen on previous journeys from Dover to London. A few miles from London we were afforded a singularly fine view. We saw the city spread out before us, her countless domes and towers, dominated by St Paul's, spread along a river of masts which looked like a veritable forest, stripped of its foliage. Greenwich lay before us, to the left the town of Deptford, with its ship-building yards, busy docks and warehouses and on our right the equally busy town of Woolwich, that enormous arsenal of English sea power, with all the stores and factories necessary to it. Around and between all this is the undulating countryside, typically English in its rich cultivated fertility and many woods of ancient trees.

We drove on to Bromley, past many villas in pleasant settings, although we did note that the larger country house was not a feature here, as at Richmond, perhaps due to the absence of the river and the fact that this part of Kent is somewhat lacking in water. Near Bromley we visited an old friend. When we were last in England some years ago, he was a merchant of moderate means with his office and small house in the City: now we found him to be the wealthy owner of Tunbridge Park. Our friend had built this elegant villa in the Italian style, the Temple of Ceres near Rome having inspired the main façade, and surrounded it with an impressive park and a charming garden.

Continuing for a few miles, we reached Knole, near Sevenoaks. This mansion, the seat of the Duke of Dorset, is of venerable age and is set in a spacious park where the oak trees, soaring to the sky, are probably even older than the house itself. It is a gloomy, straggling building whose interior furnishings are a strange mixture of the old and the new. Some rooms are completely modern, others in the style of a few hundred years ago. The apartments actually in use seem to be a mixture of both periods and it is not a happy combination.

For the student of antiquities, two rooms are of particular interest. The first still stands as King James I left it after spending a night there. There is a high carved bed in which six people could easily be accommodated. The frames of the mirrors round the walls are so heavily carved that their glass seems insignificant. Enormous armchairs weighing at least a hundredweight, are fitted with small steps to enable one to take one's place on them. The other room, whose furnishings date from the same period, is a fine example of ancient, solid splendour. The massive curtains around the bed, which itself is said to have cost twenty thousand pounds, are woven of gold and silver and would appear more likely to have been forged on an anvil than woven on a loom. The bedcover, decorated with very thick gold embroidery, seemed capable of suffocating anyone sleeping under it. Other furnishings include a beautiful toilet set of fine old embossed work, a large silver table and a massive carved cupboard, as large as a house in the Highlands, with magnificent silver vases on top of it.

There are many other rooms, containing old paintings, and a fine long gallery of family portraits and distinguished people, some caricatures and others by master portraitists. There is a very characteristic study of Cromwell and some of Luther, his friend Melanchthon, and Erasmus, all by Lucas Cranach. Also, featured in another room, are the images of famous English scholars and poets.

Travelling on from Knole we again went through interesting country, fascinatingly shaped cliffs, hilltops from which we obtained superb views, a ruined castle on a hillock, a vast stone quarry. The ruin towers over the little town of Tonbridge.

The spa at Tunbridge Wells, a short distance away, is much frequented, as it is only 36 miles from London and can be reached in a few hours. We shall not describe it in detail as we have already dealt with the niceties of the English spa on more than one occasion and anyway, it is not a particularly distinguished example. Let us, therefore, make Tonbridge the point at which we take leave of the reader who has kindly accompanied us so far on our journeys, and bid him a grateful farewell.